ABORTION

ABORTION
New Directions For Policy Studies

EDITED BY
Edward Manier
William Liu
David Solomon

UNIVERSITY OF NOTRE DAME PRESS
NOTRE DAME   LONDON

Copyright © 1977 by
University of Notre Dame Press
Notre Dame, Indiana 46556

Library of Congress Cataloging in Publication Data

Main entry under title:

Abortion.

   Includes bibliographical references.
   1. Abortion—United States—Addresses, essays, lectures. 2. Abortion—United States—Public opinion—Addresses, essays, lectures. 3. Public opinion—United States—Addresses, essays, lectures. 4. Abortion—Law and legislation—United States—Addresses, essays, lectures. 5. Abortion—Law and legislation—Germany, West—Addresses, essays, lectures. I. Manier, Edward. II. Liu, William Thomas, 1930– III. Solomon, David, 1943–

HQ767.5.U5A23   301   76–51617
ISBN 0-268-00582-6

Manufactured in the United States of America

CONTENTS

Preface   vii

Abortion and Public Policy in the U.S.:
A Dialectical Examination of Expert Opinion
    Edward Manier   1

Membership Decisions and the Limits
of Moral Obligation
    Edmund L. Pincoffs   31

The Abortion Decisions:
Judicial Review and Public Opinion
    Judith Blake   51

Abortion and the Constitution:
The Cases of the United States and West Germany
    Donald P. Kommers   83

Philosophy on Humanity
    Roger Wertheimer   117

Abortion and the Social System
    William T. Liu   137

Philosophers on Abortion
    David Solomon   159

Conclusions
    Edward Manier, William Liu, and David Solomon   169

Appendix:
Comments on the 1976 Supreme Court Decisions:
Planned Parenthood v. *Danforth* and *Bellotti* v. *Baird*
    Edward Manier   177

Index   183

PREFACE

At a Catholic university, the discussion of abortion brings into play a complex set of intellectual and social forces. Nevertheless, two conferences on abortion have already been held at the University of Notre Dame, on September 26 and 27, 1973, and March 19 and 20, 1975. A third conference is projected as a result of discussions between the president of the university, Reverend Theodore M. Hesburgh, C.S.C., and then presidential candidate, Jimmy Carter, in October 1976. This sustained discussion and analysis of the problems of abortion has taken place in the midst of a conflicting variety of campaigns and pronouncements on the subject, but the university has provided a rational and civil atmosphere for far-ranging exchanges of information and opinion throughout this period.

Universities such as Notre Dame exist, in part, to preserve and pass on a religious and moral tradition. Father Hesburgh often uses the medieval motto *fides quaerens intellectum* when he asserts that understanding will deepen faith rather than replace, dismiss or dilute it. He also argues that religious fidelity can foster a critical temper as acute and comprehensive as that found in the scientific community.

> Few institutions on earth need the climate of freedom to the extent that universities do, whatever the risk involved. Moreover, it should be said that universities since their founding in the Middle Ages have always been unruly places, almost by nature, since the university is the place where young people come of age—often an unruly process—places where the really important problems are freely discussed with all manner of solutions proposed, places where all the burning issues of the day are ventilated, even with hurricane winds at times. Again, by nature, the university has always been dedicated uniquely to criticism of itself and everything else, even, or perhaps especially in the case of the Catholic university, those things held most dear.[1]

1. Rev. Theodore M. Hesburgh, C.S.C., "The Vision of a Great Catholic University in the World of Today" (Address given at Special Convocation commemorating the one-hundred-twenty-fifth anniversary of the founding of the University of Notre Dame, December 9, 1967, p. 8.

Consistent with this position, Father Hesburgh replied to the query of an episcopal authority concerning the first abortion conference by stating:

> If this country is to find a better legal policy and practice in the matter of abortion than it now has, by Supreme Court decree, it would appear fairly obvious that we must discuss our differences with those who proposed and have promoted the present situation. If intelligent Catholics had held such discussions in the past, instead of mainly talking to themselves, we might not now be in the present deplorable situation.[2]

While Father Hesburgh has been willing to encourage and defend the academic freedom of his faculty, his own opposition to the Supreme Court's decisions on abortion has been unequivocal. He locates his defense of the right to life in the context of his commitment to the brotherhood of all men.

> If we really respect the right to life we must respect it right across the board for everyone, from the beginning of conception to the end of life. We have to be more concerned about the poor and those suffering injustice here and abroad, those deprived because of our conspicuous consumption. It is not just a little narrow crusade. We have to be concerned about this great mystery of life and cherish it deeply whether in a poor ghetto child, or a child in Sahil bloated from hunger, or an old person abandoned; black, oriental, white, or poor. We must be against violence. We must be against anything that brutalizes or extinguishes unjustly that enormously beautiful and mysterious gift of life.[3]

His position cannot be dismissed as blind or insensitive to the social cost of the prohibition of abortion.

There is one respect, however, in which Notre Dame is not yet an easy place to discuss abortion. This follows from the important sense in which abortion is a woman's issue. In the individualistic context of modern and post-modern societies, women confront the terrible prospects of unwanted pregnancy much more directly than men, and are often left alone to deal with those prospects. Notre Dame's tradition as an all-male university, only recently opened to women on the faculty and in the student body, still tends to impede a full and comprehensive discussion of abortion on this campus. Our conferences, however, have enabled us to try to remedy this shortcoming: more than half of the invited speakers at the two conferences have been women, and the first

---

2. Rev. Theodore M. Hesburgh, C.S.C., and Edmund A. Stephan, Chairman of the Board of Trustees, University of Notre Dame, Published letter to Leo A. Pursley, Bishop of Fort Wayne–South Bend, October 11, 1973.

3. Rev. Theodore M. Hesburgh, C.S.C., Sermon at Respect Life Mass, Sacred Heart Church, University of Notre Dame, January 22, 1975, p. 5.

Preface ix

conference addressed the issue of the new role of woman in a particularly direct way.

Notre Dame has provided an ideal environment for our efforts in that its relatively small size encourages and facilitates crossdisciplinary efforts. On this campus, it is difficult for philosophers, sociologists, or lawyers to conduct their inquiries without becoming aware of each other's problems, methods and results. Nevertheless, the first conference did not probe fully the conceptual and methodological difficulties associated with the multidisciplinary activity it involved. In the context of open, public discussion we found that the many heated controversies associated with abortion generated a polemical atmosphere geared to the scoring of points in partisan debate. We concluded that the second conference should be a closed, scholarly discussion, conducted without publicity, aimed at the publication of carefully reasoned position papers. Academic departments and the disciplines they foster tend to behave much like separate nations, with different languages, customs and values, all of which seem alien and nearly unintelligible to the nonspecialist. A special effort is required to resolve the many attendant problems of clear communication and reasoned criticism.

The present volume includes those conference papers which concentrated on the basic empirical, conceptual, methodological and normative issues which must be resolved *before* sound policy studies on this topic can be designed. The published papers represent the separate disciplines of comparative constitutional law, sociology and philosophy. Each of these disciplines, in addition to its unique vocabulary, presupposes its own bibliography and even its own typographical conventions for citing that bibliography. Without compromising important disciplinary traditions, we have striven to provide the reader with a uniform text. Nevertheless, we must ask for attention to the important differences in the intellectual style and content of the separate contributions, and for generous indulgence of the opportunity to digest these contributions carefully and slowly.

I am grateful for the contributions and discussions, during the first conference, of Carol Booth, M.D., Sidney Callahan, Alison Jaggar, Florynce Kennedy, Grace Olivarez, Joan Straumanis, Hans Verweyen, and Mary Yager. All three editors and the contributors to this volume are appreciative of the substantive contributions to the second conference made by Elihu Bergman, Harriet Pilpel, and Amelie Rorty, and of the expert criticism provided by Morris Janowitz, Ernan McMullin and William Petersen. My final editorial tasks have been enlightened by several post-conference discussions with Joan Aldous and David Leege.

The conferences were supported in part by grants from the Indiana Committee for the Humanities (an affiliate of the National Endowment for the Humanities) and the Ford Foundation. The Ford Foundation has provided a partial subsidy of this publication.

The editors and contributors assume complete responsibility for their contributions to this volume and do not claim to represent the position of the University of Notre Dame, its faculty as a whole, or its administration.

> Edward Manier
> Department of Philosophy, and
> Center for the Study of Man in
>   Contemporary Society
> University of Notre Dame
> June 9, 1977

ABORTION

Abortion and Public Policy in the U.S.: A Dialectical Examination of Expert Opinion

EDWARD MANIER

This book includes papers presented at a conference held at the University of Notre Dame in March 1975 as well as papers written by Donald Kommers and the three editors approximately one year later. The goal of a clear and singular focus for the book led to the selection of those conference papers considered most relevant to the interdisciplinary discussion of the normative foundations of the many social and political problems associated with the legalization of abortion. It is impossible to isolate aspects of these problems which correspond to specific academic disciplines.[1] No single discipline can expect to have the last word on abortion. All significant discussions of the subject must survive translation into the idiom of political controversy and into the technical language of other disciplines.

As a social problem in the United States, the subject of abortion has become politically explosive. The present situation is likely to become more tense and difficult before an effective resolution is achieved.[2] The issue has low saliency for voters, but charges and countercharges concerning the legalization of abortion have been ugly and intense. The most visible and energetic pro-life and pro-choice factions have portrayed each other as dogmatic and unwilling to compromise, and no current program for consensus formation offers solid prospects for the reduction of the political costs associated with any and all positions on the legality of abortion.[3] Both the ethos and the structure of our free market system, which aims to provide a full panoply of goods and services on demand, have worked in favor of pro-choice groups. Partly as a result of this circumstance, the most *visible* political action has been taken by so-called pro-life groups and the U.S. Catholic bishops.[4]

The *first* goal of this book is to set an effective context for cross-disciplinary discussion of abortion. Sociologists, philosophers, and comparative constitutionalists approach the subject of norms, rules, and values from such different perspectives that special precautions are necessary if they are to understand each other, let alone profit from each others' labors. A general discussion of the methodology of such cross-disciplinary work might be premature. Sections 1 to 6 of this Introduction are intended to clear ground for such discussion, however. The aim of these sections is dialectical and argumentative; it is to juxtapose the various positions presented at the conference as if they were confronting each other in critical dialogue. In this Introduction, therefore, selected papers from the conference are related to each other in a fashion not completely anticipated by the events of the conference itself. This technique of dialectical comparison is intended to assist in the isolation and description of the methodological and normative presuppositions of interdisciplinary discussion.

The *second* goal of this book is to illuminate the role of social scientists, humanists, and legal scholars who participate in the discussion of public-policy issues. A number of case studies have probed the role of the expert as policy advisor, attempting to devise a professional ethic to guide such activity and to formulate a strategy for making the most effective use of an important social resource of information and technical skill.[5] In all these previous studies a persistent theme has been a difficulty experienced by both the producers and the users of this resource: the difficulty of distinguishing and then reintegrating the *scientific, political,* and *normative* perspectives of various advisors.

In illustration, Robert Gilpin's *American Scientists and Nuclear Weapons Policy* dealt with events leading up to the negotiation of the first nuclear test ban treaty between this country and the Soviet Union. Gilpin found that the classic dispute which raged between opposed camps of expert advisors (personified by Hans Bethe and Edward Teller) was not wholly technical in nature. More important, he found the structure of the dispute determined by elements largely *unnoticed* by the disputants themselves. On his account, each side to the dispute assumed that its position represented that of the "objective" scientist, while opponents were seen as basing their position on political grounds. He concluded that the advisors' *nonscientific* assumptions concerning the military value of tactical nuclear weapons, the technological intentions of the Soviet Union, and the political desirability of disarmament were essential constituents of the "technical" advice they gave to their political superiors in the United States government.

The self-image of these expert advisors inhibited their perception of this fact and its importance. Components of this self-image included: (a) the belief that scientific method is superior to politics as a means of settling disputes, since science uses reason to exhibit the truth whereas politics uses force or persuasion to achieve agreement;[6] (b) the belief that science can produce new and imaginative solutions to man's problems which cut through the superficial cake of custom which holds the politician in thrall; and (c) the belief that there is some *one truth* to which all reasonable men will accede once its nature has been explained—countering the view that political life is a never-ending struggle for power among men and nations with opposed interests. Gilpin concluded that nontechnical, *normative* assumptions are not eliminable from expert technical advice concerning nuclear disarmament. The political or other value commitments of an advisor determine the problems he selects for emphasis, his judgments concerning the factual relevance of technical information to policy, and his inferences concerning the policy alternatives most in conformity with technical data. The editors agree that this thesis is true and that it can be given a more general formulation which is also true. When historians, philosophers, or social scientists seek to comment upon the formulation of public policy, their methods provide them with no fully satisfactory means for disentangling their extradisciplinary assumptions and values, political or otherwise, from a putatively objective and value-free core.[7] For reasons of this sort, Gilpin recommended that expert advisory committees be comprised of individuals with opposed political, economic, social, and moral perspectives. The confrontation of these perspectives, actually embedded in technical advice, he argued, would make the political ideas of scientific advisors apparent and accessible for evaluation by decision makers. We convened with a conference whose participants have opposed political, economic, social, and moral attitudes concerning abortion. We do not assume that the result is a solution to the problems of abortion. We hope the result will be a clearer formulation of the problems. We hope to make the normative, methodological, and substantive assumptions of all the participants in the on-going abortion debate more accessible to investigation and criticism by other scholars and to enlightened use by the public and the decision makers the public elects.

One final cautionary word is in order. The reader should remember that the subject of this book is in a rapid state of development. The United States Supreme Court continues to publish decisions concerning abortion; the subject is included or denied inclusion in political platforms; the Senate decides whether or not to initiate the process of constitutional amendment; new state laws are formulated; new fact situations arise—as in the *Edelin* case, or the increased availability of prostaglandin or other drugs; and new studies are published—as Kristin Luker's analysis of the background and the attitudes of women seeking abortion in a clinic in northern California.[8]

1. The "Official Decider" in U.S. Society

The rationalist school in philosophy sets great store by clarity and distinctness in the construction of concepts and in the representation of their meaning. In the technical but familiar vocabulary of Euclidean geometry, the expression 'isosceles triangle' is clear and distinct insofar as its unambiguous definition sets forth necessary and sufficient conditions for membership in the class of isosceles triangles. Biologists and philosophers of biology have generally denied that classes of living organisms can be delimited in this neat, dichotomous fashion. Answers to such questions as "Is this organism a vertebrate?" may be stymied by borderline cases where a decision can be made only on grounds which remain partially arbitrary and *ad hoc*. Nor is individual variability within classes of living organisms simply a brute fact. On the contrary, Darwin raised this variability to the level of theoretical principle in order to explain the origin of species of living things by descent from ancestors not belonging to the same species. Given the possibility that species of organisms give rise to one or more new species in the course of biological time, the empirical and theoretical difficulty (perhaps the impossibility) of deciding when species A becomes species B should be apparent. The difficulty of defining biological species is compounded by the continuity of developmental and evolutionary processes so that species' names are as difficult to capture with empirical precision as is the meaning of the word 'twilight.'

One might still argue that 'human being' is a special case where we have an insider's privilege. Edmund Pincoff's paper argues the contrary. He holds that the question "Is the embryo an innocent human being?" is one which cannot be given a decisive systematic answer because we cannot provide a list of conditions necessary and sufficient for membership in the class of human beings much less the class of innocent human beings. The fact that membership in the class of human beings may have decisive implications for judgments of life and death does not help settle the matter. How could one respond if an all-powerful emperor made matters of life and death depend upon a precise, rigorous, and unexceptionable definition of the first moment of twilight?

Pincoffs joins those philosophers who argue that this is not a matter that lends itself to scientific or technical resolution. We cannot rely upon the experts, he argues, to decide whether to vote the fetus up or down as a member of the class of human beings. Geneticists cannot provide a solution by telling us about the genetic characteristics of fetuses or by offering foolproof techniques for distinguishing normal from abnormal fetuses. Nor would we be closer to a solution if technology were to offer us the opportunity to scan the appearance or behavior of the fetus. Nor can we decide how to vote by getting an unequivocal answer from neurophysiologists as to whether or not fetuses feel pain, exhibit an ability to learn, or seem conscious. Social psychologists (opinion pollsters) cannot settle the matter by discovering how other people (a majority or a consensus of voters) feel about fetuses, or how they would vote concerning the membership of fetuses in the class of human beings. Nor can philosophers settle the question by any method of *a priori* investigation.

The applicability of 'humanity' to borderline cases cannot be settled by an appeal to objectively universal, necessary, and sufficient conditions for species membership. The fetus is *not* a borderline case because it possesses an undecidable mix of human and nonhuman characteristics. The status of the fetus is problematic because our awareness of the earliest stages of its development is indirect and technical, and the technical information we have concerning it is not commensurable with our ordinary uses of 'humanity.' What sort of evidence could support a decision to follow one rather than the other of these two maxims?

1. Since someone took care of me when I was a fetus, I should nurture and protect fetuses that come my way.
2. Since I'm free to take care of my body as I like, I ought to protect women's rights to do the same with theirs.

Nothing outside the *practice* of a human group can decide or determine its membership, since it is comprised of just those individuals who have reciprocal practical relations with each other.

Pincoffs places the matter in the hands of an Official Decider. He does not tell the Decider how to decide, nor does he offer advice concerning the creation of consensus on this membership decision. While he thinks that such consensus is desirable and that we are presently moving toward it, he does not describe its current status. He notes that the U.S. Supreme Court has decided the "degree of care and protection to which it [the fetus] is entitled." However, so far as the first twenty-four weeks of pregnancy are concerned, the Court's decision on this point was absolutely negative. "No care!" This implies a negative membership decision for the first and second trimester fetus. The decision means that so far as society is concerned, no justification whatsoever need be provided for killing a fetus. From this *social* perspective, then, it is not *prima facie* wrong to abort or to kill a first- or second-trimester fetus. On this analysis, in the United States, at present, a woman who secures a first- or second-trimester abortion owes her fellow citizens no explanation or justification of her actions.

We can appreciate the care and precision of Pincoffs's analysis and admit that he has significantly advanced the argument but still feel the necessity for further discussion: What is the current state of opinion (in the U.S.) concerning abortion? Are we moving toward consensus, or is opinion becoming more divided? Has the Court's decision aided or impeded the effort to reach a social consensus concerning the morality of abortion and the underlying "membership decision"? What must we think when the Official Deciders in two societies as similar as the United States and West Germany come to opposed decisions concerning abortion?

2. Public Opinion and the Direction of Social Change

A portion of the context of Judith Blake's contribution to this volume is provided by her perspective as one interested in "remobilizing the troops" to confront bureaucratic footdragging and effective collateral deterrence to the full implementation of the Supreme Court decision on abortion. In the absence of such effort, "bureaucratic and professional resistance, organized opposition, and public disapproval, ambivalence, and inattention, may well turn *Roe* and *Doe* into an empty victory in the years to come."

No less important to the understanding of Blake's position is her insistence on "above all, attempting to cope with, rather than misrepresent, the actual views of the public on this subject." As a social scientist, admitting that it is "probably possible to raise endless metaphysical and epistemological objections to the validity of questions" in polls of public opinion concerning abortion, she nevertheless holds that the methodology of asking questions is sufficiently rigorous to be adequate for the discovery of the "actual views of the public" on topics which include the time at which human life begins and the propriety and character of legal limitations on the performance of abortions. During the last decade, she has written a series of distinguished papers on public opinion concerning various methods of fertility control, a series which has established her as one of the leading critics of the prevailing view of such matters. She has also come forward with a plausible interpretation of the data gathered by a number of reputable agencies. In particular, articles which appeared in *Science* in 1969 and 1971 presented data which enabled her to describe an attitude relatively prevalent among upper-class males: "his desire for a small family, his

TABLE 1

OPINIONS CONCERNING CONTRACEPTION AND ABORTION BY SEX AND ECONOMIC STATUS.
(in percentages)

	1959–64 Approval of Birth control Men	Women	1966 Approval of free distribution of pills to women on relief Men	Women	1966 Approval of pills for teenage girls Men	Women	1969 Disapproval of elective abortion Men	Women
Econ. Status								
1	89	87	79	70	33	11	63	70
4	74	78	39	67	13	16	79	86

instrumental view of teenage sexual behavior, and his willingness to approve convenience methods of birth control."[9] This should not be misread as the construction of a stereotype; the data did *not* show unanimity in this class, and on related topics (legalization of elective abortion) disapproving attitudes ran higher than 50 percent. What the data did show was that approving attitudes were higher among upper-class males than among upper-class females, lower-class females, and lower-class males.

In 1971, her summary and interpretation of this data ventured the following hypotheses:

H_1: Upper class men have much to gain and very little to lose by an easing of legal restrictions against abortion. For some time, these men seem to have been satisfied with relatively small families extending over a limited period of their lives.... As a class they are especially vulnerable to being held financially and socially responsible for accidental pregnancies.

H_2: The majority of women and less advantaged persons derive most of their lifetime rewards from the family complex, and from the norms upholding it, and at the same time experience little that deeply challenges this institutional arrangement, (thus) they tend to support it unconditionally. In particular, they appear loathe to admit the legitimacy of laws which would allow individuals the right to "turn off" such a hallowed institution as the family through the simple mechanism of an abortion.[10]

These hypotheses, in turn, assume a methodological and theoretical background:

M_1: The methods of an empirical social science are adequate for the identification and description of social institutions and their functions in the determination of social norms.
M_2: The methods of an empirical social science are adequate for the identification and description of the functions of these same social norms in providing value ("lifetime rewards") and meaning for the lives of the members of a society.
M_3: These norms can also function in the explanation (and statistical prediction?) of the behavior (verbal replies to opinion pollsters) of the members of that society.

Since M_1, M_2, and M_3 have not been established to the satisfaction either of all social scientists or of all philosophical critics of the methodology of the social sciences, there can be no consensus concerning the warrant for H_1 and H_2. The question as to whether or not such interpretations are based in reality, whether, that is, they represent the "actual views of the public," remains undecided.[11]

Philosophers may think that any uncertainty infecting the theses H_1 to H_3 will also infect Blake's *description* of the data. However, some accurate interpretation of such data is necessary for intelligent appraisal of Pincoffs's views concerning the role of the Official Decider. In this case the Official Decider claimed that its decision was based on its own more or less accurate interpretation of the institutions of the society (including the Constitution) and of the opinions and attitudes prevalent among subclasses of the members of the society. Blake is concerned that the Court may have misread these social facts. She sees the Court's errors in this regard as fuel for a continuing dispute which threatens the effective nullification of the full reach of the Official Decider's decision. The data as she describes them make it plain that the Decider neither reflected an articulate social consensus nor functioned effectively in building a social consensus in the matter of *Roe* and *Doe*.

She finds public opinion concerning abortion, after *Roe* and *Doe*, to be deeply divided, with approval of elective abortion (as provided in *Roe*) hovering around 40 percent and disapproval hovering around 55 percent. She further notes that in January 1973, two-thirds of white American men and women thought that the law should limit abortion to the first three months of pregnancy (whereas *Roe* and *Doe* permit elective abortion up through the time of "viability," and do not require its prohibition at any time before birth). Moreover, she finds that an equal and growing percentage of the adult public hold the supporting view that human life begins no later than the end of the third month of pregnancy.

How should society proceed to attain a more stable and satisfactory basis for either social consensus or for some other means of guiding social policy concerning abortion? In this volume, Blake's response to that question is only indirect, and it involves "remobilizing the troops" and attempting to "cope" with the actual views of the public. Her earlier articles set forth two distinct political possibilities which cannot be appraised as anything other than practical political judgments concerning the best means of effecting social change and deciding what social change is desirable.

> P_1: Society should aim at the creation of a really free marketplace within which men and women, rich and poor, can receive an equitable opportunity to pursue those "lifetime rewards" which give meaning to their lives and which they value most highly.[12]

Social policy should find means for relieving coercion and for allowing lifestyles "different from marriage and parenthood to find free and legitimatized expression." Basic changes in the social organization of reproduction should lift penalties for antinatalist behavior rather than "create" new ways of life. Such antinatalist behavior already exists among us as "part of our covert and deviant culture, on the one hand, and our elite and artistic culture, on the other."

> P_2: In some instances (including racial desegregation in the public schools and the provision of elective abortion) policy should be formed by taking into account "the more positive views of a powerful minority" even if these views are then approved by only a small fraction of the members of the society.[13]

"We must bear in mind that changes far more radical than this one (the provision of elective abortion) have been effected lawfully by such minorities, even when the issues enjoyed no more public support than currently exists for elective abortion." In this instance we must look, she wrote in 1971, to the "educated and inflential . . . in spite of conservative opinions among important sub-groups such as the lower classes and women."

Blake's third hypothesis expresses the tension inherent in such combinations of liberal political philosophy and elitist theories of social change.

> H_3: To most Americans the potential gain in convenience for a few is not sufficient compensation for the probable loss of a sense of

meaning for the many, should sexual behavior and reproduction become a matter of increasing legal indifference.[14]

The cogency of this third hypothesis raises the possibility that the decision handed down by the Official Decider of the United States in January of 1973 could exact a greater social cost than its proponents admit. This leads us directly to the consideration of the decision handed down by another Official Decider in February of 1975.

3. How Many "Official Deciders" Can There Be?

Donald Kommers's discussion of the abortion decisions taken by the United States Supreme Court and by the West German Federal Constitutional Court identifies a striking divergence of opinion on the part of these two Official Deciders. The American decision, handed down in January 1973, permits abortion through the twenty-fourth week of pregnancy. Justice Blackmun wrote that the states have no legitimate interest in the regulation of abortion through the first twelve weeks of pregnancy but that the interest of the mother's health may be protected by state regulations concerning abortions performed from the twelfth through the twenty-fourth week so long as the regulations do not prohibit abortions altogether. After the twenty-fourth week, a state may proscribe abortion in the interest of the "potential life" of the viable fetus, except where appropriate medical judgment finds abortion necessary for the preservation of the life and health of the mother. The decision eschewed the question of the starting point of human life but did decide that the fetus is not a "person" within the protection of the Fourteenth Amendment to the United States Constitution.

The West German decision, taken in February 1975, differs in almost every major particular. Finding "developing life" in the womb from the fourteenth day of pregnancy, the German court rejected the attempt to assign a variable value to that life on the basis of the traditional medical division of pregnancy into three trimesters and held instead that abortion is *not* morally or legally permissible under *ordinary circumstances at any* stage in pregnancy after the fourteenth day. However, the German decision attaches no penalty to abortions performed during the first twelve weeks of pregnancy just in case the pregnancy falls under any one of three categories of special conditions: "medical indications": to preserve the life and health of the mother; "eugenic indications": to avert the birth of a seriously defective child; and "ethical indications": to terminate a pregnancy caused by sexual assault. Finally, the West German decision gave lower courts discretionary authority to withhold criminal sanctions under circumstances where abortion was the only means of averting grave hardship for the prospective mother. In this last class of situations, however, the German Federal Constitutional Court mandated a system of counseling which must positively admonish, encourage, and even assist (via appropriate programs of social welfare) the prospective mother to preserve and protect the developing life within her womb.

The juxtaposition of the papers by Blake and Kommers raises the interesting possibility that the decision of the German Court more nearly reflected current American opinion concerning abortion than did the decision of the American Court. Blake finds that disapproval of elective abortion hovers around 55 percent among the American public, but the Supreme Court permits and the Federal Constitutional Court disallows elective abortion. Again, American public opinion—by a substantial majority (67 percent)—would limit abortion to the first trimester of pregnancy and find the starting point of human life at some point no later than the end of the twelfth week of pregnancy. In both respects, the decision of the German Federal Court matches American public opinion more closely than do the conclusions of *Roe* and *Doe*. In one interesting and crucial respect, however, we are uninformed about the likely American reaction to the details of the German decision: the requirement of positive counseling and welfare assistance in instances where abortion is putatively the only means of averting grave social hardship for the prospective mother. The discussants at the Notre Dame conference (particularly Morris Janowitz) were not optimistic concerning the likelihood that the welfare system in the United States, generally perceived as already overloaded, could accept an additional burden of such magnitude at this time.

Kommers criticizes the opinions of Justice Blackmun in *Roe* and *Doe*, finding them wanting in clarity, cogency, and even consistency. Nevertheless, he finds that these decisions can be *explained* (in part) as consistent with the individualistic ethic lying at the heart of the conventional Madisonian reading of the American Constitution. Blackmun's appeal to a right of privacy to be found in the Fourteenth and the Ninth Amendments may be lacking in probity, but Kommers finds it aiming at the same value served by recent court decisions concerning legislative reapportionment ("one man, one vote") and putatively defamatory speech ("free market in ideas"). Courts in the United States allow great latitude to speech criticizing public officials, requiring that a suit for slander or libel meet the stern standard of proving defamatory intent. Consequently, the applicable standards in the "free market of ideas" permit wide variation from the ascertainable truth and protect the autonomy of individual speech as a first priority. This individualistic ethic may lessen the significance of intermediate agencies or institutions, e.g., the family, which stand between the individual and general legal institutions of the state, but its adherents are willing to pay this price in order to secure the widest possible latitude for individual discretion in speech and action. This *explanation* of *Roe* and *Doe* is not an *appraisal* or an evaluation of those decisions.

Both Kommers and Blake note the recent strong shift in elite opinion concerning abortion and the successful articulation, by powerful spokesmen from the legal and medical professions, of a liberal rationale for discretionary or elective abortion. This rationale alludes to the great social cost of strict laws which increase the difficulty of obtaining an abortion or even prohibit them altogether except in relatively infrequent circumstances. The cost of such strict laws is sometimes quantified in terms of the mortality and morbidity incurred by illegal abortions frequently performed under septic conditions or the many tragic consequences which may follow from carrying an unwanted pregnancy to term. The cost of permissive laws, on the other hand, is either very easy or next to impossible to calculate. The social cost of laws permitting elective abortion is easy to calculate and terrible to consider on the stipulation that every abortion involves the death of a human being. If this stipulation is not granted, the cost of permissive laws falls along dimensions that are nearly impossible to submit to objective measurement. How could one possibly calculate the "probable loss of a sense of meaning for the many, should sexual behavior and reproduction become a matter of increasing legal indifference"? Blake's data support the view that the more democratic procedures of American legislatures, in contrast to judicial review, were unlikely to legitimate social changes promoting alternative "antinatalist" styles of life, even during a period of peak concern for limiting the growth of the American population. However, her anticipation of the realization of "lifetime rewards" equal in satisfaction to those of marriage and parenthood, once the social penalties for "antinatalist" behavior are reduced or erased, is plausible. She and Kommers agree that the American judicial elite can invoke a legitimate tradition of constitutional interpretation in moving to promote social change which enlarges the sphere of individual liberty.

But Kommers finds the German decision intelligible and proper within a traditional "legal culture" which aims at the strict interpretation of a constitution which requires that other values must be weighed and balanced with the freedom of individual action. Such values include the inviolable dignity of human life, born and unborn, a dignity which is understood as "no more contingent on a human being's consciousness of it than on his physical ability to preserve it." Kommers insists that the articulation of this value is the result of a completely secular effort literally to reconstruct the intention of the framers of the constitution of the German Federal Republic and that in making it the majority of the Constitutional Court deliberately prescinded from all considerations of the "felt necessities" of the time as well as from all theological disputation.

Kommers's article raises a basic question for Pincoffs's account of the role of an Official Decider, a question—it must be added—which is at least as pressing and difficult for the comparative constitutionalist as for the philosopher. Is there any means of deciding among alternative Deciders? Does the difficulty or impossibility of designating a set of necessary and sufficient criteria for membership in the human species tell against the decision that "life in the sense of the historical existence of a human individual exists according to definite biological-physiological knowledge in any case from the 14th day after conception," favored by the majority of the German court? Are any procedures, whether they are the exclusive instruments of an educated elite or the general possessions of the mass of mankind, relevant for a decision concerning the comparative merits of the American and the German abortion decisions? If both the German and the American courts can be cast in the role of Official Deciders, we need some further account of what it is that such Deciders decide.

4. Abortion and the Question of Civil Rights

Given the importance of these questions, it is difficult to accept an explication which makes the numerical size of the class of human beings a function of court judgments which can vary from one jurisdiction to the next. Roger Wertheimer's analysis is more radical.[15] On his account, 'the fetus is a human being', is the crucial thesis in dispute: denied by the liberal pro-abortion faction, and affirmed by the conservative anti-abortion faction. He finds it impossible to assign *any* truth value (true, false, or an intermediate indication of probable truth) to that thesis. The human status of the fetus is the decisive issue in the abortion dispute since there is no morally acceptable way of arguing that a fetus, or even a fully conscious normal adult human being, either possesses or fails to possess some property, other than humanity itself, which makes it permissible or impermissible to kill it. Expressions such as the "family of man" or the "brotherhood of man" are drained of moral significance when it is implied that status as a brother or as a member of a family must be assigned on the basis of graded properties or even achieved by passing tests of some kind.

Wertheimer takes a critical look at the putative analogy between the abortion dispute and historical controversies centering on efforts by some race or clan of human beings to enslave some other race or clan of human beings. He finds that the slave maker attempted to justify slavery by denying the human status of the slave. Such denial of human status to members of the human species may be *explained* as the outcome of a complex set of contingencies, a "form of life" which reinforced the self-justifying rationale of the slave makers. Self-justifying pictures of institutions which enslave and falsely deny the human status of human beings are explained, Wertheimer thinks, by the slave maker's failure to develop a set of natural, normal, and healthy responses to members of the enslaved class or clan. Such failures are difficult to overcome since the errors involved are not simply errors of reasoning and often permeate the slave maker's style of life and social institutions. But the failures are *not justifiable,* and they are not incorrigible. This does not mean that racism can be obliterated, but it does mean that racists and slave makers can be shown to be responsible and morally at fault for their failure to accord human status to their victims.

On just this basis, Wertheimer denies the analogy—so frequently appealed to by both sides in the abortion dispute—between the controversies associated with abortion and those associated with slavery and racial bigotry. The controversies are alike insofar as the human status of a class of entities is in dispute but unlike insofar as the dispute *can be resolved* in one case but *not* the other. As he puts it, our "natural relations" with the fetus are extremely limited, with the consequence that any alleged "natural response" to the fetus is correspondingly unspecifiable. The basic argument or rationale advanced by each side in the abortion dispute is the exact opposite or inverse of that advanced by the other. More importantly, these arguments are of equal value, with one side stressing the obvious continuity of the process of embryological development while the other stresses the equally obvious disparity of the initial and final stages of that same process.

Judith Blake's interpretations of public opinion on abortion and the starting point of human life suggest that such opinion has roots in a complex of institutions, norms, and satisfactions which give meaning to widely differing styles of life. This implies that attitudes concerning the fetus and abortion are not simple functions of the limited set of possible relations between an adult human and a fetus. These attitudes are also influenced by the value assigned to lifestyles centered on child rearing and the family. As noted before, this interpretation raises the possibility of a serious social cost associated with the liberalization of abortion laws: "the probable loss of a sense of meaning for the many should sexual behavior and reproduction become a matter of increasing legal indifference." Blake would balance this cost by fostering social change which would remove what she sees as a prevailing set of penalties for antinatalist behavior.

In any case, it seems unlikely that attitudes toward abortion and the fetus are determined only by adult-fetus relationships, and likely that adult-family and adult-child relationships are also influential, as Wertheimer seems to acknowledge in his discussion of the importance of family relationships. These latter relations, in their turn, are embedded in a wide range of social, economic, and political institutions. Consequently, as Wertheimer would agree, it is difficult to take a first self-report of attitudes concerning the fetus and abortion at face value. Moreover, it follows that the economic, political, and social overlay which for so long clouded the central issue of slavery and racial bigotry, is still in place—unanalyzed and unappraised—so far as the abortion controversy is concerned.

There are still other leads to follow. Consider the results of a recent Gallup Poll (March 1976) concerning an anti-abortion constitutional amendment.[16] (See Table 2). The amendment described in the poll would take abortion laws in this country back to the position typical of most American states prior to the 1960s: It would prohibit abortions except when the mother's life is in danger. The hypothetical amendment alluded to in the poll had none of the subtleties of the model code embodied in the 1968 Georgia legislation overturned by *Doe* v. *Bolton*. Yet those *opposed* to the amendment amounted to no more than a 4 percent *plurality* with 6 percent undecided. Even more puzzling is the picture the poll provides of the liberal opponents of the amendment: The groups most strongly opposed are male, white, college educated, with an income of $20,000 or more, and employed in professional or administrative positions; in contrast, those groups exhibiting strongest support for the amendment are women, nonwhite, grade- and high-school educated, with incomes of less than $5,000 per year, and either manual laborers or not in the labor force. To put all this another way, it is as if those who were incurring the putatively unbearable social cost of strict abortion laws were most anxious to restore those laws to the full force they enjoyed prior to *Roe* and *Doe*.

This has the impact of a plebiscite in which slavery is supported by slaves by margins hovering around five to four, while slave owners support abolition by a greater margin, nearly three to two. These data suggest that the same individuals who presumably incur the heaviest costs when abortion is legally prohibited also express the strongest *verbal disapproval* of legalized abortion. Judith Blake explained a comparable distribution of attitudes concerning federal subsidies for the *distribution of contraceptives* to women on welfare (women of lower economic status are less in favor of such subsidy than men and women

TABLE 2
RESULT OF NATIONAL GALLUP POLL OF OPINION ON AN ANTI–ABORTION CONSTITUTIONAL AMENDMENT
(in percentages)

Question: A constitutional amendment has been proposed which would PROHIBIT abortions except when the pregnant woman's life is in danger. Would you favor this amendment which would prohibit abortions, or would you oppose it?

	NATIONWIDE			WOMEN			MEN		
	Favor	Oppose	No Opinion	Favor	Oppose	No Opinion	Favor	Oppose	No Opinion
NATIONAL	45	49	6	48	47	5	42	50	8
Sex									
Male	42	50	8	—	—	—	—	—	—
Female	48	47	5	—	—	—	—	—	—
Race									
White	44	50	6	46	49	5	41	52	7
Nonwhite	51	37	12	57	36	7	43	38	19
Education									
College	30	65	5	32	61	7	28	69	3
High School	49	46	5	51	45	4	47	45	8
Grade School	56	31	13	60	33	7	51	30	19

Region								
East	43	51	6	41	54	5	46	47	7
Midwest	52	42	6	58	38	4	46	46	8
South	49	42	9	51	43	6	46	42	12
West	29	67	4	36	60	4	20	76	4
Age								
Total Under 30	38	57	5	41	55	4	34	60	6
18–24 years	38	59	3	41	58	1	34	61	5
25–29 years	39	53	8	42	49	9	35	57	8
30–49 years	43	50	7	43	51	6	43	49	8
50 & older	52	41	7	56	39	5	46	44	10
Income								
$20,000 & over	37	60	3	38	59	3	37	60	3
$15,000–$19,999	43	51	6	50	46	4	37	56	7
$10,000–$14,999	48	45	7	48	45	7	48	45	7
$ 7,000–$ 9,999	44	48	8	44	52	4	43	44	13
$ 5,000–$ 6,999	47	48	5	48	46	6	46	50	4
$ 3,000–$ 4,999	55	32	13	59	33	8	50	28	22
Under $3,000	50	43	7	58	41	1	32	47	21
Politics								
Republican	48	47	5	54	42	4	41	53	6
Democrat	48	44	8	48	46	6	46	43	11
So. Democrat	54	36	10	—	—	—	—	—	—
Other Democrat	44	48	8	—	—	—	—	—	—
Independent	39	56	5	41	54	5	36	59	5
Religion								
Protestant	46	48	6	49	46	5	43	50	7
Catholic	52	42	6	54	42	4	51	41	8

Question: A constitutional amendment has been proposed which would PROHIBIT abortions except when the pregnant woman's life is in danger. Would you favor this amendment which would prohibit abortions, or would you oppose it?

	NATIONWIDE			WOMEN			MEN		
	Favor	Oppose	No Opinion	Favor	Oppose	No Opinion	Favor	Oppose	No Opinion
Occupation
Professional & Business	33	63	4	36	60	4	30	67	3
Clerical & Sales	45	51	4	44	50	6	46	51	3
Manual Workers	47	46	7	50	46	4	44	46	10
Nonlabor Force	50	41	9	54	38	8	45	45	10
City Size
1,000,000 & over	38	56	6	37	58	5	40	54	6
500,000–999,999	38	54	8	39	56	5	37	53	10
50,000–499,999	45	49	6	50	44	6	40	54	6
2,500–49,999	43	48	9	49	48	3	37	47	16
Under 2,500, Rural	53	41	6	57	38	5	49	44	7
Marital Status
Married	47	47	6	49	46	5	44	49	7
Single	40	52	8	45	50	5	34	54	12
Have children under 18	47	48	5	49	47	4	46	48	6
Have *no* children under 18	43	49	8	47	47	6	38	52	10

of higher economic status) by postulating a corresponding concentration of "lifetime rewards" for women of lower economic status in the activities of bearing and rearing children. However, economic status seems to account for an *even greater* portion of the variance in expressed attitudes concerning legalized *abortion*. While Blake has inferred that comprehensive social change in the direction of more equitable distribution of "lifetime rewards" would be more effective than the free distribution of *contraceptives* to women on welfare in reducing the burden of "unwanted pregnancy" for these women, this same inference remains untested in the context of efforts to decriminalize and subsidize *abortion*.

5. The Difference Between What I Say and What I Do: Opinion and Behavior

Response to the possibility or reality of abortion does not always take the form of *verbal* reply to a clear and carefully articulated question asked but once. William Liu points to different sorts of social fact: global trends toward the decriminalization of abortion and rising numbers of abortions sought and actually obtained. Within the last twenty-five years, abortion laws throughout the world have been liberalized so that fewer than 25 percent of the world's population live in countries where technically restrictive abortion laws are strictly enforced. At least two of every ten pregnancies is now terminated by abortion, and as many as one in every seven women of reproductive age in the United States has terminated at least one pregnancy by voluntary abortion. Apparently, these women are burdened neither by personal guilt nor by significant social stigma in consequence of obtaining an abortion. (Since this volume contains no analysis of the social context of the abortion decision by the West German Federal Court, the reader should take particular note of the data concerning the West German Federal Republic in Tables 2 and 3 of the article by William Liu.)

The massive social forces which either prevent incestuous relationships or stigmatize and penalize them when they occur set a standard, Liu argues, against which to measure the erosion of forces once aligned in support of the prohibition of abortion. In this context, the social system supporting the ethical prohibition of abortion seems gradually to have been reduced to a one-dimensional claim concerning the humanity of the fetus and to have both the strengths and the weaknesses of the isolated assertion that the fetus is a human being. As he points out, however, behavior risking or aborting an unwanted pregnancy is by no means one-dimensional but instead reflects *all* the basic conditions of life: "birth, marriage, death, food, disease, material possessions, housing, work, the desire to improve one's lot, and one's relationship to God and nature." Behavior which risks an unwanted pregnancy may indicate a strong attachment to the experience of being "swept away" by putatively unanticipated or irresistible romantic compulsions. Or it may reflect a cautious view of the undesirable side effects of some of the most readily available and convenient contraceptives. Or it may reflect a still deeper psycho-social preference for *stopping,* rather than *preventing,* the processes of conception and gestation. Other social or economic factors may be involved in the explanation of the *termination* of pregnancy by voluntary abortion: the desire to appear to conform to the norm of sexual exclusivity expected in marriage, a stronger preference for a social role other than parenthood, the desire to avoid economic hardship, and so on.

At present, the normative dimensions of behavior which risks or aborts unwanted pregnancy seem indefinite or conflicted, and the role played by various human values seems either *transitional* or *plural* in some deep sense which militates against the possibility of a moral consensus concerning abortion. Liu points to a possible cost associated with the discrepancy between what we say and what we do concerning abortion, and with the conflict between the various opinions, attitudes, and actions which make up the social response to the realities of sexual behavior, marital norms, ideal family size, population growth, and abortion.

Alasdair MacIntyre has suggested that the dilemma concerning abortion can be expressed in terms of two equally valid but incommensurable arguments:

> 1a. I cannot will that my mother should have had an abortion when she was pregnant with me, except perhaps if it had been certain that the embryo was dead or gravely damaged. But if I cannot will this in my own case, how can I consistently deny to others the right to life that I claim for myself? I would break the so-called Golden Rule, unless I denied that a mother had in general a right to an abortion.
> 2b. Everybody has certain rights over his or her own body. To establish such rights we need merely to show that it cannot be shown that anyone else has a right to interfere with the implementation of our own desires about our bodies. It follows that at the stage when the embryo is essentially part of the mother's body, the mother has a right to make her own uncoerced decision on whether she will have an abortion or not. Since she has a moral right, she ought also to have a legal right.[17]

MacIntyre holds that there is "no argument available, no criterion available, no rational procedure to decide between [the] rival and incompatible conclusions of these arguments." He thinks that a "liberal, pluralist moral culture," such as our own, will necessarily be confronted with incommensurable moral claims which cannot be adjudicated without requiring truly tragic sacrifice on the part of one or both contending parties. In his view, our plural culture offers no solution to the tragic "conflict of right with right" embodied in the abortion question, and "what matters most in a period in which human life is tragic is to have the strength to resist false solutions."[18]

Liu's account of the social realities of liberalized abortion laws and the extensive resort to voluntary abortion is not intended, as I read it, to suggest a solution for the moral dilemma posed by MacIntyre. Liu criticizes theologians, philosophers, and historians for dealing with abortion in an artificially simple context. But he certainly *does not* hold that an ethical dispute can be resolved by tabulating the frequency with which certain opinions and actions occur in a society. He just as obviously *does* think that the problem of abortion is seriously oversimplified if the decision to seek and obtain an abortion is automatically labeled "deviant" and "explained" merely in terms of vice or human weakness. Liu's approach to social reality generalizes the Confucian principle that harmony between the political state and the ethical order is requisite for a good society. This principle leads him to formulate the problem of abortion in terms of a social system whose elements are in balance or equilibrium so that the system as a whole operates to minimize the risk that an individual within the system will deviate from the system norms, whatever they may be.

> If abortion is wrong under all and any circumstances, then we must carefully study all and any of the circumstances under which violation of the principle may occur; and the system itself must be prepared to invoke a set of regulatory mechanisms to prevent certain conflict situations from occuring too often, lest constant repeated pressures become too burdensome for the system to bear. In the short run, such pressures may create deviant styles of response on the part of its membership. If the number of overt violations is small, the strength of the system can handle [them]. . . . In the long run, however, the system must undergo structural modification or it will break down and collapse. In the case of the absolute standard of abortion ethics, the system can be weakened considerably as is now the case, yet still maintain outward operational viability, although at a very high cost.[19]

He does regard the social realities of liberalized abortion laws and the extensive resort to voluntary abortions as evidence of the current weakness of the social system which putatively supports an absolute prohibition of abortion. But the identification of a structural weakness in a social system which gives significance and force to a particular social norm may have positive as well as negative significance for that system and its other norms. Negatively, his critique calls into question the utility of simply *reiterating* the ethical prohibition of abortion as homicide. Ample evidence indicates that if such reiteration is sufficiently graphic it may gain increased assent, measurable both in surveys of public opinion and in elections or plebiscites. Nevertheless, the countervailing pressures to risk and to abort unwanted pregnancies are *not* reduced by such advertising campaigns. They remain untouched and continue to cause personal and social conflict and suffering, and to threaten the stability of personal and social relationships. Positively, his approach leaves open the possibility of reviving those "regulatory mechanisms" which might reduce resort to abortion. Such an effort would require a thorough reconsideration of the basic social institution of the family and its social, economic, religious, and political underpinnings. Finally, Liu assumes that human social behavior cannot be systematically and rationally modified unless it has been comprehensively and accurately described and explained. He does not pretend to set the goals of social and moral change. He does *not* set an agenda for the social engineer. The impasse identified by MacIntyre remains. If this book finally offers no solution to the problem of abortion, at least it offers no false solution.

6. Philosophy, Sociology and Comparative Constitutional Law

It should now be obvious that there are many points of contact between the current work by philosophers, social scientists and legal scholars on the problems of abortion. The relationship, however, is not merely one of relevance. No one of these disciplines can do an adequate job of understanding or appraising abortion as a set of social problems unless it makes full and cogent use of the opportunities for interdisciplinary cooperation.

The reasons for this insistence upon the necessity of interdisciplinary cooperation are developed and discussed at greater length by David Solomon in the book's penultimate chapter, and they are reiterated more succinctly in its final chapter. Those readers who are not professional students of philosophy ought to take particular note of Solomon's discussion of recent and radical shifts in the goals and methods of moral philosophers. The full significance of the papers by Pincoffs and Wertheimer which appear in this volume may be missed if those papers are not seen in the context, provided by Solomon, of current philosophical literature on abortion and comparable topics. One of the larger obstacles to effective interdisciplinary communication is bound up in the task of sketching the background literature with sufficient clarity so that it can be understood by someone not trained in the discipline. Particularly with subjects as compelling and complex as abortion, an author's energy may be entirely devoted to the statement of *his* evidence, *his* analysis, and *his* conclusions. But since these statements are ordinarily directed to an audience of professional and disciplinary peers, those who do not enjoy such status may find it heavy going. As Solomon notes, this difficulty was most pronounced, at the Notre Dame conference at least, for the nonphilosophers who attempted critical response to the contributions by Pincoffs and Wertheimer. Solomon points out an effective means for alleviating this difficulty.

Finally, in order to more sharply express my own sense of the integral interconnection of the work by philosophers, sociologists, and comparative constitutionalists on this subject, I would like to offer several concluding remarks to complete this introduction.

The selection and sequential arrangement of the chapters in this volume reflect an editorial decision *to emphasize and clarify the differences* among three key disciplines involved in expert discussion of public policy on abortion: sociology, comparative constitutional law, and philosophy. Taken in isolation, each of these disciplines fails to ask questions of crucial relevance for the real political phenomenon of public policy. Berger and Luckman suggest that the special sciences deal only with an abstract and partial "reality," and that it is philosophy which must distinguish that "reality" and the real world in which we live.[20]

No one, however, certainly not Berger and Luckman, considers the academic discipline of philosophy better prepared than its sister disciplines to be the final arbiter of expert advice concerning public policy. It is just in case that 'philosophy' is used in the broader sense of a reflective and dialectical effort to analyze and appraise all modes of inquiry and human action, that anyone who would utilize scientific expertise in the formulation of public policy must accept responsibility for the *philosophical* criticism of their efforts. The participants in the second Notre Dame conference on abortion accepted that responsibility in the discussion sessions of the conference, and this Introduction has sought to throw into sharp relief the more significant differences of expert opinion evident in those discussions.

The sequence of the chapters of this volume does not reflect the division of disciplines in the modern university. Each of the chapters sets questions of great importance for each of the others. If these questions are understood and kept in mind, the significance of each separate contribution is modified. To have grouped the chapters by discipline would have been to obscure these questions and to impute more significance to the traditional division of the disciplines than would be conducive to our effort to chart a new direction for expert contributions to public policy concerning abortion. To summarize, these questions are:

    1. Granted that neither science nor philosophy can construct an objectively valid set of necessary and sufficient conditions for membership in the class of human beings, how can any one social institution (the Court, for instance) decide such an awesome membership question?

    What social facts or principles can be used to appraise decisions concerning membership in the class of human beings?

    2. What do we learn concerning the real status of norms concerning the voluntary termination of pregnancy from the "facts" that as many as two-thirds of us think that the law should limit abortion to the first three months of pregnancy, that as many as one in every seven women of reproductive age in the U.S. has terminated at least one pregnancy by voluntary abortion, and that abortions are obtained as frequently, in proportion to their numbers, by Catholic as by non-Catholic women?

    Do these "social facts" reflect real social norms? If they do not, how can we discover what those norms are?

    3. Can the comparative analysis and appraisal of decisions such as those by the West German Federal Court (1975) and the U.S. Supreme Court (1973, 1976) relate these decisions to real differences in social norms? Is it meaningful to ask if one of them is the "better decision?"

    4. What is to be made of the "fact" that lower-income and minority groups in the United States oppose the legalization of abortion? or that they oppose it more strongly than it is opposed by more privileged groups?

    If the significance of the family as a source of "lifetime rewards" varies as a function of social class so that it provides the greatest rewards to the least privileged members of society, what can justify the initiative of an elite in taking decisions which diminish the family's importance and value as a social institution?

    5. What do we know of the real intentions of those whose diverse roles involve them in permitting, prohibiting, performing, or acquiring abortions?

    What do we know of the means for resolving ethical disputes which cut so deeply across the professional responsibilities of the judiciary, the legislature, and those responsible for the delivery of health care, and which at the same time involve potentially tragic personal decisions for or against giving birth?

The following chapters point to answers to some of these questions, and the three editors have summarized the results in a closing discussion of our conclusions. These conclusions, it should be noted, take the form of an agenda for further research and discussion concerning a new direction for public policy on abortion.

NOTES

1. In 1970, Daniel Callahan emphasized and illustrated the multidimensional character of the problems of abortion in *Abortion: Law, Choice and Morality* (New York: Macmillan, 1970). Equally important, although less attentive to sociological considerations, was *The Morality of Abortion: Legal and Historical Perspectives,* ed. John T. Noonan, Jr. (Cambridge: Harvard University Press, 1970). Also see *The Abortion Experience,* ed. H. and J. Osofsky, (New York: Harper & Row, 1973).

The subject has received a surge of attention from philosophers in recent years. A number of journal articles are anthologized in three books: J. Feinberg, ed., *The Problems of Abortion* (Belmont, California: Wadsworth, 1973): M. Cohen, T. Nagel, and T. Scanlon, eds., *The Rights and Wrongs of Abortion* (Princeton, N.J.: Princeton University Press, 1974); Robert L. Perkins, ed., *Abortion: Pro and Con* (Cambridge, Mass.: Schenkman Publishing Co., 1974).

2. Recently published studies suggest that abortion "may be safe enough to equate with the pill or any other contraceptive as a routine method of birth control." See Patricia Ashdown-Sharp, "Study Discounts Risk in Abortion," *Chicago Sun-Times,* February 15, 1976, p. 3; "Abortion Last Resort, Safest Option," *Chicago Sun-Times,* February 16, 1976, p. 22 reporting an article published in *Family Planning Perspectives* 8 (January-February 1976): 6–14, "Mortality Associated with the Control of Fertility," by Christopher Tietze, John Bongaarts, and Bruce Shearer. Ashdown-Sharp asserted that the computer model of mortality associated with fertility control described by Tietze et al. "raises the politically explosive question of whether women in any numbers may wish to rely on abortion, as their preferred means of birth control instead of using it as a last resort when other methods fail."

Kristin Luker, *Taking Chances: Abortion and the Decision Not to Contracept* (Berkeley: University of California Press, 1975), argues that " 'what everybody knows' about unwanted pregnancy is not necessarily so." Her study is based on the clinical records of 500 users of an abortion clinic in northern California and upon in-depth, semistructured interviews with 50 of those women. She analyzes the decision to risk and to abort unwanted pregnancies in cost-benefit terms (Chapter 3, "The Costs of Contraception," and Chapter 4, "The Benefits of Pregnancy") and concludes that "the reality of the situation . . . is that the costs associated with contraception are often so high that abortion becomes *de facto* the only acceptable method of fertility control for many women" (p. 143). In conclusion she makes several policy recommendations. On the one hand, "since abortion has become a primary method of fertility control, it should be offered and subsidized in exactly the same way that other contraceptive services are" (p. 144). On the other (p. 147):

> This does not mean, however, that we are ready to argue that abortion should be popularized as one of several equally acceptable methods of

fertility control, with the same techniques used to encourage women to get abortions as are now used to encourage them to use contraception. Although the actual delivery of abortion necessarily reflects its present status as a major method of fertility control, it is not clear that this necessarily means we should make an ideological commitment to it as a long-term method, or that we should abandon research into better contraceptives with lower social costs for both men and women. In Chapter 6, for example, we demonstrated the magnitude of the unexpected social "spinoff" brought about by widespread use of the pill. What the social and technological spinoffs of abortion as a socially preferred method of fertility control are, we can only speculate.

The political volatility of the subject of abortion seems likely to increase as the implications of studies such as those by Tietze and Luker become more generally known and efforts to retard or accelerate the trends they describe are more fully mobilized.

3. The evidence concerning the saliency of the issue in electoral politics is not decisive. In the recent Democratic presidential primary in Massachusetts only 7 percent of the voters said it was an important consideration in deciding their vote, and of those about 40 percent voted for the right-to-life candidate, Ellen McCormack, according to a *New York Times*–CBS poll (*New York Times*, March 4, 1976, 18:3). In the Massachusetts primary Mrs. McCormack received 18,447 votes, or 3 percent of those cast for Democratic candidates (*New York Times*, March 1, 1:8); she received 9 percent of the Democratic votes in the Vermont primary (*New York Times*, March 3, 1976, 17:1); and 1 percent of those cast in the New Hampshire Democratic primary (*New York Times*, March 1, 1976, 28:3). While this strongly suggests the issue has low saliency, the complexity of Presidential primary campaigns makes it difficult to determine its impact upon individual candidates without much more careful analysis. For a brief argument that Ellen McCormack's poor showing in the New England primaries has damaged the growing political significance of the pro-life movement, see Gerhard A. Brandmeyer, "Politics and Abortion," *America*, July 1, 1976, pp. 432–33.

4. While the positions of the U.S. Catholic bishops and various "pro-life" organizations are difficult to distinguish and are often regarded as comprising only one position, important differences of principle and of political action are involved.

For example, in April 1976, the U.S. Senate voted 47–40 to kill by tabling a proposal by Senator Jesse Helms (R–N.C.), to amend the Constitution to ascribe a right to life to every human individual from the moment of fertilization. This proposal was seen as prohibiting all abortion, including that deemed necessary to safeguard the life of the mother (*New York Times*, April 29, 1976, 35:4). The Helms proposal has been supported by the U.S. Coalition for Life. National Right to Life, Inc., supports a differently worded amendment which does not identify the starting point of human life and which would permit abortion to save the life of the mother.

In contrast, the Catholic bishops' *Pastoral Plan for Pro-Life Activities* specifically avoids endorsement of specific wording for a pro-life amendment to the Constitution (*New York Times*, November 21, 1975, 19:2). Instead, the bishops have put forward four principles which, in their view, should be reflected in a pro-life amendment.

1. Establish that the unborn child is a person under the law in terms of the Constitution from conception on.
2. The Constitution should express a commitment to the preservation of life to the maximum degree possible. The protection resulting therefrom should be universal.
3. The proposed amendment should give the states the power to enact enabling legislation and to provide for ancillary matters such as record-keeping, etc.
4. The right to life is described in the Declaration of Independence as "unalienable" and as a right with which all men are endowed by the Creator. The amendment should restore the basic constitutional protection for this human right to the unborn child.

See National Conference of Catholic Bishops, *Documentation on Abortion and the Right to Life, II* (United States Catholic Conference, 1976), p. 28. These principles were incorporated in testimony given before the subcommittee on civil and constitutional rights of the House Committee on the Judiciary, March 24, 1976, by Archbishop Joseph L. Bernardin and Terence Cardinal Cooke. See *America,* December 27, 1975, pp. 454–55; and *National Catholic Reporter,* December 12, 1975, p. 12; for editorial reaction to the bishops' plan in the Catholic press.

5. R. Gilpin, *American Scientists and Nuclear Weapons Policy* (Princeton University Press, 1962); J. Haberer, *Politics and the Community of Science* (New York: Van Nostrand Reinhold, 1969); V. Gray and E. Bergman, eds. *Political Issues in U.S. Population Policy,* (Lexington, Mass.: D. C. Heath and Company, Lexington Books, 1974); S. S. Blume, *Toward a Political Sociology of Science* (New York: Macmillan, Free Press, 1974); J. Primack and F. von Hippel, *Advice and Dissent: Scientists in the Political Arena* (New York: New American Library, 1976).

6. At the Notre Dame conference, Professor Amelie Rorty of Rutgers University noted quite similar behavior on the part of philosophical disputants of the abortion issue.

> This is an area of impasse, not of argument. We have two parties bristling at the edges of moral indignation, each armed with some arguments. But most of the armament consists of the repetition of the original intuition, suitably disguised as neutral argument. Since there is basic legislation—conceptual as well as legal—at work on both sides, we are dealing with political issues, as well as with philosophic argumentation. Of course astute philosophical politicians must—as all good politicians do—imbed as much neutral argument as they can into their persuasions. But the important work is often done, as we have seen, by the initial fast footwork of using moral indignation, combined with analytic rhetoric, to place the burden of proof firmly on the shoulders of the opposition. Whoever is foolish enough to accept that burden of proof will have up-hill work all the way.

7. In particular, see "Ideology and Positivism: The Setting of the Problem," (unpublished mss. by Alasdair MacIntyre, Department of Philosophy, Boston University).

8. The further decisions of the Supreme Court, published July 1, 1976, are discussed in the Appendix below. In the case of *Singleton* v. *Wulff,* also decided on July 1, 1976, the Court had earlier declined to consider the substantive constitutional issue involved in the denial of Medicaid payments to finan-

cially needy women to cover the costs of abortion where such payments are provided to cover the costs of giving birth (*New York Times,* January 27, 1976, 12:3). In this case, a lower federal appeals court had decided that a Missouri procedure which denied payments to abortion patients while providing them for childbirth violated constitutional guarantees of equal protection under the laws. The Supreme Court decided that the lower federal appeals court had "inappropriately exercised its jurisdiction to resolve the merits of the case when the only issue raised in district court had been the [appellants'] standing to maintain suit." On the procedural issue, the Court decided that "physicians who provide needy patients with elective abortions have standing to assert impairment of their constitutional rights by a Missouri statute that precludes Medicaid reimbursement for abortions that are not 'medically necessary' " (44 LW 5181).

On March 1, 1976, the Supreme Court refused to hear a challenge to a 1973 federal statute (the "Church amendment") that permits federally aided private hospitals to decline to permit abortions and sterilizations on either religious or moral grounds (*New York Times,* March 2, 1976, 1:5).

On April 26, 1976, the Supreme Court turned down New York State's request for a stay pending the appeal of a lower court ruling requiring the state to pay Medicaid benefits for elective abortions (*New York Times,* April 27, 1976, 15:3).

For the Democratic platform, see *The Congressional Record* for July 1, 1976, pp. H7200–7213. The following paragraph concerning abortion was included: "We fully recognize the religious and ethical nature of the concerns which many Americans have on the subject of abortion. We feel, however, that it is undesirable to attempt to amend the U.S. Constitution to overturn the Supreme Court decision in this area" (p. H7204, column b).

The Republican platform, on the other hand, endorsed efforts "to restore protection of the right to life for unborn children" (*New York Times,* August 14, 1976, 18:6).

See UPI account, "Abortion Decision Upheld: Senate Unit Rejects All Proposals," and "Aid Unwed Mothers: Bayh," dated September 17, 1975, and published in the *South Bend Tribune,* September 18, 1975. According to the account, on September 17, 1975, a Senate subcommittee on constitutional amendments, under the chairmanship of Senator Birch Bayh struck down a number of proposals aimed at overturning the Supreme Court rulings on abortion handed down on January 22, 1973. On that same day, Senator Bayh proposed legislation intended to make it easier for unwed pregnant women unwilling to have an abortion to have and to raise their children. United Press International identified the following key elements of Bayh's legislation:

—Set up a nationwide network of 'life support centers' for school-age parents, providing an array of medical, social and counseling services including family planning and adoption services.
—Require insurance companies to offer maternity benefits for single women and for unmarried dependents, thus providing coverage for childbirth where only abortions are now reimbursed, and require that group medical insurance extend to part-time workers.
—Expand part-time employment opportunities and flexible hours so that young mothers can find work rather than relying on welfare.
—Boost federal spending on family planning, maternal health child care, adoption services and nutrition programs.

Senator Bayh decided that his effort to reduce the political cost of his stand against the pro-life amendments was unsuccessful, at least insofar as these costs could be calculated in the midst of the recent presidential primary, see note 3 above. Bayh continues to be critical, on the one hand, of the Catholic bishops' failure to back a specific pro-life amendment and, on the other, of the Helms proposal mentioned in note 4. See *New York Times,* November 21, 1975, 19:2, and April 29, 1976, 35:4.

For references concerning the *Edelin* case, see notes 4 and 5 of the chapter by Judith Blake in the present volume.

Prostaglandin is an abortifacient drug promoting strong contractions of the uterine musculature. Its use and availability figured importantly in the case of *Planned Parenthood* v. *Danforth* discussed in the Appendix below.

For Kristin Luker's book, see note 2 above.

9. J. Blake, "Elective Abortion and Our Reluctant Citizenry," in *The Abortion Experience,* ed., H. D. and J. D. Osofsky (New York: Harper & Row, 1973), pp. 447–67; Blake, "Abortion and Public Opinion: The 1960-1970 Decade," *Science* 171 (1971): 540–49; Blake, "Population Policy for Americans: Is the Government Being Misled?" *Science* 164 (1969): 522–29.

10. J. Blake, "Abortion and Public Opinion," *Science* 171 (1971), 544–45.

11. See Peter Winch, *The Idea of a Social Science* (London: Routledge & Kegan Paul, 1958), and Alasdair MacIntyre, *Against the Self-Images of the Age* (London: Duckworth, 1971), pt. 2.

Compare Judith Blake's and William Liu's contributions to this volume for a sense of the dissimilarity of expressed attitudes (relatively disapproving) toward abortion and the statistical indices of abortions actually performed. For a general discussion of methodological problems associated with empirical research on the correlation of attitudes and action, see John H. Barnsley, *The Social Reality of Ethics: The Comparative Analysis of Moral Codes* (London: Routledge & Kegan Paul, 1972), pp. 131–44.

In periods of fundamental social change a growing tension between traditional norms and experienced preferences might be expected to result in highly ambiguous expressions of opinion, inconsistencies between expressions of opinion and actual behavior, or in vacillating or even self-defeating behavior.

12. J. Blake, "Population Policy for Americans," *Science* 164 (1969): 529.

13. J. Blake, "Abortion and Public Opinion," *Science* 171 (1971): 548.

14. Ibid., p. 545.

15. In addition to his contribution to this volume, see his widely anthologized "Understanding the Abortion Argument," first published in the journal *Philosophy and Public Affairs* no. 1 (1971), but since reprinted in the volumes edited by J. Feinberg, M. Cohen, et al. and cited above in note 1.

16. *The Gallup Opinion Index,* March 1976, p. 20.

17. See MacIntyre's "How Virtues Become Vices: Values, Medicine and Social Context," in *Evaluation and Explanation in the Biomedical Sciences: Proceedings of the First Trans-Disciplinary Symposium on Philosophy and Medicine,* ed. H. Tristram Engelhardt, Jr., and Stuart F. Spicker (Boston: Reidel, 1975), p. 94.

18. Ibid., p. 107.

19. William Liu, discussion at Notre Dame conference, March 1975.

20. P. L. Berger and T. Luckmann, *The Social Construction of Reality* (New York: Doubleday, 1966), pp. 1, 2, ff.

Membership Decisions and the Limits of Moral Obligation

EDMUND L. PINCOFFS

Introduction

Practical philosophy, as I conceive it anyway, is concerned with the grounds for choice. The "problem" of abortion is one that requires that we make a choice, but it is often unclear what choice it is we are supposed to be making, who "we" are, and what roles we are playing at what stage of an unspecified game. Even as we begin to specify, we are in danger of begging questions at issue. If we say, or just assume, that the choice is the mother's alone, then we may concede that there is no place for a prior choice of a practice, institution, or convention that constrains the mother's choice; and we may ignore the choices that must be made by other persons immediately concerned, for example, the doctor's and nurse's choices, the choice of the father, and of the institutional figures who may later be responsible for the nurture and education of the child. If we assume that the choice is of a rule-bound practice within which, or according to which, all persons become role-players bound by the rules, then we may gloss over the mother's freedom to choose within the rules; we may think of the rules as a kind of formula that will give anyone an answer who enters in the appropriate data. And what assumption may we make concerning the interests that are at stake, when the most heated argument is just over whether the "interests" of the conceptus are interests at all, whether it is merely a potential or an actual possessor of interests?

In what follows, since I must start somewhere, my objective will be to clear some ground for a morally defensible consensus concerning the rules that should govern choice of abortion in particular cases. This assumes that there will be moral choices, that there is not just one comprehensive and exceptionless rule: never assent to or perform an abortion. My first task will be to show the moral questionability of such a rule.

Is Abortion Invariably Wrong?

I should first make it clear that I am discussing the proposed adoption of a moral rule. What is meant by this, at least, is that the rule in question is not merely a legal one, even though a moral and a legal rule can require or prohibit the same thing. It is both morally and legally wrong to steal, torture, or swindle. Abortion is legally permissible under certain conditions. The question is whether it is ever morally permissible. I assume that there are no readers or auditors who would out-Hobbes Hobbes in identifying moral with legal permissibility.

I should like to begin by raising a general question that is seldom if ever raised in discussions of abortion. It is whether *any* flat, conditionless prohibition can be *morally* justified. The sort of prohibition I have in mind is a second-level one. A first-level prohibition would be a very general prohibition, like the principle that we should never do to others what we would not have them do to us. First-level prohibitions say nothing about the *sort* of act in question. They contain no descriptive phrases. They are open, formal place-holders. Second-level prohibitions do talk about specific sorts of acts: killing, abortion, deceiving, offending, stealing, and so on. Can flat second-level prohibitions be morally justified? I will argue that they cannot.

Here too we must avoid the begging of questions. We must not define the acts prohibited in such a way that it follows from the meaning of the label given the act that it is morally wrong. In that case it would be analytic, and not illuminatingly so, to hold that the act in question is always morally wrong. It would be like saying that bachelors are always unmarried or that crime is illegal. Wanton killing is by definition a morally unjustifiable act, so of course wanton killing is always morally wrong.

To keep the argument general, let us speak of X-ing, where X is a term that refers to a sort of act that can be described in morally neutral terms. For example, X-ing might be taking another person's property without his permission, making copies of paper currency and using the copies to buy groceries, or promising a person to do something and then not doing what one has promised. Where a second-level principle is expressed by means of a term that begs the question whether the act is wrong, we will substitute a description of the act that is not question begging. Abortion cannot be held to be by definition wrong if we are meaningfully to discuss the moral viability of a flat anti-abortion rule. We must speak, rather, of the act of inducing the premature parturition of a fetus (or of an earlier stage: blastocyte, fertilized egg) in such a way that the fetus loses its life. The question is whether this act, or succession of acts, is invariably morally wrong.

Let us go back to X-ing. Suppose we grant that there is a valid moral rule that X-ing is always wrong. Then it follows that if I X, then I do wrong. Whatever I do, or whatever situation I find myself in, I may not X. If I do X, then I will have to admit that I have done what is morally wrong, I will be ashamed or feel guilty, I will have a black mark on my moral record, I will be in some way morally deficient. However, suppose there is also a rule that I may never Y. Now, either the rules against X-ing and Y-ing can conflict in a particular situation or they cannot. If they can, then I may have to choose sometime, between X-ing and Y-ing. Whichever way I choose, I will do what is morally prohibited. But at the same time I have the excuse that if I had not X-ed, I would have had to Y. So I can hardly be blamed; it seems wrong to mark up my record; and I may be distressed, but why should I feel ashamed? But, then, what sense remains in the notion that, nevertheless, X-ing is always morally wrong? How can an act be morally wrong for which the actor is not to blame, need not feel ashamed, etc? What does it mean, given *these* qualifications, to say of an act that it is morally wrong?

It follows that if there is more than one second-level moral prohibition, and if these prohibitions may conflict, so that one of them requires an act and the other requires that it not be done, then there is no clear sense to the claim that either prohibition is flat, or conditionless. They condition each other. If they can conflict then a situation may arise in which a choice which prohibition must give way must be made. For it may not be open to the agent to do nothing, or to wait for the problem to go away. Doing nothing may, in fact, itself constitute a violation of a prohibition. We are morally prohibited from being bad Samaritans and jogging right by a man dying by the roadside. But we may be morally required to jog by if we must report for duty in a general disaster.

The supposed conditionless flat moral rule is a secondary rule. It has no pretences, as a primary rule, or moral principle, might, of serving as the *sole* rule in a system of moral rules. The Golden Rule, or some formulation of Kant's Categorical Imperative, might conceivably serve as the sole rule by which a moral agent need be, or should be, guided. But the secondary rules, being descriptively fleshed out, apply only to certain situations. The rule about stealing applies only where there is loose property, the rule about forgery only where it is possible to make false documents or certificates.

Given that there are multiple moral prohibitions, can a code of such prohibitions be formulated that will guarantee that no conflict between prohibitions will arise? Unless there is some way of guaranteeing no conflict, then no rule in the code may be conditionless. True, there may be primary rules designed to resolve conflicts between secondary rules. But then the only exceptionless rule is the primary one. And no primary rule is the prohibition of a certain description of act. But how can we otherwise guarantee that secondary rules will not conflict? Surely advocates of a conditionless moral rule must give us reason to believe that the rule in question will never come into conflict with any other moral rule.

But this does not get us to the bottom of the problem. For there is something suspect in the very notion of a moral rule that has no exceptions. Can we at once be morally responsible agents and be subject to a rule that absolutely prohibits a certain description of act? To be morally responsible is, among other things, to be to blame if one does something morally wrong. Since I may be to blame, I cannot surrender to anyone else, or even to a rule, the decisions for which I must answer. I must protect the freedom I need to consider and reconsider my course of action. But to accept a conditionless prohibition is just to surrender a part of this freedom. For it might happen that later reflection will convince me that there are circumstances in which, given all of the rules that bear on the case, I *should* violate the prohibition.

It may seem as if I am insisting, in the name of moral responsibility, on a kind of loose situationism in which the agent is free to decide each case anew, according to no set standards. But this need not be the conclusion drawn from the insistence that no responsible agent may accept in advance a conditionless prohibition. Rather, the agent may leave it open to himself to reason, by conceding in advance the moral weight of certain considerations and by recognizing that any decisions at which he arrives in the future will have to take those considerations seriously. So, for example, he may decide in advance that he should not kill any human being. But in so deciding, he may tacitly or explicitly recognize that circumstances *could* arise in which he might have to decide whether the fact that he would kill someone is sufficient to overrule a course of action that he is considering, a course of action that is called for by other moral considerations. The agent may recognize that if he is ever to kill another, he must shoulder a very heavy burden of proof. But he may not rule out in advance the very possibility of shouldering that burden. To do so would be to suppose that his present moral judgment, that he should never kill, is in some way superior to all his future moral judgments when, informed by the facts and the other moral considerations that apply, he must decide whether he has a right to kill.

The moral man is indeed rule governed, but the rules are self-imposed ones. It is inconsistent with the notion of a rule that the injunction may be set aside simply at will. But it is inconsistent with the notion of a responsible moral agent that he should be barred from reasoning about a particular case and from judging what it is morally best for him to do in the circumstances. This is the tension that exists, and it must be taken seriously. We have no moral right to legislate it out of existence by the insistence that there are conditionless prohibitions.

More could be said on this theme—in particular, that it is not merely by the adoption of a code of rules that a moral man defines himself. Man may have moral ideals that are better expressed by pointing to moral models or to ideal communities than by any kind of quasi-legislation. To the extent that this is so, there may be tension between the code by which he lives and the ideals he has set for himself. He may see the code as subordinate to the ideal in that it is a set of rules that is best followed if the ideal is to be achieved. Given that this is so, it would seem that the ideal-motivated moral man would be unlikely to agree in advance to a conditionless prohibition, since in a conflict between his ideals and the prohibition, the prohibition would have to give way. This is not to deny that there is a problem of specifying morally permissible and morally impermissible ideals nor to deny that whatever ideals a man might have there are moral bounds that he should respect. But respecting bounds and taking them as beyond the reach of his moral intelligence are different matters.

Back to abortion. If, as a moral agent, one believes that there are moral rules or ideals that could conceivably come into conflict with the prohibition of abortion, then one should not, one does not have the moral right to, legislate in advance what one's course of action would be in all of the situations that may arise in the future. These situations, as moral situations, will be defined most precisely just by specifying the moral considerations pro and con abortion, given the factual circumstances. The person who accepts conditionless prohibitions might be more predictable but only at the cost of neutering himself as an agent in those future situations in which the flat prohibition may need rethinking.

The chief difficulty, then, with the notion of an exceptionless second-level moral prohibition is that it presupposes a faulty conception of moral agency. No moral agent may, by binding himself to such a rule, sacrifice his future right to exercise his moral responsibility by thinking through the implications of a conflict of second-level moral rules. This argument is, I believe, sufficient to show the moral untenability of any exceptionless second-level moral prohibition and thereby the untenability of the rule that one should never assent to or perform an abortion.

It may be useful to put the point differently. There are lots of practical decisions, only some of which are moral. If we say of a person that he has made a moral decision, it always makes sense (as it does not always for other sorts of practical decisions) to ask what his reasons are for the decision he has made. For some practical decisions, as for example to choose butter toffee rather than fudge swirl ice cream in the local Baskin-Robbins, one is under no constraint to support his choice with reasons. At most, he may give the sort of reason that brings the discussion to a halt before it can get underway. He may say that he just likes the taste of toffee better than the taste of fudge. And supposing that there is no difference in the calorie or bacteria count and that nothing matters but taste, that is the end of the discussion. Now a person can cite a moral rule as his reason for doing or not doing something. He can cite the rule that abortions should never be assented to or performed, for example. But if he does cite a rule, gives it as his reason for his moral decision, it is always open to some critic to reply that the question is whether that is the only rule by which he should be guided given the present circumstances. That kind of criticism cannot be ignored by a moral agent. He sacrifices his claim to moral agency to the extent that he refuses to morally justify his decisions; but he does refuse to justify them if he refuses to take seriously the objection that in the case in question there is reason, moral reason, to doubt whether the cited rule should govern. With apologies to Humpty Dumpty, the question is who is to be master, ourselves or the rules. But since it is we, and not the rules, that will be held responsible for the decisions we make in particular cases, we had best not allow the rules to be master. And we couldn't let any one of them be master if we tried, supposing that they can conflict. For then we must take the responsibility of deciding which master to obey and which to disobey.

A consequence of the discussion so far is that arguments to the effect that a rule has been long established or respected are at best indirectly relevant to the agent's moral choice.[1] They show the agent that since there has been general acceptance of the rule over a period of time, there is reason to believe that there are good reasons for adopting it. Not very strong reason, it is true, but some reason. But since the rule in question will presumably not be the only rule that the agent adopts, and conflicts can arise, the argument from past, or general, acceptance of the rule does not govern the decisions the agent should make in particular cases.

Is Abortion Prima Facie Wrong?

Once we recognize that there can be no exceptionless secondary moral rules, the problem of abortion comes into sharper (not sharp) focus. The issue is not whether abortion is in every circumstance wrong, but whether it is *prima facie* wrong, whether the person who orders, undergoes, or performs it must provide a morally acceptable justification, a justification that appeals to other moral considerations. Then the question is what the secondary moral rules are with which abortion may come into conflict.

The claim that abortion is *always* wrong rests on the prior claims that taking the life of an innocent human being is always wrong and that abortion is taking the life of an innocent human being.[2] But if there are no flat secondary moral rules, it is not a flat secondary moral rule that taking innocent human life is wrong.[3] It is *prima facie* wrong; and there are moral rules with which that rule may come into conflict. It may even come into conflict with itself. It may be necessary to take an innocent life (the "baby's") to save an innocent life (the mother's). Anthropological examples abound. Suppose you are an incapacitated Eskimo elder, and it is a bad year for food; your son, according to established custom, takes you out on the ice and leaves you there. Apocalyptic examples may be relevant. You are the hypnotized slave of a madman who has ordered you to release his homemade nuclear bomb on Chicago, and you can't be stopped but by killing you. We need not reach so far, however. Suppose that to avoid crashing into a hospital, the pilot smashes into a small frame house? Or that to avoid loss of the dam and the town, floodwaters must be released, even though fishermen cannot be warned in time? Hard choices must sometimes be faced in which killing must be done to minimize killing. And I do not envy the person his moral complacency who could be sure it would always be wrong to end the life of a person hopelessly ill and in great pain or of a person trapped in a burning wreck and screaming to be put out of his misery.

If I have a right that I not be intentionally killed when innocent of no wrong, it is, like other rights, contingent. It is a right that obtains so long as it is not overridden by other rights that have a stronger claim to be honored in the situation. It is a right that I might myself believe should be overridden in the circumstances or that I would believe should be overridden were I capable of objectivity.

Can it be shown, then, that abortion is *prima facie* wrong? We will assume that killing innocent human beings is *prima facie* wrong. The question, then, is whether abortion is the killing of an innocent human being.

We have reached square one, the question of the humanity of the embryo; but let us pause to assure our right to have moved even that far and to see just where we can go from here.

If embryos are human beings and are innocent (I do not take up *that* question), then, *prima facie*, no one should kill an embryo. It does not follow that no one should, under any circumstances, kill an embryo. It does follow that whoever would kill (or order killed) an embryo must have a moral justification. I will not pursue here the question what that justification might be. It is clear that it cannot consist in an appeal to what one wants, to one's inclinations, whims, or wishes, or to what is convenient. The reason that no such purported justifications will do the work is that such appeals unfairly assume that the rule in question is a rule for others, that they should be restrained by it, but that oneself is a special case—not a morally excluded case but a special case just because the person in question is oneself.

What I do want to say a little about, in the remainder of this paper, is the question what kind of decision it is that a certain class of beings are human beings. The question can be discussed in quite general terms, and it desperately needs putting in some kind of perspective. We can think, not only of the question whether embryos are human beings, but of whether robots, programmed human organisms, highly trained apes, monsters, experimental variations on human organisms, and so forth are human beings. It is a nearly universal assumption in the abortion debate that humanity can be determined on purely descriptive grounds, that once we have established that the being in question is the genetic product of human beings and that it closely resembles human beings, then it is a human being. This is, I believe, an error and the source of limitless confusion. The error consists, I shall argue, in confusing identification of a being as a member of the class of humans with deciding whether a given class of beings shall be included in the class of human beings.

In what follows, I will, in attempting to generalize, and attain perspective on, the question what is a human being, look at classes defined in such a way that the description does not vary significantly: at the class of gorillas or of "men" whose actions are the consequence of signals to brain-implanted receivers, for example. If we think of the "class" of embryos, there might seem to be a special problem, since the description of a developing being will not stay put but changes continually from day to day and month to month. But this is only to say that the "class" has not been adequately specified. What is at issue is whether an embryo at this or that stage of development is a human being; the answer for one stage may be different from the answer for another.

On the Decision that a Class of Beings Is Human

What concerns me, then, is best expressed by the question, "Is *this* (which both seems and does not seem human) a human being?" If the thing or being in question did not *seem* human, and also seems not human, my question would not arise. I presuppose the possession of the word human in our common natural language. The problem is, how, granting that we do have this word and a common understanding of its use, we can make clear to ourselves the grounds on which borderline applications of it may be decided.

By what criteria may the question whether a given individual is human be decided? Are there necessary conditions of being human? Sufficient conditions? Necessary and sufficient? I find these neglected questions intriguing. I shall argue that although there are criteria of humanity, no one of them is either a necessary or a sufficient condition of being human. And I shall suggest a kind of Hobbesian rationale of the criteria of humanity. The position I express here will be opposed not only by those who believe that there are necessary or sufficient conditions of humanity but also by those who believe that there is no rational ground for deciding what is human.

The Scope of the Problem

There are both immediate and prospective practical problems of distinguishing human beings from other things or beings. Immediate problems include, besides natural and induced abortions, monstrous births and the present-day capacity of medical men to keep organisms going in which the brain has been destroyed ("human vegetables"). Prospective problems arise from scientific advances now predictable.

Philosophers once confined their interest in the future status of humanity almost wholly to the question whether machines could think, i.e., calculate, remember, imagine, perceive, use language—in short, whether we could regard machines as human or as 'persons.' But there are other advances, now recognized by philosophers, which also raise questions about the borderlines of humanity. Biologists may learn to control hereditary characteristics. Problems could then be raised which might not be in principle beyond those of Dr. Frankenstein's but would be subject to more subtle variations. There are other possibilities, however, with which Dr. Frankenstein did not have to cope. From experiments on animals, it seems sure that there can be "men" who have radio receivers implanted in the brain and who are manipulable by whoever transmits the signals. And once this is achieved, it seems but a step to the programming of the signals, so that we have "men" whose actions seem in every respect normal except that they have been prepared, with Leibnizian glee, in advance.[4]

The general moral and legal importance of clarity concerning the borderlines of humanity cannot be overstated. Philosophers debate the analysis of moral predicates which can, theology excepted, be applied only to humans. Only human beings can have rights and obligations, be just or unjust, saintly or selfish, honest or depraved. Ethical platforms float together to sea unless they have a line on humanity. How do we proceed from common agreement in familiar cases to deal confidently with the humanoid programmed from birth (or decanting)? Can this humanoid own property, adopt children, vote, commit murder, be elected mayor, or make a contract? Can it marry? Is it entitled to education at the public expense?

Criteria of Humanity

We know what it is to raise and debate the question whether something is human, since the problem is old and recurrent; and we know what the leading criteria are to which we may appeal.

(1) One of these is *genetic descent:* that the X in question is a member of the human family, the genetic product of humans.[5] This criterion might seem so powerful as to block out any others; it might seem that if a being has the appropriate genetic ancestry it *must* be human, but this is only trivially so. Of course a human egg fertilized by a human sperm is a human fertilized egg. But it does not follow, unless the question of competing criteria is begged, that this egg is a human being. (a) It can be debated whether monstrous births, including especially parasitic monsters, are human beings. (b) Given the possibility of successful manipulation of nucleic acids, the characteristics of the genetic offspring of a human mother could be made to vary widely. How widely may they swing before the doubt is raised whether the offspring is human? (c) Is a programmed being necessarily human because born to a human mother?

These considerations weigh against the thesis that genetic descent is a sufficient condition of humanity. Is it necessary? Can nothing be human which is synthesized in a laboratory? We can suppose for the sake of argument that it would be indistinguishable in appearance, reactions, and capacities from human beings. To appeal to self-evidence is to stop our ears to a lively debate among philosophers, computer devotees, and, above all, science-fiction fans.

(2) Reflection on this debate might make it appear that *appearance* governs: whatever boasts the appropriate human appearance will qualify as human. But appearance-be-damned arguments will arise, ancestry will be appealed to as well as inappropriate behavior. If the beings speak in clicks and propel themselves by invisibly rapid vibrations of the arms, appearance will not carry the load.

Is it even a necessary support? "There are limits," we want to say. "It can look like an ape or an angel, but not like a stove or a star." To a paralyzed blind man? Why shouldn't a stove be human for him? "But why bring in a democracy of defective percipients? Should the man left only with smell be allowed a vote?" But who is to vote him down, if the stove smells human to him? In Heller's *Catch-22* the soldier-in-white's appearance goes against his humanity and raises doubts. He "was constructed entirely of gauze, plaster, and a thermometer . . . like an unrolled bandage with a hole in it or like a broken block of stone." But the nurses and the Texan believed him human, even though Yossarian demurred.

(3) Suppose our creatures (appearance right) speak German and propel themselves by walking. Check, for *behavior*. But they speak parrot-fashion, fail to avoid obstacles, do not discriminate between trees and persons. Behavior understood as typical bodily movements will not do. It is not a sufficient condition; and spastics and paralytics rule it out as necessary.

(4) What is wrong with speaking parrot-fashion, etc., is that the behavior, though typical, is uninformed by *mind,* it might be argued. Mind, it will be argued, is the criterion of humanity. What has no mind is not human. But what of beings descended from the human family, whose brain has been destroyed by a stroke? The stroke does not exclude them from humanity. It seems that it is of machines and early embryos that we demand mind as an entry-ticket, although we are not sure exactly what the ticket is supposed to look like. Is mind a sufficient condition? Philosophers who argue the question whether a machine can have a mind may believe that whatever has a mind is human, but what seems sensible in general sometimes breaks down in detail. In what sense of "having a mind" does having a mind entail being human? Heeding one's action? Careful machines will then rekindle our debates. Mental capacities? Mental reactions?

(5) Does anyone believe that some set of mental *capacities* like memory, imagination, mathematical ability will warrant anything as human? Let us go to the end of this road immediately, to the robot whose capacities are better than (but not too much better than) par. And his *reactions*. He produces imaginative works, recalls past events, calculates; but also he winces, screams, and flushes appropriately. If we know that he has been fabricated and programmed, the debate is not over. Is this because the robot might not be conscious? Is consciousness the sought criterion?

(6) *Consciousness* is not necessary, clearly enough, or we lose our humanity in sleep. "The capacity to be conscious then!" But how do we decide whether a robot is capable of consciousness if the robot's actions

and introspective reports are not conclusive? And they are not. The appeal to consciousness is a built-in argument against the humanity of robots, not an independent criterion.

An Objection and a Clarification

What I have attempted to do so far is to show that of the ordinarily accepted criteria of humanity, no one criterion appears to be either a necessary or sufficient condition of being human. At this point the following objection might be raised: "You have shown, at best, that no one of the criteria considered is, taken individually, a necessary or sufficient condition of humanity; but this is still a long way from showing that there are no necessary or sufficient conditions. For, to say nothing of the fact that you have no proof that your list of criteria is complete, you have not shown that the conjunction of the criteria you accept (ancestry, appearance, behavior, capacities, and reactions) is not a sufficient condition of humanity. In fact, this is but one of four possibilities which arise when we consider whether the conjunction or disjunction of your criteria could be either a necessary or a sufficient condition of humanity!"

What I have said does, I think, cast doubt on the possibility that the conjunction of criteria mentioned constitutes a necessary condition of humanity. For this would be to say that nothing *could* be human which did not meet *all* of the conditions mentioned, and we have seen reason to doubt this. We have seen how debates could arise over creatures which did not meet this or that criterion but did meet others.

And what I have said also, I think, casts doubt on the possibility that a disjunction of the criteria mentioned constitutes a sufficient condition of humanity. This would be to say that a given creature is human if it meets the requirements of at least one of the five criteria mentioned. But we have seen reasons to doubt whether something meeting any one of these criteria is human, for example whether something which is born of a human mother is, hence, human.

This leaves the possibilities of (1) a disjunction of the criteria mentioned constituting a necessary condition of humanity or (2) a conjunction constituting a sufficient condition. And I would in fact agree that this disjunction and conjunction do constitute a necessary and sufficient condition, respectively, of being human. But it is beyond the scope of this paper to attempt to argue for this position. To deny these two conclusions would be to assert that (1) a thing could be human which did not meet the requirements of *any* of our criteria and (2) a thing could meet the requirements of *all* of the criteria and not be human. The first of these possibilities does not seem to me at all plausible. The second envisages not merely a restriction on humanity which we do not now foresee, something which could perfectly well come about in some dark age behind a not-too-distant 1984, but it requires that this restriction not fall under the heading of ancestry or any of the other factors we have mentioned. It is hard to see what this criterion would be since our criteria are so very general and in the nature of the case seem to cover all questions concerning humanity likely to arise. Yet we have by no means proved that the list of criteria is mutually exclusive; and it is not even clear to me what such a proof would be like.

On the Claim that Something Is Human

To the philosopher who would tie down humanity to a formula, the most we can concede is that nothing can be human unless it either is of human ancestry, or resembles humans, or behaves like a human, or can do what humans can, or reacts like a human; and that anything that does in fact fulfill *all* of these conditions is human. But of course we realize that debates can arise over whether any one of these conditions *is* fulfilled. It is not at all clear how we are to specify what constitutes sufficient resemblance, or where to set the limits of human behavior, for example. In fact, it appears that *the most general characteristic of the concept of humanity is what looks like its systematic elusiveness.* That is, we do not seem to be able to specify in advance any specific way of deciding whether this or that is human. This might lead us to conclude that there is no rational ground for such decisions: that to assert that a creature is human is merely to express fellow-feeling for him, and to elicit a like feeling in others. (I will discuss that possibility later.)

Is it possible to offer a rationale of the criteria to which we appeal in deciding humanity—a connected account which would show not merely the considerations to which we appeal but the reason why we appeal to those considerations? And would such a rationale account for the elusive character of humanity? I think that at least the first, negative steps in such a rationale are reasonably evident.

Let me begin with the obvious but often overlooked question, What difference does it make whether something is human? It makes all the difference. To say that something is not human is to say that it has no place in that community (or arena) in which we hate, love, marry, contract, buy and sell, tax and pay, obligate and excuse. To say that something is human is to acknowledge that its feelings cannot be disregarded, that it enters into the place-swapping calculus of justice, that it is not merely an object with a price and a use. On the principle that future decisions must be consistent with past ones, when we decide that this new, unusual, or insufficiently considered creature is human we decide that the class of creatures meeting this same description is human. Such decisions are, then, of great moment. They must not be confused with *identifications as* human.

We may identify the creature on the raft as human by its shape and movements, and we may drop food accordingly. In the circumstances, our identification is fully warranted. Stanley, trying to find Tarzan among the apes, is not concerned whether Tarzan might *be* an ape; and the scout who identifies a human in the ape horde need only describe what he has seen. A robot might be programmed to identify animals and to identify some animals as human. Where problems of identification arise, they arise over the lack of perceptual evidence. We cannot see the raft clearly enough through the overcast and the spray; the apes hide Tarzan.

In contrast with the identification problem, the decision whether a new or insufficiently considered class is human is more like deciding *how to vote on membership requirements*. Suppose several children are proposed for membership in an organization that has been composed of adults. Collecting information about their ages won't resolve the membership question. The question does not go away when the descriptive facts are in. The seeming elusiveness of humanity comes from confusing identification problems with membership decisions. We cannot move from perceptual evidence to these decisions, but we must take into account circumstances and consequences as well.

Why could we not program a robot to *recognize* human beings? The oddness of this question arises out of the ambiguity in "recognize as human" between "identify as human," and "accord human status to." We have already granted that robots could recognize humans in the first sense; what is wrong with the notion of programming them to recognize humans in the second? To program the robot correctly we would have to know the formula by which we ourselves would vote for or against the humanity of any new creature likely to appear, under any conditions likely to obtain. And we do not know because we do not have such a formula.

Yet it does not follow from this that there are no rational grounds on which membership decisions are made. The grounds are the criteria we have isolated. But what is the ground of these grounds? Here I can only say something negative but something that is, I think, still worth saying. Consider what the consequences would be of abandoning the criterion of humanity in question. Ask whether we would be willing to accept these consequences. If not, we have a reason for retaining the criterion.

Consider, for example, appearance and genetic descent. Suppose we were to allow that something could be human no matter what its appearance: star or stove, fish or lizard, cat or camel. We cannot then assume that an X is human because it resembles humans. But how far is this to go? Must we learn the genetic pedigree before we know that neighbors, customers, pedestrians, prisoners, and players are human? This is a recipe for chaos.

Consider the consequences of abandoning genetic descent. That an X's mother is human is now no longer *evidence* that the X is human. So, presumably, we must set up testing procedures for appearance, capacity, and reaction. But where do we set the cutting score? Robots may make better grades. And the reproductive habits of robots could be bothersome. Suppose they can be mass produced and that they can mass produce each other. Then rights, contracts, taxes, obligations, adoptions, justice, marriage, voting, and honor whirl dizzyingly and settle we know not where. What has disturbed philosophers and led them to press harder and harder for some set of specifications of humanity which can never be met by a machine is not just that thinking and acting machines can be fabricated. It is that machines can be mass produced. Suppose that a thinking and acting machine, a robot, with the capacities and appearance and reactions of a human could be made only by painstaking cottage labor—at most twelve or thirteen to a couple, and usually less—a folk art with no great change in the pattern. Then why worry? But put the factories to work on robot production, with new models each year, and we do not know what kind of ride we are in for. Then the specifications drawn up to exclude machines will become the working plans of robot designers.

To drop any of the criteria of humanity is to create or make likely an intolerable situation. Institutions, practices, common understandings, would be undercut; and all that depends on social organization eroded away.

This is not an argument for some kind of status quo for the concept of humanity. If conditions were radically otherwise, we might have different ideas. If the human race should be rendered sterile by renewed nuclear interchange, and the means were at hand for the creation of a self-renewing-population of robots, I do not venture to say what judgments we should make, nor how we should regard our successors. I do not say that none of the criteria of humanity can be challenged and debated. They can. But the decision regarding which criteria to rely upon is not therefore arbitrary or whimsical. Changes are not warranted which would lead to general chaos and misery. But the status quo could conceivably be rejected on the same ground.

Still, Can't We Discover that a Class of Beings Is Human?

Yet talk about decisions where criteria compete may leave us uncomfortable. What has been shown, at best, is that Hobbesian consequences follow the abandonment of one or other criterion. What is the *motivation* for accepting this kind of being as human and refusing to accept that? Why, given the description, is it more persuasive, easier to accept, that the late rather than the early embryo is a human being? Why does appearance make a difference? and behavior? and, possibly, mind or consciousness? Why should we (or do we?) *care* that the embryo is an homunculus, that it has fingers and toes? The answer, I want to suggest, is that sympathy is a necessary condition of a being's being human but that, because sympathy extends much further, it is not sufficient.

Suppose, for a moment that we are animists. Lots of people are or have been. Then we will feel kinship with other parts of living nature. We will believe, quite seriously, that the bear or the squirrel is our brother, and we will take his interest into account when we dig into a burrow or cut down a tree. We will kill him for food only in extreme need and then with regret and apologies. We would not think of having a squirrel-fry, or a squirrel-shoot. In fact, our sympathies might extend much further to all creatures, large or small, however different in form from our own: to frogs, snails, worms, praying mantises, and ants.

Even we who are not animists draw lines, however fuzzy, on the treatment of animals. Humane societies thrive and expand. Hardly anyone can stomach the wanton torture or killing of animals. The clubbing of baby seals is abhorrent, as is the slaughter of whales and the crippling of show horses. Our sympathy, our fellow-feeling, extends much further than, in writing philosophy or sociology, we usually give it credit for extending. Inevitably, a part of what is at issue in deciding whether each of a class of creatures is one of us is the sympathy we can feel, and do feel, for those creatures. If they can suffer as we suffer, cavort and cuddle as we do, love, give birth, sing or howl, quiver with ecstasy or fear, writhe in pain, these are things we can understand, that we do too in our way. If we could feel no sympathy, if the howling and cuddling seemed entirely alien to us, as in fact it does to some of us, then no set of *descriptions* of animal genetics, appearance, or behavior would *move* us to take special account of animals, to *feel for them*. We would feel no pressure to justify causing them to suffer or killing them; but in fact most of us do feel such pressure. We don't feel that we may shoot anything flying or moving just for target practice. We give some consideration to the relative painfulness of modes of killing when we butcher. We admonish children for pulling the wings off of flies.

A class of creatures could become *valuable,* or we could come to recognize the value they have had all along; and people might then come to feel a special repugnance toward the mistreatment or waste of those creatures. The elder Cato felt this way about slaves, considering them simply instruments for the acquisition of wealth, and encouraging masters to make the most economical use of them, and to destroy them when they were aged or infirm.[6] But the recognition of *value* should not be confused with the recognition that a creature is one of us (or that we are creatures along with them). Cato could as well have been talking about the care and obsolescence of chariots. No conclusions about the rights of slaves, no statements about the obligations of owners to slaves, follow from his remarks. The careless owner is imprudent and wasteful, but only for that is he to blame.

It might be felt, and I suspect the feeling is widespread, that the degree of sympathy we feel should determine the degree of humanity we accord the embryo, and that, since we feel more sympathy for late embryos, they are therefore more human. But, thought through, this criterion would have consequences unwelcome to most persons who might put it forward. Pets would, on this criterion, have far greater claim to humanity than fetuses at whatever stage. We may know, in general, that fetuses look more and more like babies, but sympathy does not attach easily to what is unseen, to what we cannot caress, to what does not express pain or joy; but it does attach easily to what expresses delight at the prospect of a walk, ecstasy at one's return home, anxiety about missing members of the household, and fear of strange creatures or contraptions.

To decide that a class of beings is human is not, however, just to express our sympathy; it is to accord the members of that class a status. If they have that status, a great deal follows, both morally and legally. It will not do to say that they have it and they don't have it, or that they have it to a certain degree, just as it won't do to say that children both are and are not members of an organization, or that they are members to some degree. Either they are members or they are not; and creating a special category of membership for them is still not acceding to the notion that they are somewhere on a continuous scale that leads from nonmembership to membership.

Decisions concerning membership establish a convention, they express an agreement, ideally a consensus. Given some understanding of what membership implies, the choice of criteria is not arbitrary. No one can, by fastening on one criterion, legislate the others out of existence. The move to make genetic descent the sole criterion is such a move.

Hobbesian consequences follow from the move that would make a fertilized egg a child. But they follow as surely if genetic descent is excluded as a criterion.

Yet if the choice of criteria is not arbitrary, the decision whether a class of beings that both seem and do not seem human *are* human is to a degree arbitrary. Because there are questions of membership, with all of the corollaries concerning rights and obligations that follow, there must be line drawing. An arbitrarily drawn line is not therefore a rationally or morally indefensible one. It may be, and it is, morally necessary that such a line be drawn. The mother's moral decision, and the decision of others concerned, in particular cases, must be by reference to that line. *She* cannot decide the question of membership or status. That decision should reflect a consensus. Sometimes the only way to achieve consensus is to entrust the decision to an Official Decider who, within the constraints of the going criteria, just decides.

The metaphor is by this time overstrained. The Court does not decide, for example, that the embryo in the first trimester is a human being but does decide the degree of care and protection to which it is entitled. It decides the status of the first-trimester fetus. What the Court rightly perceives is that to agree with extremists that a fetus is, at whatever stage, a child, baby, human being, or, alternatively, just an organism or a part of the body is to concede too much. It is precisely to cancel out in advance just those distinctions of status on which both moral and legal consequences rest. And the mother is not left without a decision once the Court has spoken. Within the constraints established, she must still ask herself whether the being (or organism) she bears may be killed.

NOTES

1. See John T. Noonan, Jr., "An Almost Absolute Value in History," in *The Morality of Abortion,* ed. John T. Noonan, Jr. (Cambridge, Mass.: Harvard University Press, 1970), pp. 1–59.

2. Of course, understood loosely, abortion could result in live delivery. The charge against Dr. Edelin was not that he had performed an abortion but that he had killed a "male child," i.e., an eighteen- to twenty-week-old male fetus. Nevertheless, since that is what is at issue, I will assume that the abortion under dispute is a practice that results in the death of the fetus.

3. It is curious that "innocent" is used in this argument in such a way that it is *impossible* that the "individual" could have been either innocent or guilty. Does it really make sense to speak of the innocence or guilt of a sixty-four-cell organism, say, just hooking onto the wall of the uterus? Does it, then, make the same kind of sense as to speak of the innocence of the prisoner before the bar

or of the saintly mother? In the sense in question, lower animals and plants are innocent; but it is far from clear that this adds weight to the argument that *their* lives should be spared.

4. The possibilities are capable of endless ramification and popular entertainment. See Michael Crichton, *The Terminal Man* (New York: Alfred A. Knopf, 1972).

5. Note that it does not necessarily follow that a being born of a human mother is genetically human nor that what is genetically human is born of a human mother.

6. W.E.H. Lecky, *History of European Morals* (New York: George Braziller, 1955), I:301–3.

The Abortion Decisions: Judicial Review and Public Opinion

JUDITH BLAKE*

The United States Supreme Court decisions on abortion (*Roe* v. *Wade* and *Doe* v. *Bolton*), which were announced in late January 1973, overturned, to a greater or lesser degree, restrictive legislation concerning abortion in almost every state.[1] In *Roe* v. *Wade*, the Court ruled that a woman's decision to have an abortion (whatever her reasons) is encompassed by the fundamental "right to privacy." Therefore, only compelling interests can justify the state's limiting abortion. The Court held that the state does have compelling interests in protecting maternal health and preserving the life of the fetus, but these interests were judged to become sufficiently compelling to justify curtailment or prohibition of abortion only at certain durations of pregnancy.

Until after the first trimester, the mother's health does not seem threatened and hence no state regulation was deemed necessary. The decision was held to rest with the woman and her physician. After the third month, the Court decided that state regulation should be concerned with measures designed to insure the mother's health but should not be needlessly restrictive. With respect to the state's interest in preserving the life of the fetus, the Court held that a fetus is not a "person" protected by the Fourteenth Amendment and that no one could agree when life begins. Consequently, neither courts nor legisla-

---

*I gratefully acknowledge the Ford Foundation's support of the research presented in this article. I also thank Irving Crespi of the Gallup Poll for his help in the collection of the survey data. Heidi Nebel of the University of California's Survey Research Center at Berkeley and Eric Larson of International Population and Urban Research have provided invaluable assistance with data processing and compilation. I have benefitted from comments by participants at the Notre Dame conference on abortion, especially William Petersen, Harriet Pilpel, and Edmund Pincoffs as well as from colleagues at Berkeley, Le Roy Graymer, Arnold Meltsner, and Aaron Wildavsky, who were kind enough to read an earlier draft of this paper.

tures could abrogate the rights of the pregnant woman by declaring that life begins at conception. The Court maintained that the state's compelling interest in preserving the fetus begins with viability. After this point (approximately six months gestation), the state is justified in regulating and even proscribing abortion (except where it is necessary to save the mother's life). The Court explicitly refused to render a decision concerning whether the woman's right to an abortion could be limited to consent of the prospective child's father or that of the woman's own parents.

In *Doe* v. *Bolton,* the Court dealt with the question of certain medical requirements and standards for the performance of abortion. First, it struck down the Georgia requirement that restricted the performance of abortions to hospitals accredited by the Joint Commission on the Accreditation of Hospitals. The Court did allow for the licensing of facilities where abortions would be performed after the first trimester. The Court also invalidated abortion review committees and requirements that two additional physicians pass judgment on the decision of the woman's physician to abort. Additionally, it invalidated a provision that prevented migration into Georgia for purposes of obtaining an abortion.

The Court's decisions precipitated a nationwide change in the legal status of abortion that doubtless would not have occurred for many years without the exercise of judicial review. Although at the time of the decisions public opinion in the United States preponderantly supported, as justifications for legal abortion, threats to the mother's health and possible child deformity, the public clearly disfavored abortion solely as a birth control measure—that is, for no other reason than that the couple (or the woman) does not want a child to be born.[2] Hence, it seems highly unlikely that individual states could have rapidly overturned, by legislative means, severe legal restraints on abortion or that the legislative actions that might have resulted would have been as permissive as were the intended consequences of judicial review.

The Court's decisions regarding abortion thus represent an additional instance of the effort to effect rapid, though deeply controversial, social change through the exercise of judicial review. The most notable of such efforts were, of course, the desegregation decisions. Indeed, although abortion differs from desegregation in many important ways, the analogy is highly relevant when one begins to consider the matter of implementation. The issues are then seen to share the problems of noncompliance and collateral deterrence (indirect means of inhibiting the change such as, in the case of abortion, overregulation of clinics; withholding of Medicaid funds; statutes requiring that doctors supply elaborate statistical information, including the woman's name, concerning every abortion) that attend public polarization and dissent.

As opposition groups have organized themselves during the years since the Court's decisions, examples of concerted pressure against abortion have begun to cumulate rapidly. States such as Rhode Island, Nebraska, and Tennessee have been passing legislation that does not comply with the spirit of *Roe* and *Doe*. Pressures are being exerted on Congress concerning the use of public monies for abortion. A movement has sprung up to amend the Constitution in an effort to bypass the Court's decisions. Recently, the conviction of Dr. Kenneth Edelin on manslaughter charges for aborting a fetus of more than twenty weeks gestation may have significant effects on the willingness of physicians to perform abortions.[3] And, of course, efforts to prevent scientists from engaging in research on fetuses scheduled for abortion—efforts best exemplified in the recent Massachusetts legislation sponsored by William Delahunt—are a direct spin-off of increasingly organized "right-to-life" movements.[4]

If the decisions are to be fully implemented on a continuous basis, local organized efforts at collateral deterrence obviously will require equally organized vigilance by those favoring the Court's decisions. Additionally, there are at least two reasons why broadly based popular support for the issue involved in the Court's rulings would seem to be of major importance to successful implementation. First, if the content of the decisions is unpopular, or even if much of it has low saliency for the public generally, then organized opposition becomes emboldened by these facts alone. Moreover, implementation involves individuals in many echelons and branches of public service as well as numerous levels of health professionals. Both groups are exceptionally vulnerable to charges of misconduct, malpractice, and lack of integrity because they are deeply dependent on public confidence and trust. Even insofar as members of such groups are sympathetic to the Court's decisions, if public opinion does not support them, then public servants and professionals will seek to avoid compromising and morally isolating situations regarding abortion. This is particularly true since, even in the Court's view, whether a pregnancy termination is regarded as abortion or manslaughter seems to depend heavily on how the fetus is socially defined at each stage of pregnancy. As Rosoff has said:

> Pressure, sometimes vehement, from organized groups is a common fact of life on Capitol Hill. (Witness the recent campaigns for school prayer and capital punishment or against amnesty and busing.) However, members of Congress are rarely accused of being "murderers," either because of their support of Supreme Court decisions or their refusal to endorse constitutional amendments.[5]

Sensing the vulnerability of public officials and health professionals to the potential ugliness of charges regarding abortion, the pro-abortion movement has concentrated much effort on reassurance. In particular, there has been constant reference to the preponderance of public support for liberalized abortion and the atypical character of anti-abortion sentiment.[6] However, as I have shown in two previous articles using a time series of national-survey data for the population of voting age and as has been substantiated by results of the national fertility studies of 1965 and 1970 for a national sample of married women in the reproductive ages, this effort to defuse official anxieties concerning liberalized abortion has grossly oversimplified and overstated its case.[7] Not only do the claims by many supporters of the Court's decisions not accord with the bulk of survey data on this subject, but it can be shown that the empirical basis of these claims is highly suspect.

For example, survey results showing a preponderantly favorable public response to purely elective abortion, cited repeatedly by some supporters of the Court's decisions, have been based on a question whose wording is so biased as virtually to guarantee the outcome desired. I have discussed these biases in detail elsewhere.[8] Similarly, a recent effort by Rosoff to assure politicians that support of abortion is not "political suicide" involves a positive distortion of the implications of congressional polls concerning a question on attitudes toward the Court's abortion decisions. Rosoff has accumulated the results of thirty-three such polls taken in 1973-74, showing that in over half, 60 percent or more of respondents claimed to favor the Court's decisions.[9] Aside from the numerous methodological problems associated with attempts by congressmen to poll their constituents by mail, what is obscured by this apparently large-scale support for the Court's rulings is that a scant 49 percent of the public of voting age has heard of the Court's decisions *and* is correctly apprised of their general intent (whether they be to make it easier, harder, or to have no effect on a woman's ability to obtain a legal abortion). This finding stems from two questions I commissioned on a Gallup survey in April 1975 concerning public awareness of the Supreme Court's decisions and knowledge of their overall intended effect.

Now, with organized efforts to local collateral deterrence well underway, survey results showing widespread disapproval of elective abortion are of more than academic interest. Misrepresentation of the degree of public support for changes as great as were embodied in the Court's decisions threatens to boomerang. Having alleged that anti-abortionists are a politically insignificant splinter group, it is now difficult for pro-abortionists to express credible alarm over the fact that implementation is actually turning into a pitched battle—a battle requiring highly mobilized resistance if it is to be won. If anti-abortionists strike a chord only in the hearts of a few extremists and if the general public is supportive of elective abortion, why is there a need to organize vigilantly in order to insure implementation? Is not implementation what the public mandated?

In attempting to bring data to bear on this question, I must emphasize that implicit in public support for abortion is not only widespread popular sanction for elective pregnancy termination but knowledge and approval of the particular issues involved in the decisions, such as the months of pregnancy during which an abortion is permissible and allowable physical sites for pregnancy termination. These specifics are the principal foci of local efforts at deterrence, and it is the spirit in which these particulars are handled on a day-to-day basis that will determine whether abortion is elective to the extent allowed by *Roe* and *Doe,* or, for significant segments of the population, prohibited on a de facto basis. For example, given the biological time constraints, it is not difficult to see how a few roadblocks to ready access to abortion—let us say, refusal of Medicaid funds and a local requirement that the operation be performed in hospitals—could easily exclude numerous women from elective pregnancy termination. If, as a result of the Edelin conviction, physicians become more conservative regarding the time limit for abortion, this will further curtail the period during which women can attempt to overcome obstacles.

We may ask, therefore, whether the public has significantly increased its assent for purely discretionary abortion since the decisions in January 1973? Further, if we disaggregate some of the additional issues involved in the Court's decisions—issues such as the husband's consent, whether abortion should be performed outside of hospitals, when people believe that human life begins, and the timing of abortion—might we expect that the public will provide active resistance to organized anti-abortion efforts? Or did the Court's decisions so far outdistance public dispositions concerning abortion that large segments of the population may be sympathetic to organized anti-abortionists, highly vulnerable to "right-to-life" media campaigns, or, at the least, apathetic and passive concerning the issues? The present paper brings evidence from national surveys to bear on these questions.

Justifications for Abortions, 1962–74

A major issue involved in the 1973 abortion decisions concerns the Court's support for the right of a woman to obtain an abortion on no other grounds than that she does not wish to bear the prospective child. In the Court's view, legitimate limitations on her action are only medical up to the time of viability, after which states may regulate, even prohibit, abortion in the interest of preserving the life of the fetus.

What were the views of Americans concerning justifications for abortion at the time of the Court's decisions, and have these views changed since that time? In this paper, I shall use data derived from questions I have commissioned on a series of Gallup surveys.[10] The results presented here are for whites of voting age. I should call attention to the fact that two major national fertility surveys of married women in the reproductive ages (the national fertility studies of 1965 and 1970) have asked questions similar to those discussed in this section. The results have closely corresponded to those I shall present.[11] It should be noted that none of the questions relates to the actual decisions themselves but rather to issues involved in, or resulting from, them.

Between 1962 and 1974, the following questions were asked on nine Gallup surveys:

> Do you think abortion operations should or should not be legal in the following cases:
> a. Where the health of the mother is in danger?
> b. Where the child may be born deformed?
> c. Where the family does not have enough money to support another child?

Beginning in 1968, at my request, the seven surveys between 1968 and 1974 added a fourth question:

> d. Where the parents simply have all the children they want although there would be no major health or financial problems involved in having another child?

As has been noted in previous papers, the health of the mother as a justification for abortion is concurred in almost unanimously by white Americans.[12] Recent surveys in November 1973 and September 1974 continue to show that well over 80 percent approve this justification— 88 percent in the most recent survey. On the 1974 survey, 82 percent of Catholics and 90 percent of non-Catholics approved. These results represent no change since March 1972, which is the last date prior to the Court's ruling.

With regard to the issue of possible child deformity, opinion has also remained essentially unchanged. Approval characterized three-fourths of white respondents, while 19 percent actively disapproved as of September 1974.

Since medical indications for abortion constitute a small share of all reasons for actual pregnancy termination, it is important to know about public views concerning the so-called softer justifications—financial stress and the simple desire to avoid having a child. As may be seen from Table 1, public opinion in March 1972 (approximately a year before the Court's decisions were announced in January 1973) preponderantly disfavored the simple desire to avoid having a child as a justification for abortion (to be referred to here as discretionary or elective abortion). Even financial stress was disapproved as a justification by over half of all respondents. In 1972, only 27 and 38 percent approved discretion and financial stress respectively as justifications for abortions.

Ten months after the Court's decisions were announced, November 1973, we can see from Table 1 that with respect to financial stress, disapproval remained essentially unchanged from the level it had attained in March 1972—55 percent. By September 1974, however, disapproval did show a statistically significant drop bringing it below the halfway mark for the first time in our documented history.

Less compelling is evidence concerning the sense of legitimacy for purely discretionary abortion. Table 1 shows no change between March 1972 and November 1973 in disapproval of this justification and a very slight decrease in disapproval between November 1973 and September 1974—leaving overall disapproval at 63 percent in the last survey. Hence with respect to whether couples should have a right to legal abortion on the ground that they simply do not want the prospective child, the public appears to be a long distance from the permissiveness embodied in the Court's decisions.

Furthermore, the pace of change in public opinion has slackened. Although, over the time period 1962 to 1974, there was a substantial drop in disapproval of abortion for both financial and discretionary reasons (Table 1), most of the change took place prior to 1970. Since then, change has been slower, especially if one takes into account the unevenness of some of the periods between observations. Such an attenuated rate of change leads one to suspect that current levels of disapproval may not yield readily.

Are the negative views of respondents concerning elective abortion a result of the way in which the question was worded? Is there also, perhaps, an order effect involved in the sequencing of questions from hard (health) to increasingly soft (discretionary) responses?

In order to test whether the question on elective abortion greatly distorted respondent's views on the subject, I have posed the issue somewhat differently in the following question, "Do you believe there should be no legal restraint on getting an abortion—that is, if a woman wants one she need only consult her doctor, or do you believe that the

TABLE 1

Percentage disapproving legalization of abortion if the parents cannot afford, or do not want, another child. White men and women in the United States. Nine Gallup surveys, 1962–74.

	Aug. 1962	Dec. 1965	May 1968	Dec. 1968	Oct. 1969	June 1970	Mar. 1972	Nov. 1973	Sept. 1974
Money									
Men	73	71	72	63	66	50	51	53	46
Women	74	76	73	73	69	56	59	57	49
Total disapproving	74	74	72	68	68	53	55	55	47
Discretion									
Men	—	—	82	78	77	67	64	66	60
Women	—	—	88	85	81	71	70	69	65
Total disapproving	—	—	85	81	79	69	67	67	63
TOTAL RESPONDENTS	(1391)	(1428)	(1483)	(1427)	(1448)	(1394)	(1365)	(1363)	(1343)

law should specify what kinds of circumstances justify abortion?" on two Gallup surveys to date—September 1972 and September 1974. As may be seen from Table 2 disapproval of elective abortion is lower as a result of this question than as a result of the previous question (the last of the four questions in the series beginning with "Mother's Health") addressed to the same issue. For example, in September 1974, 53 percent believed the law should specify the circumstances justifying abortion as contrasted with 63 percent disapproving abortion if the couple does not desire more children. Interestingly, however, there has been no significant change during the two-year period, and disapproval of no legal restraint on abortion remained at 53 percent even as late as September 1974.

What causes the different levels of approval resulting from the two questions? One possible source of variability lies in the fact that the question regarding legal restraint was asked singly—it was not preceded by three other questions in an obvious order from health to discretionary reasons. For the purpose of testing for an order effect on question d (that is, "Do you think abortion operations should or should not be legal where the parents have all the children they want although there is no major health or financial problems involved in having another child?"), I arranged to have the series of four abortion questions asked in two orders on a split ballot. The first order was the usual one that has been used on all previous surveys. The second order was the complete reverse—the question on elective abortion was asked first and the one on the mother's health last. The results may be seen in Table 3.

It is apparent that the order effect can account completely for the difference between the question on elective abortion (question d) in the series and the single question on legal restraints. It would seem, therefore, that approval of elective abortion currently hovers around 40 percent of white Americans and disapproval around 55 percent. It seems fair to say, therefore, that at the time of the Court's ruling, and as late as October 1974, white Americans have not regarded discretionary abortion as properly a woman's private and personal decision (subject only to certain limited compelling interests by the state to be discussed below).

Roe and Doe: Beyond Justifications for Abortion

The public is not only less permissive than the Court concerning justifications for abortion, but popular opinion is far less tolerant than that of the judiciary when it comes to other particular issues embodied

TABLE 2

Responses of white men and women to the question, "Do you believe there should be no legal restraint on getting an abortion—that is, if a woman wants one she need only consult her doctor, or do you believe that the law should specify what kinds of circumstances justify abortion?" asked on two Gallup surveys, September 1972 and September 1974. In percentages.

	September 1972	September 1974
Men		
No legal restraint	40	43
Law should specify circumstances	52	50
No opinion	8	7
Total	100	100
Total respondents	(676)	(645)
Women		
No legal restraint	38	37
Law should specify circumstances	55	56
No opinion	7	7
Total	100	100
Total respondents	(689)	(671)
Total		
No legal restraint	39	40
Law should specify circumstances	54	53
No opinion	7	7
Total	100	100
Total respondents	(1365)	(1316)

TABLE 3

Responses of white men and women to four questions on abortion (ranging from "Mother's Health" to "Discretion") asked on a split ballot in usual order and reverse order, Gallup survey, January 1973. In percentages.

	Questions Asked in Usual Order					Questions Asked in Reverse Order				
	Approve	Disapprove	No Opinion	Total	Approve	Disapprove	No Opinion	Total
Men								
Mother's health	87	10	2	100 (334)	81	15	4	100 (328)
Child deformed	74	20	6	100 (334)	65	27	8	100 (328)
Money	42	52	6	100 (334)	49	45	6	100 (328)
Discretion	28	68	4	100 (334)	41	55	4	100 (328)
Women								
Mother's health	88	9	3	100 (355)	82	13	5	100 (341)
Child deformed	73	20	7	100 (355)	69	25	7	100 (341)
Money	44	50	6	100 (355)	50	46	4	100 (341)
Discretion	32	64	4	100 (355)	41	55	4	100 (341)

in *Roe* and *Doe*. With regard to the timing (in months of pregnancy) of abortion, whether the operation should be performed only in hospitals, migratory or nonresident abortion, when human life begins, and whether pregnancy termination should be lawful without the husband's consent, it is evident that the Court has far outdistanced (and, in at least one case, misread) public views on the subject of abortion.

However, the reader should be cautioned at the outset that these results do not necessarily indicate implacable opinions by respondents concerning the issues. Indeed, there are reasons (to be discussed later) for arguing that the public has not thought through many of the points under discussion. The results, nonetheless, do give some baseline concerning popular views *in the absence* of intensive media campaigns explicating and favoring the intricacies of the Court's decisions. Moreover, even if a concerted pro-abortion campaign were launched, it might do no more than counter the negative effects of organized anti-abortion campaigns. Hence, it is difficult to argue that the net outcome for public opinion would be very different from the results presented here.

During the latter part of the same week that the Supreme Court decision was announced in January 1973, the following questions were asked (at my request) on a Gallup survey:

1a. Some states have laws that say abortion cannot be performed after a woman has been pregnant a certain period of time. Do you think there should be some such time limit or do you think there should be no legal restriction concerning the time when abortion can be performed?

1b. (If should be limit)
Taking into account that a woman may not know she is pregnant until three or four weeks after conception, after what month of pregnancy do you think it should be illegal to perform an abortion?

2. Some state laws specify that abortions may be performed only in hospitals, whereas other states allow abortions to be performed in various kinds of outside medical facilities other than hospitals. Do you think that it should be legal to perform an abortion only in a hospital or would you permit the use of outside medical facilities other than hospitals?

3. In some states the laws make it easy to get an abortion, and in others they make it hard. Do you think the easy states should limit abortions only to their own residents, or should they freely allow women from other states to come and get abortions?

4. (Hand respondent card C) It is sometimes said that the morality of abortion rests on the question of when one thinks human life begins. For example, some people believe that it begins at conception, that is, when sperm and egg first meet. Others say that it begins only when the woman first feels movement inside her (what is sometimes called quick-

Judith Blake

ening), and still others say that human life has begun when the unborn baby could probably survive if it were born prematurely. Finally, there are those who hold that human life begins only with the actual birth of a baby. Which of these alternatives best expresses your views?
1. Human life begins at conception
2. Human life begins at quickening
3. Human life begins when the unborn baby could probably survive on the outside if it were born prematurely
4. Human life begins only at birth[13]

In addition to the questions cited above, on two Gallup surveys (August 1972 and October 1974), I have asked the following question:

> Do you think it should be lawful for a woman to be able to get an abortion operation without her husband's consent?

Table 4 summarizes the results of all of these questions (with the exception of question 4 concerning when life begins) for men and women separately. As for the time limitation, the majority of respondents believe that there should be legal limits (or that abortion should not be performed under any circumstances) and that these limits should be within the first trimester of pregnancy. Few respondents would allow abortion to occur beyond the third month. It is evident as well that a hospital is preponderantly regarded as the only proper site for abortions. Respondents are most liberal in allowing for abortions to be performed on non-residents of a state with permissive abortion laws. Even here, however, fewer than 40 percent of respondents would allow migratory abortion. Finally, a strong majority (approximately two-thirds) of respondents interviewed both in 1972 and in 1974 do not think that it should be lawful for a woman to be able to get an abortion without her husband's consent.

Concerning when human life can be said to begin, the Court said:

> We need not resolve the difficult question of when life begins.... It should be sufficient to note briefly the wide divergence of thinking on this most sensitive and difficult question. There has always been strong support for the view that life does not begin until live birth. This was the belief of the Stoics. *It appears to be the predominant, though not the unanimous, attitude of the Jewish faith. It may be taken to represent also the position of a large segment of the Protestant community, insofar as that can be ascertained.* (Italics mine.)[14]

The results presented in Table 5 allow two types of comparison regarding this issue. One is between responses to the same question (question 4 above) asked in January 1973 and April 1975. The other is between the April 1975 tabulations of question 4 and responses to a

TABLE 4
Views of white American men and women concerning various aspects of abortion. Gallup survey, January 1973, and (where noted in table) August 1972 and October 1974. In percentages.*

	Men	Women
Time limit on abortion		
Should be limit	55	65
No legal restriction	20	11
Abortion should never be performed/ disapprove all abortion (volunteered)	15	16
If limit, how long?		
Less than 3 months	21	24
Three months	41	49
Four months	12	12
Five or more months	12	8
Type of medical facility for abortion		
Only in hospitals	55	59
All right in medical facility that is not hospital	30	26
Abortion should never be performed/ disapprove all abortion (volunteered)	12	12
Nonresident abortion		
Limit to own residents	42	40
Allow women from other states	38	38
Abortion should never be performed/ disapprove all abortion (volunteered)	14	14
TOTAL RESPONDENTS	(662)	(696)

	Aug. 1972	Oct. 1974	Aug. 1972	Oct. 1974
Consent of husband				
Should not be lawful without husband's consent	67	66	67	61
Should be lawful without husband's consent	20	22	24	28
It depends on the woman's reasons for seeking the abortion	7	7	7	7
TOTAL RESPONDENTS	(663)	(642)	(682)	(682)

*A small proportion of men and women gave "don't know" responses and, in some cases, there were miscellaneous other responses. In order to conserve space these percentages are not included in the table above.

TABLE 5

Responses of white men and women to a question on when human life begins asked on Gallup surveys taken in January 1973 and April 1975, as well as to a question on when the unborn may be considered a human person asked on a Gallup survey in April 1975. In percentages.

	Life Begins		Person
	1973	1975	1975
	Men		
At Conception	35	42	33
At Quickening	19	15	14
At Viability	16	15	22
At Birth	19	20	19
Don't Know/Other	11	8	12
TOTAL	100	100	100
	(662)	(679)	(685)
	Women		
At Conception	50	60	53
At Quickening	24	15	18
At Viability	13	11	15
At Birth	8	9	8
Don't Know/Other	5	5	6
TOTAL	100	100	100
	(696)	(682)	(673)

different question on the same subject from an additional survey in April 1975. This question was worded as follows:

> It is sometimes said that the morality of abortion rests on the question of when, in the course of pregnancy, one believes that the unborn can be considered a human person. (Hand respondent card B.) For example, some people believe that a human person exists from conception, that is when sperm and egg first meet. Others say that it exists only when the woman first feels movement inside her (what is sometimes called quickening), and still others say that it exists when the unborn baby could probably survive if it were born prematurely. Finally, there are those who hold that a human person can be said to exist only with the actual birth of a live baby. Which one of these alternatives best expresses your views. Just read off the letter.

In both 1973 and 1975, few respondents believed that human life begins only at live birth. Less than 10 percent of women and about 20 percent of men held this belief at both dates. Most respondents, especially female respondents, claimed that life begins at conception or at quickening. Moreover, among both men and women in April 1975, higher proportions believed that life begins at conception than was the case in January 1973 at the time of the Court's ruling. In April 1975, 42 percent of men and 60 percent of women claimed that life begins at conception, whereas the 1973 percentages were 35 and 50 for men and women respectively.

It can be argued that the wording of the question on "when human life begins" biases responses toward the early part of the gestational period, in the sense that even the blastocyst is obviously neither nonliving nor nonhuman. Hence, insofar as the Court implied a concern for when the fetus may be regarded as a "person" with constitutional rights, it is perhaps more valid to present the issue to respondents according to when the unborn can be considered a "human person." The full text of this revised question is given above.

It is apparent that the revised question did affect the responses of both sexes, as may be seen from a comparison of the two tabulations for April 1975—one relating to the question on when human life begins and the other to the question on when the unborn can be considered a person. Thirty-three percent of the men and 53 percent of the women believed that a "human person" begins at conception—percentages that are lower than the 1975 results of the question on when human life begins. However, there was no change in the "after birth" response for either sex. It thus remains that high proportions of respondents—approximately 70 percent of women and 50 percent of men—believe that a "human person" exists at conception or at quickening, and a small fraction would designate personhood as occurring only after parturition.

Admittedly, it is probably possible to raise endless metaphysical and epistemological objections to the validity of questions on this topic. However, the results of the question concerning the personhood of the unborn are congruent with respondents' reluctance to allow abortion after the third month of pregnancy. It thus appears that most respondents' evaluation of when life begins is very different from the Supreme Court's assessment of public opinion. In the next section, we will see that these results hold for non-Catholics as well.

Social and Demographic Differentials in Attitudes toward Abortion

If the public generally is less permissive than the Court toward abortion, are there differentials in attitude among major subgroupings? Let us look at the situation with regard to Catholic–non-Catholic differences and, among non-Catholics, according to age and educational level.

Table 6 gives the results of religious affiliation for seven surveys, 1968–74, of the question on discretionary abortion in the series of four questions beginning with the mother's health. We see that there has been a drop in disapproval over the time period among both Catholics and non-Catholics, and Catholic levels of disapproval are higher than those of non-Catholics. But, for our purposes here, it is significant that high levels of disapproval (typically over 60 percent) characterize even non-Catholics.

Among non-Catholics stratified by age and education (Table 7), youthful respondents tend to have lower disapproval rates, but, even among the young, disapproval ran well over 50 percent as late as September 1974. In these tabulations, the smallest proportions disapproving were among college-educated non-Catholics (42 percent among men and 44 percent among women), by contrast with two-thirds of the high-school and three-fourths of the grade-school educated.

With regard to the single question about whether there should or should not be legal specifications concerning the circumstances justifying abortion, the results (not shown in tabular form) are very similar. In general, Catholic–non-Catholic responses differed little and, among most major subgroupings of non-Catholics, half, or considerably more than half, of respondents favored having the law specify the cir-

TABLE 6
Percentage disapproving legalization of abortion if the parents do not want another child. White men and women in the United States by religious affiliation. Seven Gallup surveys, 1968–74.

	May 1968	Dec. 1968	Oct. 1969	June 1970	Mar. 1972	Nov. 1973	Sept. 1974
				Men			
Catholic	85	84	80	74	72	75	69
Non-Catholic	81	75	76	64	61	63	57
				Women			
Catholic	88	88	87	78	76	80	74
Non-Catholic	88	84	79	68	68	64	61
Total respondents	(1483)	(1427)	(1448)	(1394)	(1365)	(1363)	(1343)

TABLE 7
Percentage disapproving legalization of abortion if no more children are desired. White non-Catholic men and women in the United States by age and educational level. Seven Gallup surveys, 1968–74.

	May 1968	Dec. 1968	Oct. 1969	June 1970	Mar. 1972	Nov. 1973	Sept. 1974
Men							
Age							
Under 30	76	74	66	57	53	55	56
30–44	80	77	79	69	65	68	57
45 +	82	75	77	64	63	64	58
Education							
College	72	69	63	51	49	45	42
High school	86	80	83	72	68	72	63
Grade school	81	76	79	68	67	73	74
Total disapproving	81	76	76	64	61	63	57
Total respondents	(543)	(543)	(539)	(500)	(484)	(498)	(469)
Women							
Age							
Under 30	90	84	82	68	61	59	56
30–44	89	85	80	72	67	62	62
45 +	86	83	77	68	72	69	63
Education							
College	80	76	70	56	47	42	44
High school	91	86	81	73	73	71	67
Grade school	90	84	86	70	84	83	73
Total disapproving	88	84	79	69	68	64	61
Total respondents	(548)	(511)	(512)	(530)	(495)	(486)	(468)
Total							
Total disapproving	84	79	78	66	65	63	59
Total respondents	(1091)	(1054)	(1051)	(1030)	(979)	(984)	(937)

cumstances justifying abortion. Again, the highest levels of permissiveness were among the college educated.

What of the other issues raised by *Roe* and *Doe*—the maximum pregnancy duration for abortion, when life begins, whether the operation should be performed only in hospitals, migratory or nonresident abortion, and whether abortion should be lawful without the husband's consent?

An overwhelming majority of respondents considered by religion, age, and education believed that there should be a time limit (pregnancy duration) on abortion, or that abortions should not be performed at all (Table 8). Among those who answered in terms of a time limit, relatively few (regardless of religion, age, or education) would allow abortions past the first trimester (Table 9).

Respondents doubtless have a number of reasons for the view that abortion should be confined to the early months of pregnancy. Among them would seem to be the belief that human life begins either at conception or early in the gestational process. Taken by religious affiliation (Table 10), in 1973, 50 percent of the men and 72 percent of the women, even among non-Catholics, believed that life begins at conception or at quickening. Interestingly, among both non-Catholics and Catholics, the proportions believing that life begins at conception increased between January 1973 and April 1975. As for those averring that life begins at birth, in both 1973 and 1975 slightly over a fifth of non-Catholic men and less than a tenth of non-Catholic women expressed this view, indicating considerable error in the Supreme Court's assessment of non-Catholic opinions on this subject. In fact, even the question concerning when the unborn becomes a "human person" did not significantly change the percentages by religious affiliation who answered "at birth."

If we confine our tabulations to non-Catholics alone and disaggregate them by age and educational level, we are able to see whether there is any grouping in the non-Catholic population that differs markedly from average opinion on this subject. Considered by age (Table 11), we see a definite preference, among all age groups, for the early months of pregnancy as the time when "life begins." However, younger respondents especially younger men, were most likely to favor the later periods. On the other hand, by 1975, the largest proportional increase in the "at conception" response was among those under age 30, to the extent that the percentages in this age group believing that life begins at conception equalled or exceeded the percentages among older people. There were no major differentials by age in the proportion of respondents who believed that human life or personhood begins at live birth. The difference that seems most outstanding in this table, as in the more aggregated results, is the one by sex. At all ages, women were far more likely than men to respond in terms of the early part of the gestational process and far less likely to reply that life or personhood begins at birth.

Finally, with regard to education, it is clear that college-educated non-Catholics are least likely to place the beginning of life or personhood at conception and most likely to put these qualities at viability or

TABLE 8

Responses of white men and women by religion, age, and education to the question, "Some states have laws that say abortion cannot be performed after a woman has been pregnant a certain period of time. Do you think there should be some such time limit, or do you think there should be no legal restriction concerning the time when abortion can be performed?" asked on a Gallup survey during the last week in January 1973. In percentages.

	Should Be Limited		No Legal Restriction		Abortion Should Never Be Performed		Other Answers And No Opinion		Total	
	Men	Women	Men	Women	Men	Women	Men	Women	Men	Women
Religion										
Catholic	52	58	14	8	24	27	10	7	100 (190)	100 (222)
Non-Catholic	56	69	22	13	11	11	11	7	100 (472)	100 (474)
Age										
Under 30	58	70	25	15	7	11	10	4	100 (160)	100 (172)
30–44	61	66	18	13	17	13	4	8	100 (175)	100 (213)
45 +	50	62	17	9	18	20	15	9	100 (322)	100 (302)
Education level										
Grade school	46	60	15	4	24	26	15	10	100 (104)	100 (80)
High school	56	66	19	10	16	17	9	7	100 (319)	100 (442)
College	58	66	22	19	9	8	11	7	100 (234)	100 (170)
Total	55	65	19	11	15	16	11	8	100 (662)	100 (696)

TABLE 9

Responses of white men and women by religion, age, and education to the question, "Taking into account that a woman may not know she is pregnant until three or four weeks after conception, after what month of pregnancy do you think it should be illegal to perform an abortion?" asked on a Gallup survey during the last week in January 1973. In percentages.

	Fewer than 3 Months		Three Months		Four Months		Five or More Months		No Opinion		Total	
	Men	Women	Men	Women	Men	Women	Men	Women	Men	Women	Men	Women
Religion												
Catholic	23	23	42	48	8	14	10	9	16	5	100 (190)	100 (222)
Non-Catholic	20	25	41	49	13	11	13	8	13	7	100 (472)	100 (474)
Age												
Under 30	22	17	40	49	14	19	16	13	9	2	100 (160)	100 (172)
30–44	19	29	41	50	8	9	17	9	16	5	100 (175)	100 (213)
45 +	22	26	43	49	12	9	8	5	15	10	100 (322)	100 (302)
Educational Level:												
Grade school	25	35	48	46	4	8	6	2	17	8	100 (104)	100 (80)
High school	20	27	41	50	14	12	12	6	12	5	100 (319)	100 (442)
College	20	13	40	47	11	13	14	16	15	10	100 (234)	100 (170)
Total	21	24	41	49	12	12	12	8	14	6	100 (662)	100 (696)

TABLE 10

Responses of white men and women by religion to a question on when human life begins asked on Gallup surveys taken in January 1973 and April 1975, as well as to a question on when the unborn may be considered a human person asked on a Gallup survey in April 1975. In percentages.

Religion	At Conception Life Begins[a] 1973	At Conception Life Begins 1975	At Conception Person[b] 1975	At Quickening Life Begins 1973	At Quickening Life Begins 1975	At Quickening Person 1975	At Viability Life Begins 1973	At Viability Life Begins 1975	At Viability Person 1975	At Birth Life Begins 1973	At Birth Life Begins 1975	At Birth Person 1975	Total[c] Life Begins 1973	Total Life Begins 1975	Total Person 1975
Men															
Catholic	49	53	53	16	16	12	15	15	15	12	13	12	(190)	(188)	(178)
Non-Catholic	29	38	26	21	14	14	15	15	25	22	23	22	(472)	(491)	(507)
Women															
Catholic	62	76	68	19	12	14	9	4	10	5	8	4	(222)	(199)	(186)
Non-Catholic	45	53	46	27	16	20	14	11	17	9	9	10	(474)	(483)	(487)

[a] The question was: *(Hand respondent card)* It is sometimes said that the morality of abortion rests on the question of when one thinks human life begins. For example, some people believe that it begins at conception, that is, when sperm and egg first meet. Others say that it begins only when the woman first feels movement inside her (what is sometimes called quickening), and still others say that human life has begun when the unborn baby could probably survive if it were born prematurely. Finally, there are those who hold that human life begins only with the actual birth of a baby. Which of these alternatives best expresses your views? (Asked last week in January 1973 and last week in April 1975.)

[b] The question was: *(Hand respondent card B)* It is sometimes said that the morality of abortion rests on the question of when, in the course of pregnancy, one believes that the unborn can be considered a human person. For example, some people believe that a human person exists from conception, that is, when sperm and egg first meet. Others say that it exists only when the woman first feels movement inside her (what is sometimes called quickening), and still others say that it exists only when the unborn baby could probably survive if it were born prematurely. Finally, there are those who hold that a human person can be said to exist only with the actual birth of a live baby. Which one of these alternatives best expresses your views? (Asked middle of April 1975.)

[c] Percentages do not add to 100 in this table because of "don't know" and "other" responses not shown here in order to conserve space.

TABLE 11

Responses of white non-Catholic men and women by age and education to a question on when human life begins asked on Gallup surveys taken in January 1973 and April 1975, as well as to a question on when the unborn may be considered a human person asked on a Gallup survey in April 1975. In percentages.

	At Conception			At Quickening			At Viability			At Birth			Total[b]		
	Life Begins[a] 1973	1975	Person[b] 1975	Life Begins 1973	1975	Person 1975	Life Begins 1973	1975	Person 1975	Life Begins 1973	1975	Person 1975	Life Begins 1973	1975	Person 1975
Men															
Age															
Under 30	28	40	28	17	14	10	21	16	30	28	25	21	(107)	(126)	(119)
30–44	30	41	25	21	11	10	19	16	32	19	24	23	(118)	(122)	(116)
45 +	29	36	26	22	16	17	12	15	20	21	22	22	(244)	(240)	(270)
Education															
Grade school	33	45	26	27	15	19	8	5	17	11	18	18	(78)	(73)	(77)
High school	31	41	29	23	16	14	13	13	22	21	20	20	(212)	(257)	(249)
College	26	31	21	16	10	11	22	23	32	27	31	25	(178)	(159)	(180)
Women															
Age															
Under 30	38	60	53	22	7	19	23	20	16	11	12	11	(104)	(114)	(122)
30–44	50	50	50	24	18	18	11	16	16	11	6	11	(143)	(141)	(125)
45 +	43	52	41	31	19	21	11	10	18	8	9	9	(219)	(224)	(238)
Education															
Grade school	42	65	46	38	20	16	6	2	9	10	0	5	(50)	(54)	(43)
High school	50	57	53	27	17	18	9	12	15	7	8	9	(292)	(274)	(284)
College	33	42	33	21	12	25	28	24	23	15	15	13	(130)	(155)	(159)

[a] See Table 10 for wording of questions.
[b] Percentages do not add to 100 in this table because of "don't know" and "other" responses not shown here in order to conserve space.

at birth. In this regard, they tend to be quite sharply distinguished from those at lesser educational levels. College-educated non-Catholic men are markedly more likely than any other subgrouping to regard life or personhood as coming late in the gestational process. Nonetheless, only a minority (on the average less than 30 percent) of even this special subgrouping in the population believes that either life or personhood begins at live birth.

In sum, it seems fair to say that major support for the view that life begins at birth cannot be found among any subgrouping we have considered within the non-Catholic population. This is true even among men who, on average, tend to be much more likely than women to place life and personhood late in the process of gestation. Concerning the increase between 1973 and 1975, in virtually all subgroupings, of the percentage of respondents believing that life begins at conception, we can only speculate that "right-to-life" campaigns—which emphasize this point—may have been having some effect on public opinion.

The issues discussed so far in this section had wide exposure prior to the Court's decisions. However, many problems involved in the decisions, or resulting from them, relate to technicalities with which the general public is likely to have only marginal familiarity. Hence, given a lack of knowledge or thought concerning the specific application to abortion, responses may be highly stereotyped in terms of whatever facet of the problem seems most generally reasonable or normatively relevant. For example, as we have seen, the question concerning whether abortions should be performed only in hospitals or in medical facilities other than hospitals elicited a preponderance of responses favoring the hospital site. Yet, as events have turned out, according to Weinstock and his colleagues, "90 percent of the increase in the number of abortions reported between the first quarter of 1973 and the first quarter of 1974 was accounted for by specialized nonhospital abortion clinics." Clinic abortions now exceed the number performed in hospitals, and there has been a large increase in the number of legal abortions performed in physicians' offices. Hospitals, on the other hand, have responded slowly to the Court's decisions, and this delay has particularly characterized public hospitals on which the poor are heavily dependent.[15] Yet in spite of the increase in nonhospital abortions, abortion-related mortality has declined significantly since 1973.[16]

It is thus possible that the high overall response favoring hospitals already reported in this paper and the strong bias in favor of hospitals even when the data are disaggregated by age and education (Table 12) indicate that the public was responding in a general way to the notion

TABLE 12

Responses of white men and women by religion, age, and education to the question, "Some state laws specify that abortions may be performed only in hospitals, whereas other states allow abortions to be performed in various kinds of outside medical facilities other than hospitals. Do you think that it should be legal to perform an abortion only in a hospital, or would you permit the use of outside medical facilities other than hospitals?" asked on a Gallup survey during the last week in January 1973. In percentages.

	Only in Hospitals		All Right Outside Hospitals		No Opinion		Total[a]	
	Men	Women	Men	Women	Men	Women	Men	Women
Religion								
Catholic	68	71	29	29	3	0	100 (153)	100 (178)
Non-Catholic	60	65	35	31	5	4	100 (427)	100 (434)
Age								
Under 30	54	57	43	41	3	2	100 (153)	100 (160)
30–44	61	63	36	35	3	2	100 (153)	100 (189)
45 +	67	76	28	20	5	4	100 (270)	100 (256)
Educational Level								
Grade school	66	85	26	9	8	6	100 (84)	100 (64)
High school	73	71	25	26	2	3	100 (279)	100 (387)
College	47	48	49	49	4	3	100 (214)	100 (158)
Total	62	67	34	30	4	3	100 (581)	100 (612)

[a]This table omits those respondents who volunteered that they would not approve abortion under any circumstances.

TABLE 13

Percentage giving a negative response to the question, "Do you think it should be lawful for a woman to be able to get an abortion operation without her husband's consent?" White men and women in the United States by religious affiliation, age, and educational level. Gallup survey, August 1972 and October 1974.

	Men Aug. 1972	Men Oct. 1974	Women Aug. 1972	Women Oct. 1974	Total Aug. 1972	Total Oct. 1974
Religion						
Catholic	76	76	69	75	72	76
Non-Catholic	63	62	66	57	65	59
Age						
Under 30	63	61	70	59	67	60
30–44	74	73	69	63	71	68
45 +	65	65	64	62	64	64
Educational level						
Grade school	67	73	72	78	69	75
High school	73	72	70	64	72	68
College	58	56	55	48	57	52
Total disapproving	67	66	67	61	67	64
TOTAL RESPONDENTS	(663)	(692)	(682)	(682)	(1345)	(1374)

that an operation should be performed in a hospital. Popular predispositions, therefore, even those of almost half the college educated, favored restrictions concerning the site for abortions that *Doe* v. *Bolton* attempted to abolish. As noted already, these results do not mean that public views on this subject could not change in favor of the *Doe* v. *Bolton* ruling. The responses do show, however, that *of themselves* Americans seized upon a restrictive, highly medicalized view which, in practice, serves to deter ready access to abortion. Such a view thus provides implicit support for organized anti-abortionists, who attempt to deter access to abortion through local restriction in defiance of *Roe* and *Doe*.

Disaggregated results of the question concerning the husband's consent (Table 13) are similarly illustrative of what may be, in many cases, conventionalized responses. Admittedly, unlike the hospital issue, the problem is complex from the point of view both of familial norms and individual equity. But this fact could argue that, given widespread public awareness, responses might have been sharply differentiated among groups who viewed their interests as opposed. For example, it is not unreasonable to expect that when asked to consider this issue in 1972, younger and more highly educated women would have been influenced by the general notion of women's rights, even though the abortion decisions had not yet made the husband's consent a matter of widespread practical import. Yet, as late as 1972, more young women were disapproving than young men, and there was no significant difference by sex among the college educated, well over half of whom disapproved. In fact, with the exception of the college educated, two-thirds to three-fourths of respondents disaggregated by age, education, and religion disapproved allowing abortion without the husband's consent. Thus, although this period was one of great public ferment concerning women's rights, even segments of the public that we know were proportionately sympathetic to the women's movement did not necessarily make the relevant transfer to an issue such as abortion without the husband's consent but instead responded conventionally.

In late 1974, by which time the decisions had been made and the issue had been dealt with specifically by leaders of the women's movement, there is evidence of a substantial drop in disapproval among young women and some decline among those having a high school or college education. No similar response is evident for comparable men. It thus appears that, in this case as in others, proponents of *Roe* and *Doe* cannot rely even on interested and educated segments of the public to support ready access to abortion unless organized groups provide intellectual and ideological assistance. Left to themselves and with numerous other problems to distract them, the public is in no sense prepared to counter organized efforts to block implementation of *Roe* and *Doe*.

The issue of migratory abortion provides a good example of a problem—freedom of movement among the states—whose general nature apparently has had high saliency for some groups in the population (Table 14). The young and the college educated are strongly differentiated from the rest of the population in approving freedom to seek an abortion in another state—for example, approximately 60 percent of the college educated but only about 25 percent of those having a grade-school education would allow migratory abortion.

Summary and Conclusion

During the past twenty-five years, judicial review had been increasingly invoked as a means of effecting rapid social change. Whether, in fact, judicial decisions have helped to accomplish the intended changes more rapidly than would otherwise have happened is impossible to gauge. One thing is clear, however, In matters that are deeply controversial and that involve detailed compliance by more than a few strategically located individuals, implementation of court decisions is notoriously vulnerable both to the normal process of bureaucratic footdragging and, as well, to purposive collateral deterrence by organized opposition. The effort to implement the desegregation decisions is, of course, the prime example of the power of such inhibitions.

Like the desegregation decisions, the Supreme Court rulings on abortion (*Roe* v. *Wade* and *Doe* v. *Bolton*), handed down in January 1973, were highly controversial. Moreover, although the abortion decisions do not involve such a massive problem of compliance as has been engendered by desegregation, their implementation nonetheless does engage, directly and indirectly, numerous public officials and health professionals at local levels all over the country. To make liberalized abortion readily available to all segments of the population desiring such a service would require a widespread commitment by public servants and members of the health professions to comply with both the letter and the spirit of *Roe* and *Doe*.

There are many reasons intrinsic to the professional orientation and structural location of these groups that have been inimical to full, nationwide implementation of *Roe* and *Doe*. For example, since health professionals are conditioned to the preservation of life, widespread resort to abortion, to the extent implied by *Roe* and *Doe*, is repugnant to

TABLE 14

Responses of white men and women by religion, age, and education to the question, "In some states the laws make it easy to get an abortion, and in others they make it hard. Do you think the easy states should limit abortions only to their own residents, or should they freely allow women from other states to come and get abortions?" asked on a Gallup survey during the last week in January 1973. In percentages.

	Limit to Own Residents		Allow Women From Other States		No Opinion		Total[a]	
	Men	Women	Men	Women	Men	Women	Men	Women
Religion								
Catholic	54	47	38	45	8	8	100 (190)	100 (222)
Non-Catholic	46	46	46	45	8	9	100 (472)	100 (474)
Age								
Under 30	34	35	59	59	7	6	100 (153)	100 (157)
30–44	51	49	41	46	8	5	100 (152)	100 (186)
45 +	56	52	36	35	8	13	100 (259)	100 (246)
Educational Level								
Grade school	66	63	25	23	9	14	100 (104)	100 (80)
High school	54	50	39	41	7	9	100 (319)	100 (442)
College	36	32	55	61	9	7	100 (234)	100 (170)
Total	48	46	44	45	8	9	100 (569)	100 (596)

[a] This table omits those respondents who volunteered that they would not approve abortion under any circumstances.

many physicians and, apparently, to proportionately even more nurses. It is hardly surprising, therefore, that the medical establishment (as exemplified in the country's network of hospitals) has responded sluggishly to the increased demand for abortions. Equally, since allegations leveled at public officials who support the Court's decisions can be exceptionally ugly and distasteful, public servants generally have not gone out of their way to ensure availability of abortion to all women who fall within the purview of the Court's decisions.

Such inhibitions have been exacerbated by the rise, since the Court's decisions, of an organized national "right-to-life" movement which includes numerous active and aggressive local branches. The movement is committed not only to passing an anti-abortion amendment to the Constitution but, of more practical and immediate import, to localized collateral deterrence of access to abortion as defined and upheld in *Roe* and *Doe*.

The present paper suggests that, on balance, public views concerning the problems raised by *Roe* and *Doe* (and emanating from the decisions) serve to bolster bureaucratic and professional conservatism as well as organized anti-abortion efforts. First of all, with respect neither to the justifications for abortion nor to issues such as the timing of pregnancy termination, when life begins, and the legitimate physical site for abortion does the public fully concur in the content of the decisions. In many cases, responses are at a great distance from the decisions.

Second, with respect to some issues, this lack of concurrence may involve deeply held convictions. For example, trend data concerning justifications for abortion seem to indicate that somewhat more than half of the population genuinely disapprove elective abortion—abortion for no other reason than that the woman does not want the prospective child. There has, to be sure, been a decline over time in disapproval of elective abortion, but the decline has slackened off since 1970. Hence, with regard to one of the essential elements of *Roe* and *Doe*, a majority of the public still is not supportive of the basic "right" upheld in the decisions and, in fact, may be more than superficially antagonistic to its affirmation.

Finally, even when large-scale divergence from the Court's views exemplifies lack of saliency rather than public conviction, the effect is nonetheless negative to abortion, even if only temporarily so. Something would have to be done to change the widespread view that abortions should be performed only in hospitals or that a woman should not be able to get one without her husband's consent, since these are not issues of everyday concern. Moreover, if something *is* being done by anti-abortionists to capture public support concerning issues about which there is some confusion and indecision, then one cannot assume that clarification of opinion will necessarily move in a direction favorable to the Court's decisions. We are, for example, witnessing an apparent increase in the proportion of respondents who believe that "life" and "personhood" begin at conception.

The present paper suggests that leaders of the pro-abortion movement must rapidly face up to the truth regarding public views on abortion. Claims that anti-abortionists are a morally and politically isolated group, whose effects can readily be contained and nullified by the strong majority support for elective abortion, are oversimplified and misleading. Moreover, from a practical standpoint, this erroneous definition of the situation incapacitates the pro-abortion camp from mounting concerted opposition to increasingly organized "right-to-life" efforts. On the one hand, pro-abortionists have undercut their own potential role in warning that organized effort is necessary to combat collateral deterrence and influence public opinion. On the other, by misrepresenting the potential influence of opposition to abortion as well as the actual level of public support for it, they have systematically undermined the credibility of any warning that might be sounded. Basking in the warm afterglow of the Court's decisions, the movement has collectively repressed the drubbing it took in the Michigan elections of November 1972. Then, by dint of ignoring and denigrating "right-to-life" activity, supporters of liberalized abortion, in a matter of weeks, managed to snatch defeat from the jaws of victory.

Admittedly, in having to efface the rosy picture it has been attempting to create for the benefit of highly placed public officials, the pro-abortion movement may suffer some loss of credibility. But this seems like a relatively small and short-run price to pay for the immense long-run advantage of remobilizing the troops and, above all, attempting to cope with, rather than misrepresent, the actual views of the public on this subject. Without such an effort, bureaucratic and professional resistance, organized opposition, and public disapproval, ambivalence, and inattention may well turn *Roe* and *Doe* into an empty victory in the years to come.

NOTES

1. At the time of the decisions, only four states—New York, Alaska, Hawaii, and Washington—had abortion statutes that conformed to the Court's decisions, and even in these cases, the last three of the states mentioned above had residency requirements which became invalid under *Doe* v. *Bolton*. Fifteen additional states had relatively updated abortion laws (conforming in greater or lesser degree to the legislation suggested by the American Law Institute).

The remaining states had highly restrictive older laws which required complete revision in order to comply.

2. Judith Blake, "Elective Abortion and Our Reluctant Citizenry," in *The Abortion Experience*, ed. Howard J. Osofsky and Joy D. Osofsky (Hagerstown, Maryland: Harper and Row, 1973), pp. 447–67.

3. Barbara J. Culliton, "Abortion and Manslaughter: A Boston Doctor Goes on Trial," *Science* 187 (January 31, 1975): 334–35.

4. Barbara J. Culliton, "Fetal Research: The Case History of a Massachusetts Law," *Science* 187 (January 24, 1975): 237–41; and "Fetal Research (II): The Nature of a Massachusetts Law," *Science* 187 (February 7, 1975): 411–13.

5. Jeannie I. Rosoff, "Is Support of Abortion Political Suicide?" *Family Planning Perspectives* 7 (January/February 1975): 13–22.

6. See, for example, Rosoff, "Is Support of Abortion Political Suicide?" and Richard Pomeroy and Lynn C. Landman, "Public Opinion Trends: Elective Abortion and Birth Control Services to Teenagers," *Family Planning Perspectives* 4 (October 1972): 44–55.

7. See note 3 above and Judith Blake, "Abortion and Public Opinion: The 1960–1970 Decade," *Science* 171 (February 12, 1975): 540–49; Elise F. Jones and Charles F. Westoff, "Attitudes toward Abortion in the United States in 1970 and the Trend Since 1965," in U.S. Commission on Population Growth and the American Future, *Demographic and Social Aspects of Population Growth*, ed. C. F. Westoff and R. Parke, Jr. (Washington, D.C.: U.S. Government Printing Office, 1972), pp. 569–85; and Elise F. Jones and Charles F. Westoff, "Changes in Attitudes toward Abortion: With Emphasis Upon the National Fertility Study Data," in *The Abortion Experience*, ed. Howard J. Osofsky and Joy D. Osofsky, pp. 468–81.

8. See note 3 above.

9. See note 6 above.

10. These surveys use nationwide probability samples of adults of voting age. The Gallup corporation is one of the highest-rated and most experienced commercial survey units in the country. In evaluating results from these surveys, as compared, for example, with results from the national fertility studies, the reader should be aware that the latter also were conducted by commercial survey corporations.

11. See note 3 above.

12. Ibid.

13. As has been mentioned, no reference was made in these questions to the Supreme Court decisions on abortion.

14. *The United States Law Week*, January 23, 1973, p. 4227.

15. Edward Weinstock, Christopher Tietze, Frederick S. Jaffe and Joy G. Dryfoos, "Legal Abortions in the United States Since the 1973 Supreme Court Decisions," *Family Planning Perspectives* 7 (January/February 1975): 23–31.

16. "Abortion-Related Deaths Down 40 Percent Since 1973 Supreme Court Rulings Overturning Restrictive State Abortion Laws," *Family Planning Perspectives* 7 (March/April 1975): 54.

Abortion and the Constitution: The Cases of the United States and West Germany

DONALD P. KOMMERS*

1. Introduction

On January 22, 1973, the United States Supreme Court substantially curtailed the power of the American states to prohibit or limit the right of a woman to procure an abortion.[1] On February 25, 1975, the West German Federal Constitutional Court ruled that the German parliament, by permitting abortions within the first three months of pregnancy, violated the constitutional rights of unborn children.[2] These decisions provide us with an uncommon opportunity to compare the constitutional law of different nations on abortion. That the highest tribunals of two robust constitutional democracies and secular political cultures should decide the question of the unborn child's right to life under the constitutions of their respective countries differently should excite the wonder of us all, no matter where we may stand in the abortion controversy.

This paper seeks to restate and assess the reasoning in support of the doctrinal result in the German and American cases and then to

---

*This chapter first appeared in *The American Journal of Comparative Law* 25 (1977): pp. 255–85 and is reprinted here by permission of the author and the *Journal*. This material is a revised version of a paper originally prepared for delivery at the April 1-3, 1976, meeting of the Western Political Science Association, in San Francisco. The author wishes to thank Professor Dr. Hans Verweyen (Essen University, West Germany) and Professor Walter F. Murphy (Princeton University) for their valuable comments and suggestions on an earlier draft of the paper. He is also grateful to Mr. Michael J. Wahoske, research assistant in the Center for Civil Rights of the University of Notre Dame Law School, for his generous assistance and meticulous workmanship.

relate those results to the legal culture and constitutional values of the two countries. Yet we cannot wholly separate the two decisions from their political contexts or from the debate, intense in both countries, about the role of the judiciary in their respective systems of government. In both countries the very propriety of judicial intervention in the policy-making process on abortion has been severely deplored. In fact, the issue of the judiciary's role in the making of abortion policy received considerable stress by the dissenting justices of both tribunals. Thus we cannot afford to ignore the issue here.

Democracy and constitutionalism, although capable of creatively coexisting within the same political order, are principles with a frequent aversion for one another. The tension between these principles is clear in the abortion cases. The ruling in both regimes represents a judicial veto of legislative policy. In the United States and West Germany, however, judicial authorities are empowered to review statutes on constitutional grounds and, if they find in a case properly before them that an act of the legislature is in conflict with the constitution, they may nullify the act or refuse to enforce it. In a regime of judicial review—such as West Germany and the United States—authority of the judiciary to void legislation raises serious questions about the relationship between courts and legislatures, particularly since the line separating constitutionality and unconstitutionality is thin and often the source of lively dispute between fair and reasonable men. A full comprehension of the abortion decisions will require some further mention of this relationship in the two political systems together with some discussion of the legal rules governing the jurisdiction of the deciding tribunals.

2. Background

A. The United States

Roe v. *Wade* and *Doe* v. *Bolton* involved litigants in Texas and Georgia who challenged on federal constitutional grounds their respective state statutes limiting the right of a woman to obtain a legal abortion.[3] These statutes were typical of most state laws on abortion. The Texas law prohibited abortion unless procured by medical advice for the purpose of saving the life of the mother.[4] When *Wade* and *Bolton* were decided, the criminal abortion laws of a majority of states were similarly restrictive. For the most part, these laws were carbon copies of state statutes enacted in the early nineteenth century.

Georgia's statute, patterned after the American Law Institute's Model Penal Code,[5] was of more recent vintage. Revised in 1968, it limited legal abortions to situations where (1) a continuation of the pregnancy would endanger the life or seriously and permanently injure the health of the pregnant woman, (2) the fetus would very likely be born with a grave, permanent, and irremediable mental or physical defect, or (3) the pregnancy resulted from forcible or statutory rape. Among the statute's procedural and evidentiary provisions was the requirement of a written medical opinion by a physician stating that an abortion is justified under the statute along with the written concurrence in that opinion by at least two other physicians licensed to practice medicine in Georga.[6]

Prior to the Supreme Court's holding in these cases, abortion was a criminal offense in all the American states. Historically, the social judgments which these laws embodied enjoyed a firm mooring in the nation's moral consciousness. But within a relatively short period of time, roughly during the 1960s, public support for restrictive abortion laws seemed dramatically to erode, although still today's public opinion polls show substantial minority support for such laws. More important was the reversal in educated American opinion, particularly within the legal and medical communities, which probably laid the foundation for the liberalization of some state abortion laws, notably that of New York, effectively allowing abortion on demand up to the twenty-fourth week of pregnancy.[7]

Another striking instance of this shift in influential opinion was the 1972 report of the President's Commission on Population Growth, which recommended that abortion be readily available in all the states.[8] Yet in spite of such pronouncements and in the face of mounting opposition to restrictive abortion statutes, state legislators generally held firm in their conviction that existing laws were not only a fair accommodation between the interests of pregnant women and unborn children but also a reflection of predominant moral feeling among their constituents. *Wade* and *Bolton* came to the Supreme Court within this general context of continuing state legislative support of policies proscribing abortion. *Wade* involved a pregnant single woman, *Bolton* an indigent, married, pregnant woman, both of whom sought declaratory judgments that their respective state abortion laws (Texas and Georgia) were unconstitutional.

Some commentators have strenuously argued that the Supreme Court exceeded its rightful authority in reaching the merits of *Wade* and *Bolton*, for the female litigants had already terminated their pregnancies—rendering their cases moot in the eyes of the Court's critics—and were in no immediate danger of losing their liberty or being deprived of a federal constitutional right.[9] According to this view, the parties had no "standing to sue" and were therefore incapable of invoking the Court's jurisdiction.[10] However, the Court remarked in *Wade* that litigation involving pregnancy, which is "capable of repetition" is an exception to the federal rule that an actual controversy must exist at the time a case is decided on appeal.[11] In *Bolton* the Court held that even licensed physicians consulted by pregnant women have standing to sue because they are within reach of the law's criminal provisions. These physicians "should not be required to await and undergo a criminal prosecution as the sole means of seeking relief,"[12] asserted the Court. Thus, the abortion cases were capable of judicial resolution.

Some of the Court's critics have noted that this apparent stretching of the standing rule is the result of significant enlargement of the Court's own perception of its institutional role. They would probably agree with Richard A. Epstein's assertion that "the Supreme Court today views constitutional litigation as a means of settling great conflicts of the social order."[13] On the other hand, as de Tocqueville once reminded us, all great political conflicts in America tend eventually to resolve themselves into constitutional questions.[14] Failing to achieve their objectives by political means, proponents of liberalized abortion laws naturally gravitated to the judiciary, seeking victory on more favorable terrain. For purposes of this analysis, however, it is not the victory that is important but rather the Court's own capacity to persuade a reasonably open mind of the validity and propriety of its ultimate ruling.

B. West Germany

The German case provides an intriguing contrast to the American situation. First, although West Germany is a federal republic composed of ten states, excluding West Berlin, the making of abortion policy falls exclusively within the jurisdiction of the national government. Unlike the bulk of criminal law in the United States, the Penal Code, Section 218 of which provides penalties for illegal abortion, is national law. Originally based on the Prussian Penal Code of 1851, the current code was adopted by the German Reich in 1871.[15] The code provisions on abortion under inspection here were associated with a major effort in Germany to revise and reform the criminal code as a whole. The Revised Penal Code went into effect on January 2, 1975.

Second, the Basic Law of 1949 (*Grundgesetz*) confers on the Federal Constitutional Court explicit and far-reaching powers of judicial review. Among these powers is the Court's authority to resolve "differences of opinion or doubts on the formal and material compatibility of federal law or land (state) law with this Basic Law."[16] This is known as an abstract judicial review proceeding (*abstrakte Normenkontrolle*), which can be initiated only by the federal government (chancellor and cabinet), a state government, or one-third of the Bundestag's members.[17] The proceeding is called "abstract" because no concrete controversy involving adverse parties engaged in litigation before the regular courts is required, as in the United States, to trigger the exercise of judicial review. Thus politicians and governments may draw the Federal Constitutional Court into their political conflicts almost at will, risking the possibility of the Court blunting government by majority rule well before the democratic process is fully played out.[18] Thus a defeated legislative minority of 100 delegates or more is able, as happened in the abortion case, to transfer a controversy directly from the legislature to the Constitutional Court if the statute, once duly promulgated, is challenged on constitutional grounds.[19] Such a capability would on first impression appear anomalous in a parliamentary democracy powered by a responsible party system, committed to majority rule.

Yet the Federal Constitutional Court has been one of the strongest guardians of the democratic process in West Germany, seeking to insure, for example, that the system of political representation operates to guarantee public policies reasonably in accord with the "general will."[20] Since it has been alleged in some circles that the decision-making process here violated the principle of democratic responsibility, we should recapitulate the steps leading to the parliamentary approval of the Abortion Reform Act of 1974.[21]

In contrast to the United States, where long-standing abortion statutes were not the subject of *extended* legislative discussion prior to their sudden invalidation by the Supreme Court, the new German policy had long been preceded by a lively national debate. Like most American state laws, the Germany Penal Code since the mid-nineteenth century had placed a ban on abortion however and whenever performed. The old abortion statute included the following provisions:

1. A woman who destroys her fetus or permits it to be destroyed by another, shall be punished by imprisonment, and in especially serious cases by confinement in a penitentiary.
2. The attempt is punishable.
3. Any other person who destroys the fetus of a pregnant woman shall be punished by confinement in a penitentiary, and in less serious cases, by imprisonment.
4. Anybody who supplies a pregnant woman with a drug or object designed to destroy the fetus, shall be punished by imprisonment, and in especially serious cases by confinement in a penitentiary.[22]

Subject to considerable official scrutiny during the time of the Weimar Republic, this law was relaxed in its severity by a 1927 decision of the Supreme Court (*Reichsgericht*), which held that an abortion procured for medical reasons (*medizinische Indikationen*)—that is, when necessary to preserve the life and health of the pregnant woman—was not punishable under the law.[23] An abortion procured by legitimate medical means to preserve the mother's life is an "extra-legal emergency" (*uebergesetzliche Notstand*), said the Court, and can be justified within broad principles of the criminal law.[24]

In the 1950s another comprehensive review of abortion policy took place, culminating in the German Draft Penal Code of 1962.[25] The draft code continued to treat abortion as a punishable offense but lowered considerably the maximum penalty. In addition, the proposed code permitted the destruction of the fetus by a physician "if according to medical knowledge and experience, danger of death or of undue and serious injury to the body or health ... of the woman can be averted only by the abortion."[26] Under considerable pressure to liberalize abortion policy, parliament nevertheless failed to enact these provisions into law. Indeed, there was considerable parliamentary sentiment in favor of decriminalizing abortion within the first twelve weeks of pregnancy, mainly because of the feeling among legislators that penal sanctions were of little use in deterring abortions.

Between 1965 and 1972, parliament considered several abortion reform bills, but none commanded anything close to majority support.[27] Finally, in April 1972, a special committee on criminal law reform held public hearings on two major proposals, one offering an "indications" solution and the other a "term" solution as a means of liberalizing the old abortion law.[28] The first proposal, introduced by the federal government, would have allowed an abortion in four situations: to preserve the life and health of the mother ("medical indications"); to avert the birth of a seriously defective child ("eugenic indications"); to terminate a pregnancy caused by a sexual assault ("ethical indications"); and to unburden the woman of extremely harmful consequences that would arise in the event of the child's birth ("social indications"). In the last two situations an abortion would have been permissible only in the first trimester of pregnancy, subject to the sole condition that the operation be performed by a licensed physician after the woman has submitted to professional counseling.

The second proposal—a term solution—would have rested a decision to abort a fetus entirely with the woman and her physician within the first three months of pregnancy. But even the governing coalition of the Social Democratic party (SPD) and the Free Democratic party (FDP) headed by Chancellor Willy Brandt felt that this measure, failing adequately to protect unborn life, was too extreme. The Christian Democratic Union (CDU) and its conservative Bavarian affiliate, the Christian Social Union (CSU), were in opposition to both bills. Thus, abortion policy in West Germany, unlike the United States, became the subject of partisan controversy, with the ensuing parliamentary strife mirroring the fierce clash of opposing groups in the society at large. But a domestic economic crisis resulted in the premature dissolution of parliament, and with the calling of new federal elections in November 1972 the legislative debate on abortion came to a sudden close.

Surprisingly, abortion reform was not debated by the contesting political parties in the 1972 election campaign.[29] Social Democrats, needing Catholic votes, were especially reluctant to raise the issue, although Free Democrats occasionally spoke out in favor of a liberalized abortion law. As a consequence, the Brandt government, even though returning to power with a substantial parliamentary majority, could not easily claim to have a popular mandate for an abortion reform policy, and none was introduced by the government in to the newly elected parliament. Instead, four separate bills proposed by individual legislators and party groups were referred to a special committee on penal law reform. These bills included proposals ranging from a policy of abortion on demand in the early months of pregnancy, favored by a small group of SPD–FDP delegates, to an abortion policy restricted to medical indications, favored by Christian Democrats. None received majority support in the special committee, whereupon, in an unusual move, all four bills were sent to the floor of the Bundestag.

The new Abortion Reform Act of 1974, which was backed by a majority of SPD and FDP delegates, amended the Penal Code in the following ways: First, termination of a pregnancy would no longer be punishable during the first twelve weeks after conception if performed by a licensed physician with the consent of the pregnant woman (Section 218a); second, destruction of the fetus would be permissible after the first twelve weeks if warranted by medical or eugenic indications and procured prior to the twenty-second week of pregnancy (Section 218b); finally, the person or physician terminating the pregnancy—not the pregnant woman—would be punishable under the act (Section 218d). Criminal penalties would continue to operate with respect to abortions performed after the third month of pregnancy, except in those instances where medical, eugenic, or ethical indications would justify the fetus's destruction.[30]

We should note that those Germans who might have wished a stout parliamentary defense of the pregnant woman's right to interrupt a pregnancy would recoil before the SPD–FDP's rationale in support of the Reform Act, for the new policy was ostensibly based on a theory of deterrence. Whatever the feeling toward abortion outside parliament, the legislative reform was not predicated on any presumed right of women flatly to terminate their pregnancies. The counseling section of the new law was simply regarded as a more effective method of turning pregnant women away from abortion and of protecting unborn life than resort to criminal sanctions. This strategy was adopted in the awareness that women, despite criminal penalties, were resorting increasingly to illegal abortion. Thus the decriminalization of abortion in the early months of pregnancy was no ringing affirmation of a female bill of rights; it merely represented an attempt by parliament to adjust the legal order to an evolving social reality.

Even so, the act came under instant attack, which was both political and constitutional. On the political side some Christian Democrats suggested—and this ties in with the earlier-mentioned argument based on democratic theory—that there was no mandate in support of the abortion statute. And the haste with which the bill was finally passed precluded any meaningful consultation between the government, charged under the Basic Law with the primary responsibility of setting policy guidelines,[31] and the parliament. Moreover, as the Constitutional Court itself acknowledged, the bill failed to command majority support upon first balloting in the Bundestag and was finally accepted by fewer than an absolute majority of delegates as the less objectionable of two proposals which survived an earlier ballot taken to eliminate those bills with least support. Thus, the bill finally approved was not the first, nor in many cases the second, choice of legislators voting for it. From the point of view of democratic theory, then, opponents of the bill could suggest that the statute did not bear the clear stamp of legitimacy marking a policy generated within a parliamentary democracy.

The more serious challenge to the Abortion Reform Act was constitutional. The ink had barely dried on the act when the state governments of Baden-Württemberg, Bavaria, Rhineland-Pfalz, Saarland, and Schleswig-Holstein—half of the German states—together with 193 members of the Bundestag—all Christian Democrats—filed petitions with the Federal Constitutional Court challenging its validity under several provisions of the Basic Law. On June 21, 1974, the Court responded by issuing a temporary injunction enjoining the application of the law pending a full determination of its constitutionality.

3. The Courts Speak

A. The American Decision

There are several interesting steps in the Supreme Court's argument in *Wade* and *Bolton*. Speaking through Mr. Justice Blackmun, the Court first explored the historical origin of American state abortion laws. Its rather detailed excursion through history includes a description of abortion policy as reflected in Greek and Roman law, the Hippocratic oath, common law, English statutory law, and American law, followed by an analysis of the evolving policy and current attitudes of the American Medical Association, the American Public Health Association, and the American Bar Association. Without indicating precisely the relevance of its historical overview to the doctrinal point made later in the opinion, the Court then hastened into a discussion of the reasons justifying American criminal abortion statutes. After noting that most were passed in the latter half of the nineteenth century, the Court concluded that they were intended mainly for the purpose of protecting the woman from a dangerous medical procedure as well as for the purpose of preserving prenatal life.[32]

Justice Blackmun then turned to a consideration of the right to privacy. Acknowledging that the Constitution does not explicitly mention any such right, he affirmed its existence by implication, citing several decisions in which the Court has found in varying contexts at least the roots of that right under assorted provisions of the Constitution. The conclusion of the Court deserves to be quoted in full:

> This right of privacy, whether it be founded in the Fourteenth Amendment's concept of personal liberty and restrictions upon state action, as we feel it is, or, as the District Court determined, in the Ninth Amendment's reservation of rights to the people, is broad enough to encompass a woman's decision whether or not to terminate her pregnancy. The detriment that the State would impose upon the pregnant woman by denying this choice altogether is apparent. Specific and direct harm medically diagnosable even in early pregnancy may be involved. Maternity, or additional offspring, may force upon the woman a distressful life and future. Psychological harm may be imminent. Mental and physical health may be taxed by child care. There is also the dis-

tress, for all concerned, associated with the unwanted child, and there is the problem of bringing a child into a family already unable, psychologically and otherwise, to care for it. In other cases, as in this one, the additional difficulties and continuing stigma of unwed motherhood may be involved. All these are factors the woman and responsible physician necessarily will consider in consultation.[33]

However, cautioned the Court, the right of personal privacy is not absolute. At some point in pregnancy, wrote Justice Blackmun, "a state may assert important interests in safeguarding health, in maintaining medical standards, and in protecting potential life."[34]

Crucial to the outcome of the abortion cases was the question of whether the Fourteenth Amendment protects the unborn fetus from indiscriminate destruction.[35] Justice Blackmun answered by declaring that the fetus is not a "person" within the Fourteenth Amendment's protection. Taking judicial notice of the historical conflict among theologians, philosophers, and physicians over the issue of the fetus's personhood, the Court simply asserted: "We need not resolve the difficult question of when life begins."[36] When, then, does the state acquire a legitimate interest in protecting "potential life"? Approximately at the end of the second trimester of pregnancy, when the fetus has become viable, answered the Court. At this stage, the state "may, if it chooses, regulate, and even proscribe, abortion except where it is necessary, in appropriate medical judgment, for the preservation of the life or health of the mother."[37] At the end of the first trimester the state may begin to regulate the abortion procedure in the interest of promoting the health of the mother, but it may not constitutionally prohibit abortions altogether. During the first trimester the state is powerless to assert any legitimate interest in regulating abortion: At this stage the woman's right to privacy is predominant; the abortion decision "must be left to [her and] the medical judgment of the pregnant woman's attending physician."[38]

Dissenting opinions were written by Justices White and Rehnquist. In one of his strongest dissents ever, Justice White described the majority opinion as "an exercise in raw judicial power," one which effectively upholds, and imposes upon the states, a policy of abortion on demand. "The Court simply fashions and announces a new constitutional right for pregnant mothers and with scarcely any reason or authority for its action, invests that right with sufficient substance to override most existing state abortion statutes."[39] In White's view, the Court had merely substituted its values with respect to the ordering of priorities between mother and unborn child for those of the states, a policy which "should be left with the people and to the political processes the people have devised to govern their affairs."[40] Justice Rehnquist, in an opinion which questioned the plaintiffs' standing, also attacked the sweeping invalidation of all restrictions on abortion during the first trimester of pregnancy. He denied that the right to privacy was involved in these cases and reproached the majority for ignoring the history of the Fourteenth Amendment whose adoption discloses, according to the justice, no understanding in the minds of the framers that unborn children were not to be regarded as "persons" within its protection.[41]

Three justices concurred in the majority opinion. Chief Justice Burger, displeased with the dissenting justices' wide interpretation of the majority opinion, rejected the contention that the rule in the cases permits abortion on demand. Justice Douglas, hedging against a too narrow interpretation of the rule and meeting Justice White's argument about the ordering of priorities between fetus and mother, found Georgia's statute constitutionally defective precisely "because it equates the value of embryonic life immediately after conception with the worth of life immediately before birth" and because the statute fails to include the psychological as well as the physical "health" of the woman as a permissible reason for the right of a woman to interrupt her pregnancy prior to viability.[42] In Douglas's view, the right of a woman to procure an abortion was well within the marital privacy cases on contraception. The concurring opinion of Justice Stewart was a reluctant acceptance—a capitulation following his long resistance, beginning with the *Connecticut* birth control case, to the doctrine of substantive due process—of the prevailing view that social policy is now subject to judicial review on substantive grounds.[43] Rather than scouring the Constitution's hidden recesses for a nonexistent right of personal privacy, he squarely holds on the basis of his reading of the precedents, that the right of a woman to procure an abortion is part of the "liberty" protected by the due process clause of the Fourteenth Amendment.[44]

B. *The German Decision*

On February 25, 1975, after eight months of judicial deliberation, the Federal Constitutional Court invalidated Section 218a of the Abortion Reform Act, and in effect directed parliament to reestablish abortion as a crime under the Penal Code. Until the enactment of a valid law, the Court announced that the following rules would govern German public policy on abortion: First, abortion would be permitted during the first twelve weeks of pregnancy under Section 218b of the Reform Act for medical or eugenic indications; second, the termination of pregnancy by a licensed physician during the first twelve weeks after conception would not be punishable if the pregnancy resulted from a criminal assault; finally, the courts would have discretionary authority to withhold criminal sanctions with regard to the termination of pregnancy by physicians during the first twelve weeks in those situations where abortion is the only remaining measure reasonably expected to relieve pregnant women of a "grave hardship."[45]

In striking at the heart of the act, the Court invoked Article 2, Section 2, of the Basic Law, which says: "Everyone shall have the right to life and to the inviolability of his person," what the Court calls an "objective value decision"—indeed the most fundamental value—of the German constitution. When read in tandem with Article 1, Section 1, directing the state "to respect and protect" the dignity of man, Article 2 incorporates an affirmative duty on the part of the state to secure and preserve human life. In sharp contrast to the U.S. Supreme Court, the German tribunal met head on the question of when human life begins: "Life in the sense of the historical existence of a human individual exists according to definite biological-physiological knowledge in any case from the 14th day after conception."[46] The Constitutional Court likewise rejected the notion, accepted by the Supreme Court, that the human fetus is divisible into three equal parts signifying gradation of personhood or humanness. "The process of development which has begun at that point in time is a continuous process," said the Court, "which cannot be sharply demarcated and does not allow a precise division of the various stages in the development of human life."[47] Thus the Basic Law's command to respect human life—a command likewise reflected in the abolition of capital punishment under Article 102—fully extends to the fetus within the mother's womb.

Broadly interpreting Article 2, the Court construed 'everyone' as everyone living, meaning unborn life as well as born life. That developing life or germinating life is indeed protected by Article 2 the Court found abundantly supported in the deliberations leading to the Basic Law's adoption.[48] Indeed, the Court found buried in the legislative history of the act an assertion by its main supporters—the Social and Free Democratic parties—that the "legal value of unborn life is to be respected in principle equally with that of born life."[49]

If this motivation was predominant, why then did the Court strike down the statute? Because, according to the justices, the state failed adequately to balance the interests of the unborn child with those of the mother. The justices acknowledged that pregnancy falls within that sphere of private relations constitutionally protected by Article 2, Section 1, of the Basic Law, which says: "Everyone shall have the right to the free development of his personality in so far as he does not violate the rights of others or offend against the constitutional order or the moral code." As this wording indicates, the free development of personality is a qualified right and in the case of pregnant women, noted the justices, it is qualified by the existence of another life about to become "an independent human being." The Court thereby rejected any theory which would treat the decision of a woman not to become pregnant in the first instance on the same level of constitutional protection as her decision to destroy a fetus once pregnancy has occurred. "A balance which guarantees protection of unborn life and secures the right of a pregnant woman to procure an abortion," declares the Court, "is not possible since the termination of pregnancy always means the destruction of human life."[50]

Yet the Court was not prepared to rule that the Basic Law requires the protection of unborn life regardless of the cost to the mother. Some balancing between the rights of mother and fetus is permissible, even while the Court noted—majority and minority justices alike—that under the Basic Law "dignity" as used within the meaning of Article 1 ("The dignity of man shall be inviolable") inheres equally in born and unborn life and is no more contingent on a human being's consciousness of it than on his physical ability to preserve it.[51] Hence *developing* human life has dignity, and this dignity must be taken into account, *especially* in the light of the developing fetus's inability to defend itself, when a pregnant woman's claim to the protection of her own dignity would result in terminating the developing life within her.

Accordingly, when balancing the right of the mother to the free development of her personality (Article 2, Section 1) and the right of the unborn child to life (Article 2, Section 2), the Court insisted that "both constitutional values be perceived in terms of their relationship to 'human dignity,' which is the heart of the political value system under the Constitution."[52] The rights of the unborn child and mother may be balanced, emphasized the justices, presumably in certain cases to the ultimate detriment of the unborn child, *so long as* the rightful claims of both are pondered within a framework—clearly demanded by the Basic Law—of respect for the supreme value of human life.

At issue in this constitutional litigation is whether a life-regarding framework of evaluation is provided by the counseling provisions of the Abortion Reform Act. Under Article 1 of the Basic Law the state is obligated to respect and defend the dignity of man. This duty of the state, declared the Court, is "comprehensive" (*umfassend*), for it not only proscribes state infringement upon "developing life" but also requires the state affirmatively to protect such life against illegal assault by private parties, including the pregnant woman herself. To defend human life as the ultimate value upon which all other rights depend is thus a fundamental responsibility of the legal order under the Basic Law.[53]

But simply to assert that the supreme value of human life is at stake is to beg large questions. Why are *penal* sanctions required to safeguard unborn life? And which governmental body or state agency shall be entrusted with this fundamental responsibility? The Court conceded that it is the legislature's responsibility ordinarily to determine the means by which fetal life is to be protected, subject only to the recognition that in the first instance developing life "is entrusted by nature to the protection of the mother."[54] Minimally, in the Court's view, the state must seek to reinforce the mother's own determination to protect unborn life, even if that requires the enactment of social welfare measures to support a private decision to preserve the fetus.[55]

The Court did not argue that the right of the unborn child to life must always prevail over the right of the mother to self-determination. Nor did it insist that a law protecting postnatal life apply with equal rigor to prenatal life. The justices acknowledged that under the Basic Law the unborn child's right to life may impose a burden upon the mother far in excess of the normal travail associated with pregnancy. They conceded that penal measures are an inadequate response to situations where pregnancy leads to "grave hardship."[56] Indeed, a proper balancing of rights requires the state to respect a morally conscious decision to terminate a pregnancy whose continuance would *seriously* and *unreasonably* impinge upon the ability of a woman to preserve her own personhood. In removing such cases from the reach of the criminal law, however, the state must not neglect its duty to protect life; indeed the state is obligated to admonish the pregnant woman of the necessity to preserve the right of life of the unborn, to encourage her to continue the pregnancy, and to support her through practical aid in cases of special difficulty. In all other cases, admonished the justices, abortion must remain a punishable offense within the German legal order for the very reason that when the termination of pregnancy results from mere whim or is unmotivated by a severe condition of distress, it assumes the character of an arbitrary act clearly subversive of the highest value of the Basic Law. But even here, the decriminalization of abortion is justified under the Basic Law only when other equally effective sanctions are applied and only when the law clearly marks abortion as an illegal act.

In the Court's mind, the Abortion Reform Act satisfied neither these criteria nor the level of protection demanded of the state under Articles 1 and 2 of the Basic Law. The justices found Section 218a of the Reform Act constitutionally defective, first, because it failed expressly to embody an official disapproval of abortion during the first twelve weeks of pregnancy and, second, because the counseling plan failed to incorporate a pronounced pro-life orientation. When read together with a supplementary statute, enacted after parliament's approval of the Reform Act, extending the coverage of the state's obligatory health insurance program to the costs of an abortion, Section 218a was considered to be an unlawful encouragement to women wishing to terminate their pregnancies. A valid abortion policy, suggested the Court, must affirm the dignity of unborn life. Indeed a formal statutory condemnation of abortion is necessary to foreclose any inference that the destruction of fetal life during the first twelve weeks of pregnancy is morally or legally a permissible act.[57] In *ordinary* circumstances, noted the Court, "abortion is an act of killing that the law is obligated to condemn."[58]

Yet the state is not absolutely required to protect unborn life through penal sanctions. "The decisive factor," said the Court, "is whether the totality of measures protecting unborn life, be they socio-legal or penal in character, is a real safeguard corresponding to the importance of the legal value to be secured."[59] On the other hand, punishment must be exacted for the procurement of an abortion if no other means is adequate to protect the life of the unborn child. The penal sanction must be proportionate to the legal value threatened with extinction. Thus, as a general principle, "the elementary value of human life requires criminal law punishment for its destruction."[60]

Even a statutory affirmation of the sanctity of unborn life would have been insufficient here because of other fatal defects in the counseling plan under the Abortion Reform Act. Although a woman was required to go to a counseling center and confer with a physician, she—in the Court's reading of the statute—effectively had the option under the act of destroying the fetus no matter what the reason. Moreover, the plan provided no assurances that the woman would be motivated to carry on her pregnancy. Informational services alone, imparted neutrally by a counseling center, are not sufficient. Nor is the advice of physicians adequate; they would be functioning outside of their expertise when acting as counselors, for they are not trained to proffer professional advice or help in cases requiring an assessment of social need. Indeed, the very physician consulted by the woman wishing to abort a fetus was entitled under the act to give the required counseling; such a person, the Court surmises, is not likely to work toward the goal demanded by the constitution.[61]

To satisfy the spirit of the Basic Law, hinted the justices, the counseling centers themselves would have to be prepared to provide material relief, moral encouragement, and other forms of direct assistance to pregnant women.[62] Positive programs of this kind might in the eyes of the Court begin to approach the threshold of constitutionality. Whether such agencies would in fact meet constitutional standards was not decided in this case, however. Actually, the thrust of the case is to affirm the necessity of penal sanctions if unborn life is to be adequately safeguarded within the German legal order.

As noted earlier, the Abortion Reform Act was predicated on the notion that preventive measures would be more effective in protecting fetal life than penal sanctions. But it was the justices' conviction that the inadequacy of the old law was owing mainly to its failure to discriminate between abortions arbitrarily procured and those warranted by legitimate indications, causing a rising number of illegal abortions. The abortion case would now happily end this confusion and put the state on notice that certain terminations of pregnancy are clearly criminal acts demanding prosecution and punishment.

The Court also seemed impressed with predictions, buttressed by statistics concerning the effects of liberal abortion policies in England and East Germany, that if the Abortion Reform Act were validated the incidence of abortions would rise appreciably. The Court was cognizant of the trend toward more liberalized abortion policies in other western countries and cited the examples of Sweden, Austria, England, and France. However, disregarding the fact that these policies were sharply controverted, the justices pointed out that the legal standards of these countries do not apply to West Germany.[63]

The Court closed its argument by noting that the Basic Law must be understood "in the light of the historical experience and the spiritual-moral confrontation with the system of National Socialism," which stripped men of their dignity and denied the value of human life. Out of the death and destruction of the Nazi era arose a new Constitution—the Basic Law—which reaffirmed "human life" as the highest value of the political order. Moreover, the Federal Constitutional Court was created to insure that this value and other fundamental principles of the Basic Law would be observed by all organs of the state. Thus, in nullifying the Abortion Reform Act, the Court was doing nothing less or more than upholding the Republic's constitution.[64]

The Abortion Reform Act was invalidated by a 6-to-2 vote of the First Senate of the Federal Constitutional Court. (The Constitutional Court is composed of two divisions, called senates, with mutually exclusive jurisdiction and personnel. Each senate is staffed by eight justices.) Justices Wiltraut Rupp von Bruenneck and Helmut Simon wrote a common dissenting opinion. The minority opinion did not take issue—indeed it affirmed—the majority's conclusion that human life is a primary value of the legal order and that there is a constitutional duty on the part of the state to protect unborn life. Striking the same note as the dissenting opinions in the American cases, the minority rebuked the Court for ignoring the principles of judicial restraint by substituting its judgment of how best to protect the value of human life for that of the legislature. The question is not *whether* but *how* the value of human life is to be protected, remarked the two justices. "This question," they insisted, "is a matter of legislative responsibility."[65]

The minority argument proceeded as follows: The traditional role of the Federal Constitutional Court has been one of protecting the rights of citizens against state encroachment. But here, in an unprecedented step, the Court seized upon an objective value decision of the Basic Law—namely the state's duty to protect human life—as a basis for requiring the legislature to criminalize abortion and therefore effectively to *invade* the sphere of personal liberty.[66] This was contrary to the spirit of the Basic Law and at variance with the original intent of the framers. While required constitutionally to justify the imposition of a criminal penalty for certain conduct, the legislature was under no obligation to justify the replacement of a criminal statute with a social policy deemed more effective than punishment as a means of realizing a given constitutional value. The principles of political democracy and separation of powers placed such a decision squarely in legislative hands. Furthermore, it was a fundamental misconstruction of the Basic Law to suggest that any particular solution to a social problem is constitutionally required.[67] The social system was being ordered here, and to transfer this function from the legislative to the judiciary was to convert the Court into a "political arbitration board for choosing between alternative legislative proposals."[68] This was not to say that the Court is never justified in reviewing legislation implementing or promoting an objective value of the constitution, for the "Court could oppose the legislature when the latter has completely disregarded a value decision or when the nature and manner of its realization is clearly defective."[69] But the Abortion Reform Act was reasonable, having been adopted after an exhaustive parliamentary investigation, and fully consonant with the policy of other "western civilized states."[70]

The minority chided the Court for paying insufficient attention to the complexity of the social problem surrounding abortion. Social change and changing social values (abrupt and direct in the area of sexual morality), the high incidence of illegal abortions, the unenforceability of existing penal sanctions, and the discriminatory effect of not enforcing these sanctions were among the problems addressed by the legislature. On the basis of its findings, the minority noted, the legislature sought to structure a workable remedy for protecting unborn life. But that remedy was also fashioned in awareness of the moral dilemma confronting women who consider abortion as a means of escaping mental strain or social hardship. The minority underscored the "uniqueness of the interruption of pregnancy."[71] In its view the destruction of a fetus in the early months of pregnancy is of a different order than ordinary homicide, for the latter can be deterred in no other way than through criminal law. It is the unique unity of "actor" and "victim" that may warrant other than criminal means to preserve unborn life.[72] The objective values of the Basic Law do not preclude the legislature from devising measures to protect life that are based on the traditional distinction, rooted in European legal history and the canon law of the nineteenth century, between born and unborn life. Furthermore, the mother's unique relationship to the fetus requires an immense investment of psychological and physical energy if a child is to be cared for adequately. It is nature which tells a mother that she must secure and protect the life of the child *en ventre sa mere*. Hence a criminal statute is not necessary "by nature" (*von Natur aus*) to secure protection of unborn life and, more importantly, may not be the most effective way of achieving this objective.

Justice von Bruenneck (the only woman on the Court) introduced a female perspective into the minority argument by her reference to the "natural feelings of the woman,"[73] which in her view is legally relevant to the legislature's decision to adopt a "term" rather than an "indications" solution to the abortion problem. She advanced a psychological argument in referring to the "growing maternal relationship" that "corresponds to different embryonic stages of development."[74] Her point was that this relationship is far stronger in the later stages of pregnancy than in the first trimester. Thus she regarded the equating of an abortion in the early weeks of pregnancy with intentional murder as morally naive and legally untenable. Drawing upon theology, she also supported her view by reference to canon law and the theory of ensoulment, which in the nineteenth century held abortion performed up to the eightieth day after conception to be free from punishment.[75]

Still, in the end, the objective of the statute was to protect life and the burden was upon the court to show that the Abortion Reform Act was deficient in this respect. The minority pointed out that the legal protection of life is never complete or foolproof—a trivial observation since the same could be said of any area of law—and that the counseling scheme of the Reform Act had weaknesses. But then any solution to the problem was likely to be at best a "patchwork" (*Stueckwerk*). The old criminal law was a patchwork; the new Reform Act was a patchwork; but at least it was based on the hope that more rather than less protection for life will be the result.[76]

4. The Abortion Cases: An Analytical Overview

Let us restate the main constitutional rulings and principles of the German and American abortion cases. The American case holds that the right to privacy, founded upon the Fourteenth Amendment's concept of personal liberty, is broad enough to encompass a woman's decision whether or not to terminate her pregnancy. A zone of privacy is created within which the decision to procure an abortion is exclusively that of the pregnant woman and her physician. Accordingly, the state has no legitimate interest whatever in preventing abortions from occurring within the first trimester of pregnancy. Its only interest is seeing to it that abortions are performed under circumstances that insure adequate surgical procedures and care for patients. Yet the right to procure an abortion is not absolute, and so, following the first trimester of pregnancy, the state may begin to assert important interests in maintaining medical standards. It may assert these interests because an abortion performed in the second trimester is a greater medical risk than one performed in the first trimester. It is only in the last trimester, when the fetus becomes viable and potentially able to survive outside of the womb, that the state may promote its interest in protecting future life, but even during this period the unborn child may be destroyed, medical standards permitting, to preserve the life or health of the mother. What we have here is a constitutional policy on abortion based on the Court's conclusion that a fetus or unborn child is not a "person" within the meaning of the Fourteenth Amendment.

The German case holds that "developing life" in the womb is an independent legal value protected by Article 2 of the Basic Law. Life within the meaning of the Basic Law begins on the fourteenth day after conception, approximately at the stage of implantation. Abortion after that stage of development is an act of killing and the law must so indicate. Under the constitution, the state is duty-bound to protect and foster this life—i.e., the fetus or unborn child *in utero*—and under no circumstances is the state permitted to destroy this life. The affirmative duty of the state to protect the fetus must be exercised even against the wishes of the mother. Thus, the right of the child in the womb generally takes precedence over the right of the pregnant woman to self-determination or to the free development of personality. It is not absolutely necessary that criminal law be used as the sole instrument of protecting fetal life; measures other than punishment are permissible. The crucial requirement is that the totality of measures designed to protect unborn life be appropriate to the significance of the legal value safeguarded by the constitution. If that value can only be protected by the threat of punishment, then punishment is indeed constitutionally required. Yet, the Basic Law does not require extraordinary sacrifice on the part of the woman, nor does it imply that the woman's constitutional right to self-determination is wholly subordinate to the welfare of the fetus. Thus, a pregnancy may be terminated if necessary to protect the woman's life or to guard against the serious impairment of her health. In addition, abortion is free of punishment in those situations where the woman can be expected to undergo serious social hardship. It is clear that such hardship must be out of the ordinary and far in excess of the burdens ordinarily associated with pregnancy. Finally, any counseling system designed for women contemplating abortion must incorporate a positive attitude toward life and seek to persuade and, if necessary, materially to help women see their pregnancies through. `

A. Legal Cultures

How shall we evaluate these two decisions? An explanation of their differing doctrinal positions requires some consideration of the legal culture and socio-political values of the two countries, especially West Germany. The socio-political values to which we refer are clear enough and will be discussed further below. The concept of "legal culture" is inexact and rather limited as an explanatory device; nevertheless, if cautiously employed, it can be a useful analytical tool. Here we use the concept of legal culture to describe "a set of deeply rooted, historically conditioned attitudes about the nature of law, about the role of law in the society and the polity, about the proper organization and operation of a legal system, and about the way law is or should be made, applied, studied, perfected, and taught."[77]

Clearly there is no space here to explore in detail these several aspects of Germany's legal culture. But we will mention a couple of ideas on law and the judicial role that loom important in German legal theory and which seem relevant to this analysis. First, owing in part to the nineteenth-century movement for codification of German private law and in part to the intense drive for a powerful national state, law has come to be regarded as a highly unified and logically arranged system of rules governing nearly every aspect of human relations. In this view, law is architectonic; it "texturizes" the entire society, giving it unity of direction and purpose. This conception of law is one reason the state stands out as a rich and living reality in nineteenth century German jurisprudence. It is also the reason why the *Rechtsstaat* (law state) is a pivotal concept in German constitutionalism, embodying the notion of equal justice under law.

Under the taught tradition of German law, law is exclusively statutory in nature, and it is the solemn duty of an independent judiciary to apply that law in strict conformance with the legislative or, more accurately, "general" will. The taught tradition has also influenced the process of constitutional interpretation in West Germany and judicial role perceptions. The German justices tend to be less sociological in their approach to constitutional interpretation than their counterparts on the American Supreme Court. The Basic Law's meaning is to be discerned from the literal text of the constitution read in the light of the founding fathers' intent. Those justices who take a broader view of their role tend to emphasize the objectivity of the judicial decision-making process. Consider the following remarks by former Justice Gerhard Leibholz:

> In the procedure in which it is to be determined whether a statutory norm is in conformity with the Constitution or not, we are concerned with an objective procedure. Corresponding to this characteristic of the norm control procedure, the declarations of the Federal Constitutional Court of Germany have an effect *erga omnes*. It is consequently not surprising that the Court decisions, insofar as they contain a determination that a law is not (or is) in conformity with the Basic Law or other federal law, are published by the Federal Minister of Justice in the *Bundesgesetzblatt* (Federal Gazette). In other words, the decisions of the Federal Constitutional Court have statutory force. In addition, such decisions claim a fundamentally retroactive effect. They apply *ex tunc* and not *ex nunc*. The decision on unconstitutionality of a statute by the Federal Constitutional Court of Germany results, in principle, in its absolute nullity.... This norm control is, therefore, of basic importance for the entire constitutional jurisdiction,

for under it the ancient tension between the law of nature and positive law,—between justice and law,—arises. With the help of a constitutional examination of statutes, the norm control system is designed to counter the point of view that "right" can be fully incorporated in a statute. In the certainty that there is a higher law which finds expression, in particular, in the catalogues of basic rights in the constitutions, constitutional norm control finds its ultimate justification.[78]

The emphasis here upon legal certainty is strong and explains why the authority to nullify legislative statutes is vested exclusively in the Constitutional Court; it also explains the high value Constitutional Court justices attribute to unanimity on the Court, even though since 1971 the justices have been legally empowered to publish dissenting opinions. (The abortion case is one of those rare instances in which first Senate justices have published their dissenting views.)

While the legal order broadly reflects community feeling and values—the *Volksgeist* according to Savigny—constitutional interpretation in West Germany does not respond to the immediate "felt necessities" of the time. Those "felt necessities," whatever they may be—and they are not manifest in the abortion dispute—cannot be allowed, in the German view, to nullify or attentuate the central values proclaimed by the constitution. The German decision mentioned two elements of contemporary experience, the widespread incidence of illegal abortion and the Nazi slaughter of defenseless and innocent persons; but in the end these considerations seemed not to loom very large in the reasoning of the Court, although the Court did note that the founding fathers had the Nazi experience in mind when they included a right to life in the Basic Law.

B. Religion

Students of the American judicial process, particularly those of the behavioral persuasion, would be inclined to find the causes of the abortion decision in the background characteristics and personal beliefs of the German justices. Indeed one might suppose, as has been suggested, that the German Court's mind was influenced by the religious affiliation of the justices and particularly by the Catholic presence on the Court. Yet only three of the eight justices who decided the case are Catholics. Exactly half of the justices in the majority, including President Ernst Benda, who occupies a crucial place in the decisional process, are Protestants. It might be added that the principles of the abortion case are incompatible with the prevailing view among Catholic theologians, which holds that ensoulment takes place with fertilization, whereas the Court held that the fetus assumes the character of personhood at the point of implantation, which occurs fourteen days after conception. In addition, the Court held that abortions are constitutionally permissible in cases of severe hardship (social indications), whereas the prevailing Catholic theological position holds that the direct and purposeful destruction of the fetus is never permissible. Ironically, it was the minority opinion that appealed to theology and canon law in partial support of its conclusion that the destruction of the fetus in the early months of pregnancy does not constitute conduct deserving of criminal punishment.

Whatever the personal beliefs of the justices, the German decision is distinguished by the fact that it does *not* explicitly rely upon the theology of any particular denomination or religious tradition. In the main body of the Court's opinion there is no reference to theological thinking or religious belief. Rather, *constitutional* reasoning is the predominant mode of analysis and the main strength of the German decision; the Court's argument is based exclusively on its analysis of legislative history, constitutional language, judicial precedents, and the intent of the constitution's framers. The Court did not find any utility or relevance in reciting, as did the U.S. Supreme Court, the history of religious or philosophical reflection about the beginning of life. Biological knowledge and human experience were, for the German Court, sufficient to decide this case. "Life in the sense of the historical existence of a human individual," to reiterate the Court's argument, "exists according to definite biological-physiological knowledge, in any case, from the fourteenth day after conception.[79]

The terms 'life' and 'human dignity,' which appear in the text of the Basic Law, were of course interpreted in the light of the nation's experience and culture, which obviously includes religious influences. But then constitutionalism itself has an ultimate religious basis. Carl Friedrich teaches that the very idea of "constitutionalism is rooted in certain basic beliefs, the belief in the dignity of man and the belief in man's inclination to abuse power. These beliefs rest upon religious convictions."[80] Few Americans or German justices would deny the religious dimension of constitutionalism. The point to be made here is that this religious dimension is ultimate rather than proximate and broadly cultural rather than narrowly denominational. And so, when the German justices probed the concept of 'human dignity' to discern the juridical meaning of 'life,' they were engaging no more and no less in religious reflection than was Justice Brennan when he asserted in *Furman* v. *Georgia* that capital punishment is "inhuman" and fails to "comport with human dignity," or when Justice Marshall opined in the same case that it offends the "conscience of society."[81] Or, to put the matter differently, the presuppositions of *Roe* v. *Wade* are no less religious than those of the German abortion case. After all, the value of privacy is squarely rooted in the historical belief in man's spirituality, out of which grew a theory of personal autonomy.

C. Social Philosophies

A more plausible explanation for the German decision is to be found in certain normative aspects of the Basic Law. The constitution might be said to be normative in the sense that it protects certain kinds of values and community interests. The Basic Law embodies a conception of political order that includes an ethical *minimus consensus* rooted in the moral tradition of the West. Whereas American constitutionalism emphasizes a rugged individualism in the exercise of personal freedom, German constitutionalism has a larger communitarian thrust with a corresponding limitation upon the exercise of political freedom. This difference between American and German constitutionalism is one of emphasis, yet important to an understanding of the varying constitutional policies of the two countries.

The argument is in need of amplification. If we accept here the conventional, Madisonian view of American constitutionalism, we will regard the political order as a democracy unencumbered by any substantive definition of the public interest and encouraging a pluralism of private interests and moral persuasions. Politics is a method by which group interests are served, and freedom is a value primarily in the service of the individual. In this sense, American constitutionalism fails to incorporate a specific notion of the common good or a concept of authority responsible for directing men toward goodness.

The German notion of freedom, on the other hand, if this interpretation of the Constitutional Court's jurisprudence is correct, includes the classical proposition that men fulfill themselves in community with others. There is, of course, a private sphere which the Basic Law protects. Certain rights of the human person are beyond the reach of the state, for human dignity can subsist, in the modern German constitutional view, only when men are allowed to achieve moral freedom and to act on their moral convictions. But the constitution sets boundaries to the exercise of freedom. For example, "Everyone shall have the right to the free development of his personality," but only "insofar as he does not violate the rights of others or offend the constitutional order or the moral code" (Article 2, paragraph 1). Freedom of speech is likewise "limited by the provisions of the general laws, provisions of law for the protection of youth, and by the right to the inviolability of personal honor" (Article 5, paragraph 2). Freedom to teach "does not absolve from loyalty to the Constitution" (Article 5, paragraph 3). The right of association is guaranteed, but activities "directed against constitutional order or the concept of international understanding are prohibited" (Article 9). The one principle which can in no way be encroached upon is "human dignity"; indeed, under the terms of Article 79, Article 1 (which proclaims "the inviolability of man's dignity") is beyond parliament's amendatory power. The Basic Law also sets up a "social" federal state (Article 20) and underscores the values of marriage and family life while placing mothers under "the care and protection of the community" (Article 6). Political parties are even instructed to "participate in forming the *political will of the people*" (Article 21, italics supplied). These constitutional norms are part of the living fabric of German constitutional law and fairly accurately reflect values anchored in Germany's social and political traditions.

Free-speech jurisprudence offers an illustration of opposing constitutional policies based on the different orientations of the German and American constitutions. Perhaps the strongest current in the broad stream of American free-speech theory is the Holmesian "free trade in ideas" view—"that the best test of truth is the power of the thought to get itself accepted in the competition of the market."[82] The doctrine is pragmatic and relativistic. Authority does not guide men toward truth; rather the market determines it. And as the market changes, so does truth. In American theory it is not the purpose of political discourse to arrive at truths by which *permanently* to live; at least those truths may not be incorporated into public law in such a way as to forbid any person or group from attacking them verbally or to foreclose changing them by political means. The individualism implied in the American theory is manifested most clearly by Supreme Court cases effectively immunizing citizens against libel suits arising out of false allegations against public officials and public figures.[83]

The Basic Law requires political man to observe certain traditions of civility when making public utterances. German constitutional theory regards political discourse as an exercise in *reasonable* debate and as a means of achieving the public good. This requires that men speak the truth. The constitutional value of "personal honor," allied as it is to the concept of "human dignity," permits actions against newspapers and individual citizens for their false and misleading statements about public officials and ordinary citizens.[84] Indeed, public officials are entitled to special protection under West German libel laws, whereas the reverse is true in the United States. Utterances about public officials in the United States, however distorted or untruthful, may not constitutionally be punished by state libel laws unless it can be shown that the utterances are made with actual malicious intent, which is difficult to prove since to do so one must show that the statement was made "with knowledge that it was false or with reckless disregard of whether it was false or not."[85] In Germany, free speech is limited by the necessity to preserve public order and to maintain the community's respect for the authority of the state as reflected in the personhood of its high officials. The prevailing American theory of free speech seems consistent with the Supreme Court's vision of the political order. As the one-man, one-vote principle put forth in the apportionment cases so forcefully shows,[86] political man is an autonomous agent in an atomistic society, for he speaks *for himself* and he votes *alone*.

D. Abortion Depoliticized

Thus, although the logic of *Roe* v. *Wade* leaves much to be desired, the result of that case seems very much to be a logical extension of American constitutionalism. The effect of that decision is to deny the individual states the right to consider, in shaping their abortion policies, the community's interest in protecting the fetus. In effect, the Court was saying that the question of whether a woman has the right to procure an abortion is not an issue to be effectively considered in the public realm. Thus, oddly enough, free speech cannot be used here to influence the development of public policy. The decision seems perfectly consistent with Madisonian liberalism: the constitutional order is to serve the individual and his interest. In the Supreme Court's *Weltanschauung*, society is not viewed as fundamentally communitarian in nature. Just as the apportionment cases see the individual voter as an autonomous political agent, *Roe* v. *Wade* sees the human person as an autonomous moral agent. A woman is thus entitled to separate herself from the community while the community is rendered powerless to act in its common defense for the purpose of safeguarding shared values. It is the Fourteenth Amendment concept of "liberty" that is given overwhelming significance in *Roe* v. *Wade,* to the virtual exclusion of countervailing considerations that might have been deemed to inhere in the related concepts of person and life. As one writer noted: "The basic assumption of the whole [American] system is very clear: no partial community may impose its substantive vision of the good life on the whole community. On the level of the whole, our unity is formal, not substantive."[87]

In another sense, however, the Supreme Court did underscore the importance of unity, although not the unity of a community glued together by a moral consensus. In the Court's view, this moral consensus does not exist, and the Court is probably correct here. It appears that Justice Blackmun's dreary recitation of the history of moral and philosophical thinking about abortion was actually intended to illustrate this lack of consensus. What other reason could there have been for his long prologue to the merits of the case? Surely it provided no theological or scientific basis for dividing pregnancy into three periods and formulating different constitutional rules pertaining to each. The Court's interest seemed to lie in the promotion of social peace—a policy of "live and let live"—best achieved through the constitutional right of privacy.

In a pluralistic society composed of a multitude of belief systems, the Court seems intent on keeping certain issues—those likely to be religiously or theologically divisive—out of the forum of *effective* public discussion. By not allowing the abortion question be legislatively determined, the Court has effectively "depoliticized" the issue. If the people's representatives are incapable of acting on an issue after its exhaustion by discussion, it makes no sense, *politically,* to talk about it. *Lemon* v. *Kurtzman,* where the Court invalidated a Pennsylvania statute reimbursing church-related schools for costs of teachers salaries and textbooks in specific secular subjects, is an even clearer illustration of the Court's attempt to "depoliticize" a public issue and, incidentally—to return to the anticommunitarian theme—to erode the significance of religion as an intermediating agency between the individual and mass society. Remarked Chief Justice Burger: "Ordinarily political debate and division, however vigorous or even partisan, are normal and healthy manifestations of our democratic system of government, but political division along religious lines was one of the principal evils against which the First Amendment was intended to protect. The potential divisiveness of such conflict is a threat to the normal political process."[88] Thus is social peace achieved.

This analysis is a rather circumspect way of saying that the result in *Roe* v. *Wade* not only conforms to the individualistic ethic at the heart of American constitutionalism but is also understandable in the light of the pluralistic nature of American society. But then so is German society pluralistic, both religiously and socially, just as there is a wide variety of views in the population on whether abortion should be permitted. On the other hand, the clearly dominant opinion in the German legislature and Federal Constitutional Court is that under the Basic Law the state has a duty to protect unborn life and, what is more, to instruct the people that the taking of unborn life is an offense against human dignity, although these institutions are in disagreement over whether this objective is best achieved by criminalization or decriminalization of abortion. But as the German justices have said on numerous occasions, the Basic Law is not a "value-free" constitution; rather, it stands for values that "all state authority" is obligated to protect for the sake of the community or, as the constitution puts it, "the free democratic basic order."

At the risk of exaggerating the actual difference between judicial role perceptions and methods of constitutional interpretation in West Germany and the United States, I want to suggest that the German decision is also compatible with a legal culture that emphasizes a taught tradition of analytical jurisprudence. In the abortion case the German justices were governed by their own rationality and not by the existing mores of society. The decision did not essentially rest on sociological analysis, although this is not to suggest that a sociological analysis would necessarily have led to a contrary result.

Measured by any logical test that we would wish to apply, the constitutional reasoning in the German case is more tightly argued and more analytically precise than the argument advanced in *Roe* v. *Wade*. The German opinion is carefully crafted and composed in measured language, leaving little room for doubt or ambiguity with regard to its meaning. On the other hand, the privacy argument in *Roe* v. *Wade* is confusing and even contradictory. In the end, the American decision does not lend itself to a clear and unambiguous interpretation. Justice Douglas was even impelled to write a concurring opinion to hedge against a too narrow interpretation of the Court's opinion, studiously avoiding, for example, any reference to "potential life," a concept that Blackmun introduces as a limitation of privacy. Chief Justice Burger, on the other hand, concurred in what amounted to a near dissent by warning against a too broad interpretation of the opinion and by deploring Blackmun's use of current medical knowledge in support of the opinion. Of course, eroded *logic* is one of the costs of the high value that the justices as well as Americans generally place on the practice of individualized opinion writing on the Supreme Court. In Germany, such personalized expressions of opinion remain a clear exception to the rule. The law—certainly the highest law of the land—ideally speaks with one voice in Germany's legal culture, underscoring both the authority and the unity of the law.

E. *The Democratic Process*

Finally, we return to the relationship between the judiciary and the legislature. The American Supreme Court has sought to democratize the political process mainly by standing watch at the ballot box and by insuring that each citizen's vote is counted equally, as well as by protecting free speech. The Court has succeeded in installing what might be called a regime of numerical majoritarianism. It is unconcerned with the quality of political representation once the voting is over. And yet, despite its expectation and apparent belief that the one-man, one-vote principle will bring public policy more in accord with the will of the electorate, the Court is as ready as ever to strike down legislation no matter how representative of the popular will.

As seen through the eyes of the German justices, the democratic process is more elaborate than the American conception. Law in Germany is an expression of community feelings and expectations. Those expectations and feelings are crystallized through a democratic political order powered by elections and political parties. Under the Basic Law, the latter "participate in forming the political will of the people" (Article 21), a will that finds its eventual representation in the will of the state when it is converted and refined into public law by parliament and other state organs.

One reason why these remarks about the democratic process are relevant here is that in the abortion case the court seemed somewhat troubled by the series of quick votes, in the absence of meaningful parliamentary debate, leading to the passage of the Abortion Reform Act in the Seventh Bundestag. The Court seemed distressed by the failure of the Seventh Bundestag to heed the recommendations of the Sixth Bundestag, during which time there was much public and parliamentary debate on abortion, and to abide by the life-regarding principles which, in the Court's view, informed those recommendations. The constitutional ruling in the abortion case seems in part to have been attributable to the Court's belief that the political will of the people had not found adequate expression in the Abortion Reform Act. In effect, the Court turned back the clock to where the Bundestag had been in its deliberations when parliament was suddenly dissolved in 1972 and actually seemed to be inviting the Bundestag to return to the apparent consensus that had been achieved prior to 1972.

The German and American abortion cases are both products of political regimes in which judicial review plays a central role in the process of government. The enlightened conscience of a future generation may condemn *Roe* v. *Wade* in tones that we now reserve for the despised Dred Scott case. Or it may regard *Roe* v. *Wade* as another step on man's road to freedom. Or men may take a middle position, much like the German Court, and seek a balancing of rights. Whatever the future may hold in this regard, the magnitude of the power that certain constitutional democracies have conferred on their courts of law must be clear to the men of this generation. The reversal of legislative policies as important to society as American state anti-abortion laws and the German Abortion Reform Act is a very serious matter. But the judicial overriding of legislative policy on the ground of constitutionality is apparently one of the prices that citizens within a constitutional regime that confers such authority on its courts are willing to pay.

NOTES

1. See 410 U.S. 113 (1973) and 410 U.S. 179 (1973).
2. Judgment of Feb. 25, 1975, 39 BVerfG 1-95 (1975). The decisions of the Federal Constitutional Court are reported in *Entscheidungen des Bundesverfgassungsgerichts* (1952-   ). The official abbreviation of these reports is BVerfG.
3. Supra, note 1.
4. See Tex. Pen. Code Ann., Arts. 1191–96 (1961).
5. Model Penal Code, Proposed Official Draft Sec. 230.3. (American Law Institute 1962).
6. Ga. Code Ann., Sec. 26-1202 (1972).
7. N.Y. Pen. Law, Sec. 125.05 (McKinney Supp., 1971).
8. See *Population and the American Future,* The Report of the Commission on Population Growth and the American Future (Washington, D.C., 1972), p. 142. Leo Pfeffer offers an interesting, if not wholly convincing, explanation of this startling shift of opinion: "Partly it is to be found in changing standards of morality (manifested, if not to some extent caused, by Supreme Court decisions practically making pornography legal) which now seem to accept permarital sexual relations; partly the woman's liberation movement and its claim that a woman has the right to decide what will happen to her own body; partly in the recognition (though hardly new) that realistically the choice is not between legal abortions and no abortions, but between safe legal ones and dangerous, sordid, illegal ones. All this is true, yet it is probable that a major factor here, as in the case of contraceptive birth control, is the taxpayer's revolt against rising welfare rolls and costs. Legalization of contraception not having worked to an acceptable degree, and other measures . . . proving too Draconian for public acceptance, permissible abortion, encouraged by the state, is the next logical step." *God, Caesar, and the Constitution* (Boston: Beacon Press, 1975), pp. 99–100.
9. See Richard A. Epstein, "Substantive Due Process by Any Other Name: The Abortion Cases," *The Supreme Court Review 1973* (Chicago, 1974): 160–67.
10. *Baker* v. *Carr,* 369 U.S. 186, 204 (1962). There is a rule in American constitutional law that federal courts are powerless to adjudicate a case unless it is "presented in an adversary context and in a form historically viewed as capable of judicial resolution." This means that the judicial power of the United States can be invoked only in a concrete case (i.e., a real controversy, not a contrived or friendly suit) by a litigant who has sustained or is immediately in danger of sustaining an injury under federal law or the Constitution. Such a constraint is one way of confining the political and social roles of the federal judiciary, consistent with the constitutional principle of separation of powers.
11. 410 U.S. 113, 125 (1973).
12. 410 U.S. 179, 188 (1973).
13. Epstein, "Substantive Due Process," p. 161.

14. Alexis de Tocqueville, *Democracy in America*, trans. Henry Reeve, abrg. Geoffrey Cumberlege (London: Oxford University Press, 1952), p. 207.

15. See *German Penal Code of 1871*, The American Series of Foreign Penal Codes no. 4 (South Hackensack, N.J. and London: Fred B. Rothman, 1961) Sec. 218, p. 114.

16. See Basic Law for the Federal Republic of Germany (*Grundgesetz*), Art. 93, Sec. 1, par. 2. The provisions of the West German Basic Law relating to the authority and organization of the Federal Constitutional Court have been implemented by the Federal Constitutional Court Act of March 12, 1951 (*Gesetz ueber das Bundesverfassungsgericht*), *Bundesgesetzblatt*, I (1951), p. 243. (Hereafter the Act is cited as BVerfGG.) For a fuller discussion of the Court's authority see Donald P. Kommers, *Judicial Politics in West Germany: A Study of the Federal Constitutional Court* (Beverly Hills and London: Sage, 1976), pp. 100–03.

17. BVerfGG, Sec. 13(6). There are fourteen other types of proceedings which the Court may hear under the law and the constitution. Each requires special procedures and litigants. In only one of these proceedings—the constitutional complaint—may an individual citizen invoke the Court's jurisdiction. All other cases are brought by agencies, branches, or levels of government.

18. But in fact the Constitutional Court has exercised this jurisdiction very cautiously. Frequently, the Court will simply sit on a case and not decide it in the expectation that the initiating party will withdraw the case or that the dispute will be resolved politically before the Court decides.

19. In addition, the Abortion Reform Act was challenged in the Federal Constitutional Court by the governments of Baden-Württemberg, Saarland, Bavaria, Schleswig-Holstein, and Rheinland-Pfalz.

20. See Donald P. Kommers, "Politics and Jurisprudence in West Germany: State Financing of Political Parties," *The American Journal of Jurisprudence* (1971), pp. 215–241.

21. The Fifth Statute to Reform the Penal Law of June 18, 1974 (*Bundesgesetzblatt* I, p. 1297).

22. *German Penal Code of 1871*, p. 114.

23. Judgment of March 11, 1927, 61 RGSt (*Entscheidungen des Reichgerichts in Strafsachen*) 242.

24. 39 BVerfG 6.

25. *German Draft Penal Code*, The American Series of Foreign Penal Codes no. 11 (South Hackensack, N.J. and London: Fred B. Rothman, 1966), Sec. 140(1), p. 91.

26. Ibid., Sec. 157(1), p. 97. It is of some comparative interest to note that similar provisions were contained in the Model Penal Code proposed by the American Law Institute in 1962. See Model Penal Code, Proposed Official Draft (The American Law Institute, 1962), sec. 230.3. Needless to say, the provisions of the Model Penal Code would be invalid under the constitutional standards of *Roe* v. *Wade*.

27. These details of the parliamentary debate are drawn from the Federal Constitutional Court's own account of the legislative history leading up to the passage of the Abortion Reform Act of 1974. See 39 BVerfG 6–18.

28. "Indications solution" (*Indikationsloesung*) and "term solution" (*Fristenloesung*) are commonly used expressions in Germany when referring to abortion policy. These terms are awkward in English but we shall use them here anyway. An indications solution means that a pregnancy may be interrupted at

any time for reasons defined by law; a term solution means that an abortion would be permitted, for whatever reason, within a given stage of pregnancy, usually within the first trimester. There has been great controversy in Germany over which is the better or more equitable solution to the abortion controversy.

29. For a detailed account of the 1972 election campaign, see Arnold J. Heidenheimer and Donald P. Kommers, *The Governments of Germany*, 4th ed. (New York: Thomas Y. Crowell, 1975), chap. 5.

30. Basic Law for the Federal Republic of Germany (1949), Art. 65.

31. See Fifth Statute to Reform the Penal Law of June 18, 1976 (*Bundesgesetzblatt* I, p. 1297).

32. 410 U.S. 113, 130–50 (1973).

33. Ibid., p. 153.

34. Ibid., p. 154.

35. According to Section 1 of the Fourteenth Amendment: "No State shall make or enforce any law which shall abridge the privileges or immunities of citizens of the United States; nor shall any state deprive any person of life, liberty, or property, without due process of law; nor deny to any person within its jurisdiction the equal protection of the laws."

36. 410 U.S. 113, 159 (1973).

37. Ibid., p. 165.

38. Ibid., p. 164.

39. 410 U.S. 179, 221–22 (1973).

40. Ibid., p. 222.

41. 410 U.S. 113, 172–77 (1973).

42. 410 U.S. 179, 209–21 (1973).

43. *Griswold* v. *Connecticut*, 381 U.S. 479 (1965).

44. 410 U.S. 113, 167–71 (1973).

45. 39 BVerfG 2–3 (1975). The Court's authority to issue such orders or regulations is derived from BVerfGG, Sec. 35. It provides: "The Federal Constitutional Court is authorized to designate who shall implement its judgment; in individual cases it may also regulate the manner of its execution."

46. 39 BVerfG 37. The German text reads: "Leben im Sinne der geschichtlichen Existenz seines menschlichen Individuums besteht nach gesicherter biologisch-psysiologischer Erkenntnis jedenfalls vom 14. Tage nach der Empfaengnis (Nidation, Individuation)."

47. Ibid.

48. 39 BVerfG 38–41.

49. Ibid., pp. 40–41.

50. Ibid., p. 43.

51. Ibid., pp. 42–43.

52. Ibid., p. 43. See also 34 BVerfG 202, 223 (1974).

53. Ibid., p. 44.

54. Ibid., p. 45.

55. Ibid., p. 50.

56. Ibid., p. 48. By "grave hardship" the Court is referring to a severe condition of social, economic, or psychological distress.

57. Ibid., p. 53.

58. Ibid., p. 46.

59. Ibid.

60. Ibid., p. 47.

61. Ibid., pp. 62–63.
62. Ibid., p. 61. Counseling centers so equipped were actually recommended by 16 criminal law scholars in an "Alternative Draft" considered by parliament and which, according to the Court, was actually the basis of the counseling idea.
63. Ibid., pp. 66–67.
64. Ibid., p. 67.
65. Ibid., p. 69.
66. Ibid., p. 71. It is important to note the customary distinction in German constitutional law between objective values and subjective rights. Both are derived from the list of fundamental rights in the Basic Law (Articles 1 through 19). Objective value decisions (*objective Wertentscheidungen*) are generally norms of political order which govern the exercise of state power; they require affirmative action (*actives Handeln*) by the state on a continuing basis since the construction of a socially just political order is a permanent task (*staendige Aufgabe*); as such this duty falls naturally and logically, under a system of divided power, to the legislature. Subjective rights, called "defense rights" (*Abwehrrechte*) by the two justices in the minority, are those which individual persons seek to vindicate against incursion by specific state actions; they are rights with an identifiable content; most notably, they are rights amenable to judicial resolution because of the availability of concrete standards of judgment developed over time on a case-by-case basis.
67. 39 BVerfG 71–73 (1975).
68. Ibid., p. 72.
69. Ibid., p. 73.
70. Ibid., p. 69.
71. Ibid., p. 78.
72. Ibid., p. 79.
73. Ibid., p. 80.
74. Ibid., p. 81.
75. Ibid.
76. Since this article was written, the German Bundestag has amended Section 218 bringing it into line with the Court's directive. The new version of Section 218 provides for a comprehensive counseling system for women contemplating abortion. See Fifteenth Penal Law Change of May 18, 1976 (*Bundesgesetzblatt* I, p. 1213).
77. Henry W. Ehrmann, *Comparative Legal Cultures* (Englewood Cliffs, N.J.: Prentice-Hall, 1976), p. 8.
78. Gerhard Leibholz, "The West German Constitutional Court," chap. 5 in *Federalisme et Cours Supremes et L'Integration des Systemes Juridiques,* ed. Edward McWhinney and Pierre Pescatore (Brussels: UGA, 1973), p. 57.
79. 39 BVerfG 37.
80. Carl J. Friedrich, *Limited Government: A Comparison* (Englewood Cliffs, N.J.: Prentice-Hall, 1974), p. 123.
81. 408 U.S. 238 (1972).
82. *Abrams* v. *United States,* 250 U.S. 616, 630 (1919).
83. See *New York Times* v. *Sullivan,* 376 U.S. 254 (1964). See also *Curtis Pub. Co.* v. *Butts* and *Associated Press* v. *Walker,* 388 U.S. 130 (1967), *Garrison* v. *Louisiana,* 379 U.S. 64 (1964), and *Gertz* v. *Robert Welch, Inc.,* 418 U.S. 323 (1974).
84. See Judgment of Feb. 24, 1971, 30 BVerfG 173.
85. See *New York Times Co.* v. *Sullivan,* 376 U.S. 254, 280 (1964).
86. See generally *Baker* v. *Carr,* 369 U.S. 186 (1962), *Wesberry* v. *Sanders,* 376

U.S. 1 (1964), *Reynolds* v. *Sims,* 377 U.S. 533 (1964), *Avery* v. *Midland County,* 390 U.S. 474 (1968).

87. John H. Schaar, "Some Ways of Thinking About Equality," *The Journal of Politics* 26 (1964): 891.

88. *Lemon* v. *Kurtzman,* 403 U.S. 602, 622 (1971).

Philosophy on Humanity

ROGER WERTHEIMER*

People often disagree about how a person should act. Yet they agree that whether a person should perform some act depends upon what kinds of things are affected by the act and how those things are affected. For most of us, whether and how an inanimate thing is affected is generally not *in itself* a consideration; we think such effects provide reasons for acting (or refraining) only insofar as they relate to effects on something else such as a human being (e.g., the agent or the object's owner). But, for most of us, the beneficial and harmful effects of a person's act on a human being are *in themselves* relevant considerations; we regard an act's harming some human being (the agent or others) as itself a reason for a person to refrain from the act. That is, we accord an inanimate thing a *dependent moral status*, and a human being an *independent moral status*. The moral status of animals is controversial, but most people believe that, whether independent or not, an animal's moral status is *inferior* to a human being's. Though an act's having harmful effects on an animal may itself be a reason for refraining from the act, the reason is of a lower order than the reason provided by an act's having an equivalently harmful effect on a human being.[1]

The Standard Belief

Let us call the kind of moral status most people ascribe to human beings *human (moral) status*. The term refers to a kind of independent and superior consideration to be accorded an entity, not to the kind of entity to be accorded the consideration, so it is not a definitional truth that human beings have human status. But most people believe that being human has *moral cachet*: viz., a human being has human status in

---

*I gratefully acknowledge the support for this work provided by the Guggenheim Foundation.

virtue of being a human being (and thus each human being has human status). Call this the *Standard Belief*. That most people accept it is an empirical fact.

Though establishing this fact requires the services of social science, we are already familiar with a sufficiency of evidence, enough to remove most doubts on the matter without further surveys by removing confusions about the data. Among the best batches of data we have is what people say and do and feel regarding the issue of the morality of abortion. Presumably it's common knowledge that few people do or would say: "What difference does it make whether a fetus is a human being? What's that got to do with the morality of abortion?" People disagree over whether and when abortions are morally objectionable primarily, if not solely, because they disagree over whether and when a fetus is a human being. The other pertinent facts are not much disputed (e.g., facts about the other properties of fetuses and facts about the consequences of aborting and not aborting). So too with the pertinent moral principles: while people may disagree somewhat about what overriding considerations may letigimate killing a human being, most people believe that killing a human being is in principle wrong and that, if a fetus is a full-fledged human being, it may be destroyed only for those reasons that justify destroying any other human being.[2] The very structure of this familiar controversy evidences a shared assumption: the Standard Belief.

That structure and thus its value as evidence here may be challenged. Pro-abortionists often insist that the dispute is due, not to differing beliefs about the humanness of the fetus, but to an allegiance to some consideration anti-abortionists deny or deemphasize, such as the mother's rights regarding her own body and welfare. That insistence, however sincere, is rarely reliable testimony. Usually, whatever the alleged moral consideration, it applies in two conceivable cases differing only in that the victim is a fetus in one case and a week- or year- or ten-year-old child in the other. And if, as is usual, the pro-abortionist judges the cases differently—if, for example, he would sanction a mother's destroying her fetus solely because it threatens her with an emotional or economic breakdown, while he balks at her exterminating her week-old (or year- or ten-year-old) offspring for the sole same reason—then usually that is good reason for presuming that his beliefs about abortion depend upon his beliefs about the differences between fetuses and children. And usually it can be shown, and (what is not the same thing) often the pro-abortionist will come to admit that the morally relevant difference for him is that children are human beings and fetuses are not. Sometimes he will first maintain that some other difference (e.g., independent existence) is the morally relevant one, but when he imagines a child similar to a fetus in the alleged relevant respect (e.g., an incubated infant), usually he continues to condone annihilation of the fetus but not the child. And further inquiry usually reveals that his alleged relevant respect actually operates as (part of) his reason for calling a child, but not a fetus, a human being.

But now, there are no simple or foolproof procedures for determining what someone believes; they all require a knack, skill, and sensitivity for their application, and none is infallible. And not just because people may lie or be self-deceived. The difficulties are those involved in explaining a phenomenon, for to ascribe a belief to someone is to explain certain facts about him, to make sense of certain patterns in his behavior (including, but not confined to, his speech behavior). What even the most intelligent and sincere of persons *claims* to accept as moral principles usually turns out to be a hodgepodge of rules inconsistent with each other and with his own considered judgments on particular cases. Sometimes we may say he holds contradictory beliefs; other times that what he *really* believes is what he would agree to after proper reflection that clears away confusion or what explains the largest and/or most significant aspects of his behavior. No doubt the criteria for "proper" reflection and for explanatory power are problematic. And so too the distinction between what someone presently believes and what he will agree to on the basis of his present beliefs is difficult to draw and apply if only because attempts to determine what someone believes (e.g., by his reflecting on contrasting cases) may alter his beliefs. Still, there is a clear enough sense in which, whatever else they may believe, most people accept the Standard Belief. That belief is here ascribed to them, not primarily because it matches their reports of their belief on the matter, but because it provides the best account of why they believe that all humans and no animals have human status and why their arguments over abortion and many other issues take the form they do, and so on. (The "and so on" refers to numerous and diverse facts, only some of which will get mentioned.)

Again, to ascribe a belief is to explain. Whether or not the ascription is made *on the basis of* the person's behavior (self-ascribed beliefs generally are not), the ascription must be testable against the person's behavior for it to be able to explain and make sense of that behavior. Now, to explain the actions of a creature in terms of its beliefs (desires and the like) is to explain them as the actions of a rational (or at least intelligent) creature—and to do that one must presuppose a theory of rationality. For a person's behavior is evidence of some belief only given the assumption that he has certain conative and affective structures and capacities (e.g., certain desires) and also certain information-gathering (perception) and storage (memory) structures and capacities as well as certain physical structures and capacities for action. It is also evidence that the world in which he acts has certain physical structures and capacities. But even given this background of facts, his behavior is evidence only within a theory of rational behavior, a system of principles that state what someone would be believing, given the background assumptions, if he behaves in certain ways. Those principles are principles of rational thought and action. So what and how we do think is determinable only by assuming principles about what and how we ought to think. For that matter, determining any of the background facts or any fact at all presupposes the same assumption: an understanding of the physical world requires an understanding of our mental structures and capacities if only because without the latter one cannot discriminate appearance from reality, the self from the not-self.

The Factunorm Principle

Now a theory of rationality serves two functions. Its principles may be regarded as statements of natural laws with which to describe, predict, and explain the behavior of an entity given certain background conditions and the assumption that the entity is a rational creature (i.e., an entity operating in accordance with those laws). The same principles may be regarded as norms which a rational creature can conform to or violate and by which his activity can be assessed for its rationality. We may "assume" that we are rational (that we can and sometimes do act in conformity with rational principles) if only because we cannot do otherwise: to doubt or deny that oneself is rational is as self-defeating as doubting or denying that oneself exists, for in the very act of doubting or denying, one evidences the contrary. Now, a theory explains what is evidence for the theory, and what is explained by the theory is evidence for the theory. Thus, what and how we do think is evidence for the principles of rationality, what and how we ought to think. This itself is a methodological principle of rationality; call it the *Factunorm Principle*. We are (implicitly) accepting the Factunorm Principle whenever we try to determine what or how we ought to think. For we must, in that very attempt, think. And unless we can think that what and how we do think there is correct—and thus is evidence for what and how we ought to think—we cannot determine what or how we ought to think. Of course, we are fallible; sometimes we are mistaken in what or how we think. But that does not undermine the Factunorm

Principle, for it is itself something we learn only by thinking and accepting that principle. And if we can learn of our mistakes we can learn from our mistakes, and thus, by thinking and accepting the Factunorm Principle, we can alter and improve what and how we think, gradually approximating what and how we ought to think. That capacity is the essence of rationality. One essential step in this process is learning that oneself is not special in this regard, that what and how anyone thinks may be evidence for what and how anyone ought to think. Another step is learning that what and how we think in certain circumstances is not much evidence for what and how we ought to think: As a part and prerequisite of the total learning process we continuously develop, refine, and apply an elaborate variety of criteria for evaluating the evidentiary value of the process and products of thought and thus for identifying those we have the best reason to trust and that are most likely to be correct (e.g., the person is mature, sane, calm, sober, of at least normal intelligence, possessed of the requisite subsidiary information, without relevant biases, etc.). Thus, when we speak here of common belief or what most people believe, we attend only to those beliefs we cannot find suspect for some relevant defect in the personal history of the belief. And we speak of what *most* people believe just because we have also learned that in disagreements between two groups of persons similar in the other relevant respects, the judgment of the larger group is more likely to be correct; however, while uncertainty increases as the difference in size diminishes, unanimity does not supply certainty. Any such belief, no matter how many people believe it, could be mistaken; and even if something is a necessary truth, we do not necessarily believe it. What and how we do think is *evidence* for rational principles, but a rational principle is not true *because* of what and how we think. A rational principle isn't true in virtue of anything: there neither need be, nor is, nor can be, any *foundation* for rational principles.[3]

Put it this way. The goal of philosophy is, as Socrates said, self-knowledge. For philosophy is, in essence, rationality reasoning about rationality. It is the process and product of creatures who are their own paradigms of rationality exercising the very capacities for which they deem themselves rational in the attempt to chart the processes and products of the proper exercise of those capacities. But philosophy is not introspective psychology; it is a normative science. The self that the self seeks to know is not, per se, the actual self but the ideal self, the ideally rational self, for it seeks to know how it ought to act (e.g., think); how it does act is of interest only insofar as that bears upon how it ought to act. But the self that seeks to know is, ineluctably, the actual self, and its experiences are, ineluctably, its actual experiences, and the only objects it can experience are, ineluctably, the phenomena of the actual self and the rest of the actual world. The ideal self, the norms defining the ideal self, and the norms of rationality, are not possible objects of experience. The problem of self-knowledge, then, is not just whether and how the actual self can identify the ideal self using only the resources of the actual world but also whether and how the actual self can identify the actual self or anything in the actual or ideal world when information is available only insofar as the operations of the actual self accord with the operations of the ideal self—and when the actual self, in all its operations is fallible. So if the existence of the ideal self is understood on the model of the existence of the actual self, if rational principles need a foundation in some independent reality, than all true knowledge would be impossible short of some metaphysical-mystical leap. Since there need be no such foundation, knowledge of rational principles is (in principle) attainable through a dialectical process within and between actual selves over time. For, after all, what we are searching for is only an understanding of our search.

Moral Philosophy and the Standard Belief

All this—the Factunorm Principle and the rest plus more that could be said—is but an elaboration of two "assumptions": we are rational, and it is rational to believe what is believed by rational persons. Of course, not every philosopher acknowledges the Factunorm Principle, let alone the rest of the foregoing. But many have expressed acceptance of that principle, particularly those intent on developing a substantive moral theory, a system of norms of rationality regarding moral matters. By their conscious practice and often by explicit statement, most such philosophers acknowledge that a reason for thinking that some moral belief implied by a theory is true (false) is that the belief is accepted (rejected) by most people. Certainly for most of the most important moral philosophers, conformity with common belief is a test and a touchstone if not the bedrock of moral theory. This is an empirical fact easily established; the texts are public and unequivocal.

That fact, taken with the fact that the Standard Belief is a common belief, might suggest that most if not all philosophers accept the Standard Belief. Yet the fact is they all reject it.[4]

The inevasible question then is: Why do philosophers deny the Standard Belief?

The answer is hard to come by because the question has gone unasked. Philosophers don't explain their denial, for they hardly ever express it; it lies implicit in and entailed by what they do say. Mostly they don't discuss the Standard Belief at all or even demonstrate any awareness of its existence.

The answer is hard to come by as well because objections to the Standard Belief are hard to come by. I know of but two complaints that have ever been raised. One is that the belief that humans have a unique inherent value or dignity is *hubris* and nonsense. The other is that the belief that being a member of the human race is morally relevant is like the belief that being a member of the Aryan race is morally relevant. Both of those claims are true. The trouble is, no one has troubled himself to explain precisely how either of those claims constitutes an objection to the Standard Belief. If it's not obvious now that there is some trouble here, an explanation is forthcoming.

In any case, even if there exists an effective refutation of the Standard Belief, there exists no reason to think such a refutation has motivated philosophers to reject that belief. And even if it has, still, philosophical and common belief do collide here on a most fundamental moral issue, and we need to understand how that fact has passed unnoticed instead of being, as it should be, a philosophical *cause célèbre*. Philosophers must in general suppose either that their theories imply or are at least consistent with the Standard Belief or that in denying the Standard Belief they conform with common belief. Either or both possibilities must be regularly realized, for otherwise it seems inexplicable that the Standard Belief is routinely rejected with nary a word about it or with words betraying no cognizance of its centrality in common belief. These two possibilities come to much the same, for the mistakes in both cases share the same cause, a mistaken or misapplied methodology that throws doubt on the philosophers' conceptions of what the common belief is, on how their theories contrast with it, and, at the same time, on the truth of what these theories affirm.

Let us begin by clarifying the contrast between philosophical and common belief. And let us first remove a verbal similarity that masks a substantive difference, for many a philosopher has *said* (in so many words) that being human has moral cachet. But what he *means* is that being a *person* has moral cachet, that a human being has human status only because and insofar as a human being is a person. By contrast, most people believe a person has human status if the person is a human being.

The term 'human being' is correctly applied to all and only the members of our biological species. That specification is informative but incomplete without criteria for species membership. Being of human parents conceived is a partial criterion; it is explainable without circularity by referring to paradigm cases, but it provides neither a necessary condition (for, e.g., it excludes the original species members) nor a sufficient condition (for, e.g., it includes human terata whom we regard not as human beings but as some unfortunate kinds of mutants). But then, the abortion argument supplies sufficient evidence that no neat set of necessary and sufficient conditions for being human is generally agreed upon—which is to say there is no such set. For reasons not discussable here, it would be extraordinary if there were such a set of conditions. But disputes about what a human being is or which things are human beings do not indicate the existence of any linguistic divergences; on the contrary, such disputes require for their intelligibility that the disputants mean the same thing by the term 'human being'.

In common speech 'person' has various meanings; often it seems freely interchangeable if not synonymous with 'human being' or at least applicable to all human beings though perhaps not only human beings (gods are called persons). But in philosophy 'person' is a theoretical term defined differently in different subspecialties (e.g., ethics, philosophy of mind) and by different theories within each subspecialty. Moral theories generally intend it to be interchangeable with some term like 'entity having human status'. It may be defined by that term, thereby presenting the problem of determining which (ostensibly nonethical) properties are necessary and sufficient for having that status, or it may be defined by some set of (ostensibly nonethical) properties and then the problem is to determine whether those properties are necessary and sufficient for having that status. The two tactics come to the same. Theories differ over what the essential properties of persons are, but usually they select one or more cognitive or affective capacities such as rationality or sentience or a free will or a sense of justice—but never humanness. However, though 'person' is defined without reference to human beings, since a normal adult human being is the natural paradigm of both a person and a human being, philosophers follow the common practice of freely interchanging 'human being' and 'person'.

The conflict over the Standard Belief is also obscured by significant agreements on which things have human status. Most philosophers grant that no animal has human status (and thus that no property possessed by an animal has moral cachet or that animals do not possess such a property in sufficient degree) and that most human beings and certainly all normal adults have human status. Indeed, many theories seem intended to accord human status to all and (among known things) only human beings. But whatever their intent, none succeeds. They fail in different ways and for different reasons. Most make too stringent a requirement; typically they hold that only some developed (exercisable) capacity has moral cachet, thereby excluding humans whose allegedly relevant capacities are undeveloped, deformed, or defunct. When the requirement is reduced to the possession of the original, native capacity alone, still humans with the relevant congenital defects are left out. And here the requirement may be too weak as well as too strong, for normal "infrahuman" fetuses[5] may qualify while congenital defective adults do not. In other theories the requirement is just too weak, for while every human may qualify, some animals and/or "infrahuman" fetuses qualify as well as and sometimes better than some humans. Here, though the moral status of every human may be independent, it is not superior to that of some nonhuman beings. The reverse of this occurs in theories that first account for the moral status of some primary group (usually normal adults) and then admit the rest of the race through their relations (e.g., affectional bonds) to members of the primary group; every plausible suggested relation makes the moral status of the secondary group dependent upon the primary group (e.g., the effects of an act on the interests of an infant get considered only because and insofar as the affections of his parents and other normal adults are affected by effects on his interests). Moreover, with many of the suggested relations, members of the primary group could be so related to a nonhuman thing, thereby fitting it for the secondary group.

We need not examine individually each of the many theories (each with its own minor variations) to conclude that each fails to accord human status to all and only human beings. We need only reflect upon the gross disparities between various human beings and upon the close resemblances between some animals (or 'infrahuman" fetuses) and some human beings to see that no property, not even a complex disjunct property, is possessed by all humans and no animals (or "infrahuman" fetuses) and is plausibly thought to have moral cachet. No property, that is, other than being human.[6]

More importantly, all this is ultimately beside the point, for the opposition over what has moral cachet is not itself and does not entail an opposition over which things have human status. The latter conflicts are unavoidable while the former persists. The Standard Belief is consistent with virtually any traditional theory's position regarding which particular things have human status; one need only claim, as many have tried to, that the entity in question—be it fetus, congenital idiot, or whatever—is not (or is) a human being. (The plausibility of the claim may vary from case to case [and audience to audience] but the forms of argument employed are remarkably constant: e.g., fetuses are likened to parts of their mothers, mongoloids to terata, the permanently comatose to vegetables, slaves to animals, etc.) The Standard Belief is a general principle, and disagreements on principles are evidenced not so much by disagreements over judgments on particular cases ("verdicts") as by differing forms of reasoning employed in reaching those verdicts. Divergencies in verdicts attract more attention because of their more obvious practical import. But it is of more subtle and profound importance that, when arguing about abortion, euthanasia (without consent), infanticide, racial discrimination, and many, many other issues, nonphilosophers find it natural or necessary to claim on one basis or another that the creature in question is (or is not) a human being so that they can then conclude that the creature should (or need not) be regarded and treated as befits one with human status. Philosophers may reach similar verdicts by ascribing moral cachet to some property roughly coextensive with being human, and, since that property may sometimes be relevant in arguments over the humanness of a creature, they may employ similar bases in reaching those verdicts. Still, philosophers employ those bases differently, for *their* arguments bypass the issue of the creature's humanness as essentially irrelevant. Understandably, a philosopher might misconstrue this situation supposing either that his theory entails the Standard Belief and thereby conforms to common belief or that it conforms to common belief while denying the Standard Belief. But actually all such theories entail competitors to the Standard Belief and thereby reject common belief. In fine, a theory lacking the Standard Belief is comparable, not to a theory that would punish arsonists more severely than murderers, but to one that determines whom to punish and how severely without employing the notion of desert at all.

Principles and Verdicts

Traditional philosophers are liable to be misled about such matters because they practice a curious kind of doublethink: while regarding the verdicts of common belief as data against which to test their theories, they have not treated the principles of common belief as an independent form of evidence. Theorists have been concerned to formulate principles which, when taken with the facts of any situation, generate the same conclusion a competent moral judge would reach when faced with the same facts, but beyond this they have displayed little concern over whether their principles reflect the reasoning by which a competent moral judge reaches his conclusions. At minimum, theorists rarely mention the relevant evidence, so there's little reason to think they have been moved by it or have even noticed it.

This practice is indefensible. The philosopher cannot, with consistency, respect our verdicts without respecting our operative principles, our forms of reasoning. For, first our verdicts include judgments about people's motives and characters as well as about their actions and institutions; and if as I assume, a moral theory is meant to provide us with a system of reasons we could employ when deciding how to act, then those reasons must be measured against our verdicts regarding a man's motivation and character and thus regarding his principles as well as against the verdicts on the actions directed by those motivating principles. Secondly and more directly, it makes no sense to regard our verdicts as data for testing putative rational principles unless one takes those verdicts to be the output of the operation of rational principles. Any plausible reason *for* accepting our verdicts as evidence for or *against* presumed norms will rely on those verdicts being evidence *of* rational norms.

No doubt, unless a difference in principles is *possible, determinable,* and *important* independently of differences in the verdicts they imply, none of this matters.[7] Such a difference is as possible as extensional equivalence with intensional dissimilarity. The difference can be of the form: 'In situation A, do X' versus 'In situation B, do Y' where A and B regularly coincide; or 'In situation A, do X' versus 'In situation A, do Y' where doing X and doing Y regularly coincide. Besides, the implied verdicts of different principles would count as the same for the purpose of a moral theory as long as their differences were marginal as judged by the considerations bearing on the assessment of the theory: e.g., the divergencies were restricted to fact situations possible only in a world quite unlike ours in very general respects or to fact situations for which no one verdict is firmly and confidently accepted by most people.

Now I have already said that a difference in principles is evidenced, independently of any difference in verdicts, by a difference in the forms of reasoning employed in reaching the verdicts. This difference will seem unimportant if one takes it to consist solely in that people with different principles are disposed to utter different sound patterns when justifying their verdicts. But surely that can't be the whole difference, for if it were there would cease to be any difference in the meanings of the different utterances. Surely, even if we were certain someone would invariably do the right thing though always for the wrong reasons, we would still care what his reasons were, and we could still consider them the wrong reasons. Or rather, to turn this around, in an important respect a person can't do the right thing for the wrong reason, for *what* someone is doing depends not just on his bodily movements in the physical world but also on the intentions, motives, and reasons with which he acts—what he takes himself to be doing— and thus on the concepts and principles with which he explains and justifies his behavior. The acts motivated by different principles may satisfy the same verdicts and be physically the same while the nature and character of the conduct—what act is performed—may differ just in virtue of the acts' being motivated by different principles. Our principles define our acts as well as direct them; they change the meaning of the movements we make as well as moving us to make changes in our movements.

This difference in the meaning of the movements is not made manifest in the movements themselves. Rather, for persons to have different principles is, in essence, for them to regard different facts as relevant to their own and other people's lives and conduct or for them to regard the facts as relevant in different ways. This is not (necessarily) a difference in the facts or verdicts the persons can be brought to believe or deny, but rather in what they *are naturally disposed* to and *actually do* believe and deny. The difference is in the items and aspects of their world they notice, attend to, consider, in what and how they perceive, think about, understand.[8] And those differences are as much a cause as a consequence of differences in what persons care about, are interested in, appreciate, and desire, in what and how they love and fear. Such differences are manifested directly and indirectly (via their bearing on motivation and intention) as differences in behavior, much of which is left unregulated by any of a person's principles.

So the conduct evidencing acceptance of a principle need not be conduct in accordance with the principles. That most people believe that being human has moral cachet is revealed not just by the way they argue about issues such as abortion. It is reflected as well in the fact that they perceive, regard, and identify themselves and each other principally and essentially, not as accords with any of the prime philosophical categories, but as human beings. Of course, we do not always so identify ourselves, for the properties of a thing that serve to identify it vary with the purposes for which the identification is made and thus also with the background of beliefs with which it is made. However, the beliefs involved here are rational beliefs and the purposes are not the special purposes we happen to have on special occasions but the general purposes we have in virtue of being rational and thus being capable of self-identification and requiring it. Our reasons for identifying ourselves as human beings are our reasons for accepting the Standard Belief.

A Notion of Human Status

As a step toward understanding this, let us take as a rough statement of a notion of human status the dictum, G: You$_1$ are to do unto others$_a$ as you$_2$ would have others$_b$ do unto you$_3$. The dictum is addressed to you$_1$, any rational agent, because, like any rational principle, G is addressed and applies to all and only those who can listen and apply it—rational agents. So too, the others$_b$ are all the other rational agents, and when G is addressed to any of them, you$_1$ are one of the others$_b$. However, while you$_1$=you$_2$=you$_3$, neither you$_2$ nor you$_3$ need be rational agents; you$_2$ need only be what might be called a subjunctively rational creature. So too the others$_a$ need not be rational agents; they need include all but not only the others$_b$. The others$_a$ comprise the class of those with human status; or, rather, they plus yourself$_3$ comprise that class. The question of what has moral cachet is the question of how the others$_a$ are to be identified. To ask it is to ask what it would be rational for you$_2$ to identify yourself$_3$ as so that you$_3$ are among the others$_a$ when G is addressed to any of the others$_b$. That is, it would be rational for you$_1$ to accept and act upon G only if you$_2$ filled in G by identifying the others$_a$ in such a way that you$_3$ could not be excluded from the others$_a$ when the others$_b$ act upon G. And for that very reason it would be irrational for you$_1$ to accept any of the philosophical alternatives to the Standard Belief because, although you$_1$ are rational, you$_1$ are not necessarily rational and so you$_3$ could become or have been nonrational. Any of your$_1$ cognitive or affective capacities could become or could have been different without altering your$_1$ identity, so the individual whose interests are your$_1$ own could remain constant while those principles would not require the consideration of his (=your$_3$) interests. By contrast, being human is an essential property of anything possessing it. You$_1$ could not be or have been other than a human being and still be identifiable as you$_3$.[9] The Standard Belief is a common belief because it enables all and only those known creatures to whom G can be addressed to rationally accept G, for it ensures that each and every one of them has a rational claim to the consideration of his or her interests throughout his or her lifetime.[10]

Various aspects of all this need further attention. Consider first the paradigmatic moral question: How would you like (or have liked) it if somebody did (or had done) that to you? The applicability of that question and the arguments employing it is as broad and as narrow as the criteria for personal identity; the question and arguments can make sense in all and only those situations in which you could still be you. That is to say, among other things, that a rational principle is a law-like generalization and thus must be interpretable as sustaining subjunctive and contrary to fact conditionals. This helps explain what might otherwise seem odd—that in assessing the rationality of the Standard Belief and its alternatives, *what you could have been but no longer can become is just as relevant as what you presently are and what you still can become.*[11]

Next consider the prime argument of the anti-abortionists. Its power derives from the fact that any human being is identifiable as the same entity as far back as the zygote and no further. Its weakness is that while the zygote is undeniably the same entity as the later adult, it no more follows that the zygote is the same human being than it follows that the still later corpse is the same human being. When and how to date the inception and demise of the human being as distinct from the human body is a further question, and as things stand the question regarding inception has no correct answer. Yet it may seem that since you have interests in protecting your body come what may or might have been, it would be rational for you to replace the Standard Belief with a principle identifying yourself in terms of your body—e.g., being of woman conceived has moral cachet. After all, that too is an essential property of yourself, and how would you like it if someone had blinded you for life by wounding you while in the womb? To this the pro-abortionist can properly reply that, first, while *you* have interests regarding your body, your body and its parts have no interest of their own, and in its earliest stages a fetus is only a body and not a self at all; *it* doesn't have any interests, so if that body is destroyed before any self is formed, no one's interests need be harmed. Second, even in the later stages when the fetus seems undeniably a creature—even here where the anti-abortionist's argument is unquestionably compelling—though there may some sort of self with interests of its own, that self is not a human self and is not identical with the self of the eventual human being;[12] so if the fetal creature is destroyed before it becomes a human being, no human being's interests need be harmed. And to someone who insists on saying that in destroying a fetal body or fetal creature one is harming the interests of a *potential* human being, suffice it to reply that you₂ have no good reason to accord human status to nonexistent human beings, however potential they may be, because one thing you₂ could never be identical with is anything that never exists. (N.B., such "entities" are not made of the same stuff as *future* human beings.) The structure of this whole argument is highlighted by the contrast between destroying a fetal body or creature and "merely" damaging one, thereby damaging a later human being. For the true anti-abortionist the former is clearly the more serious crime; for the pro-abortionist the latter is. For both, as the aptness of the pro-abortionist's rejoinders reveal, the logic of their positions requires the Standard Belief.

Next consider the moral status of animals. Though each of us is essentially a primate, an animal, and a living thing, none of us is a nonhuman thing and neither is any other known rational creature. Doubtless some animals are quite clever and can act for a reason, but none is rational, none is among the others_b who can accept and act upon a rational principle like G. That might seem beside the point, since though they may never master a few cute cognitive tricks many humans never do either, and the interests and sufferings of animals are as real as ours. To this it should be said that to suffer, even to suffer a harm at the hands of another, is not ipso facto to suffer a wrong. More, to deny animals human status is not to deny them every substantial moral status, though precisely what the proper status is for each kind of thing is an enormous and enormously difficult question that may have no complete answer. In any case, since none of them can accord human status to any of them, let alone to us, and since none of us is one of them, none of us can have the reason to treat them as we are to treat ourselves that we have for treating ourselves that way. This is not sheer selfishness on our part, for, be it noted, if the argument for the Standard Belief goes through, it does so whatever our desires and interests may be as long as we have some at all (and that we do is presupposed by our being rational creatures.) Obviously, insofar as the interests of animals move our sympathies we have reason to protect them, but even if we were carried away to fulfill their interests as fully as our own, that wouldn't sustain an independent moral status for them.[13]

But now, suppose we could and did sharpen the wits of a gnu in a zoo enough so that it sued for its emancipation with as much eloquence as you please. Would we be obliged to manumit it? And every other gnu too? Nice questions these.[14] But let us avoid them for now except to note that the Standard Belief affirms only that being human is sufficient for having human status and thus that no property inessential for being human is necessary. The Standard Belief does not deny that being human is not necessary or that some other properties may be sufficient. Common belief does affirm both of these claims, but it does so in a complex way contrary to philosophical convictions. For example, whatever may be true of our gnu, we would probably think it proper to accept as moral equals extraterrestrial travelers who, except for their origins, differed from human beings no more than Tibetans differ from Teutons. On the other hand, it's far from clear that we would feel constrained to accord moral equality to a realization of the typical sci-fi monster—an argute fifteen-and-a-half-foot purple praying mantis oozing goo from every orifice—but our responses to such stories suggest that we might well not, especially if the creature has substantial homnivorous or sadistic impulses, which, after all, are compatible with the philosophers' pet properties. However, the realm of imagination is a treacherous place to investigate the structures of common belief: beliefs about what people's beliefs are regarding some conjecture are usually conjectures, and frequently people have no belief regarding the conjecture. Far better to look into the hard data history richly supplies, especially that regarding racial discrimination.

Egalitarian and Racist Beliefs

We need to look there anyway since it may seem objectionable that our account is tantamount to a justification of racism. For the fact that humanness is an essential property does not distinguish the Standard Belief from other principles that pick out essential properties defining natural kinds to which we belong. We have explained why principles that would place us in more inclusive kinds than humanity (e.g., primates, animals, living things) won't do, but we have yet to object to principles that place us in more exclusive kinds. Clearly, the progenitors you have are the only ones you could have had, and for all that has been said so far, you could identify yourself by your race, tribe, clan, ancestral line, or family. And just as clearly, people throughout history have done precisely that, have lived by the correlative moral principles, and have thereby lived in a variety of complex caste systems.

But let us be clear here. It's hardly an objection that our account justifies principles such as: being an Aryan (or an Apache or a McFarland) has moral cachet. After all, each such principle happens to be true, for they are all implied by the Standard Belief and they are *all* mutually compatible. The Standard Belief is only the most general expression of these, its "corollaries." What is objectionable is the distinctively racist or caste belief that Aryans (or whatever) are a *superior* kind of creature, that they have an inherent *value* or *worth* lacked by non-Aryans, and that in virtue of this *difference in value* Aryans are entitled to accord full human status to themselves and to deny it to non-Aryans. But there is no *logical* connection between this distinctively racist belief and the Standard Belief or its corollaries. There is, however, a connection made through the *psychodynamics of rationality,* and we shall come to that. But let us first recognize that it is anything but an objection that our account uncovers the rational structures underlying and motivating racism and caste systems and that it helps explain the pervasive power of the fact of lineage, of common blood, of membership in a family, ancestral line, clan, tribe or race. Egalitarians engaged in counteracting the evils of caste systems may require a rhetoric that derogates those systems by explaining them as products of rank irrationality unalloyed with any elements of rationality other than that guiding the crassest self-interest. But a philosopher is untrue to his trade when he uses the excuse of the political ideologue to explain away those complex social forms with all the wisdom of a village atheist. His overeager egalitarianism serves no one, least of all himself, for by failing in his proper study he thereby risks irrelevance.[15] He also risks—to put it kindly—unintended irony when he helps himself to such metaphors as "the family of man" or "the brotherhood of man" while defending principles that would drain those slogans of all rhetorical force.[16] The literature of philosophy is rife with such ironies. Perhaps the supreme irony is that egalitarian philosophers who reject the Standard Belief and all racist beliefs happily embrace the claim that human beings have an inherent value and dignity. Yet that claim stands to the Standard Belief in precisely the same relation as racist beliefs stand to the corollaries of the Standard Belief, and it is just as false and ultimately incoherent as those racist beliefs.

NOTES

1. Reasons may differ in kind and degree, and most of us think the superiority of our moral status involves both sorts of differences. Aside from those who attribute some supranatural feature to an animal (e.g., sacredness or the possession of a human soul), even vegetarians and antivivisectionists generally acknowledge not only that we may require a *greater* sacrifice from a person to prevent harm to a human being than to prevent an equivalent harm to an animal, but also that an animal *may*, but a human being *may not*, be destroyed when he is unable and others are unwilling to care for him. (In any case, a human's having a superior status is compatible with, e.g., the propriety of rescuing a drowning pet poodle instead of a drowning Adolph Hitler, since a thing's moral status is not the only morally relevant fact about it.) Since the particular form of the superiority of the moral status accorded human beings will not be at issue here, it need not be specified.

2. A fuller treatment of these and related matters touched upon herein appears in my "Understanding the Abortion Argument," in *Philosophy and Public Affairs* 1, no. 1 (Fall 1971): pp. 67–95.

3. Apparently a failure to appreciate this has led many philosophers to deny the Factunorm Principle for fear that it entailed subjectivism or relativism and thereby required an inappropriate foundation for rational principles. On this, see my *The Significance of Sense* (Ithaca, N.Y.: Cornell University Press, 1972), pp. 160–72. The main thrust of that work is to show that if the Factunorm Principle is applicable for any rational principle it applies to moral principles as well.

4. Anyway, all (save one) that I know of. But different philosophers reject it in different ways, some by accepting (explicitly or implicitly) some incompatible alternative, some by denying (explicitly or implicitly) that it and its alternatives could be genuinely true or false.

5. An "infrahuman" fetus (a human fetus that is not [yet] a human being) might have a moral status comparable to an animal's, independent but inferior

to a human being's. For many people, a human fetus has, in virtue of being a *human* fetus, an independent status superior to any animal's, yet, in virtue of being a human *fetus*, its status is inferior to a human being's.

6. This claim has a class of pseudo-exceptions, *species-normal properties:* a property (indirectly) attributable to every member of a natural kind if it is (directly) attributable to any normal member of that kind. It is fully proper to say that human beings are, e.g., rational bipeds, albeit some things properly called human beings can't reason or have one or three legs due to congenital malformation or subsequent deformation. A mongoloid, no matter how idiotic, is still a human being, and, in the species-normal sense, a rational creature. A natural kind (species) is specifiable by the properties of its normal members without regarding its abnormal members. (More specifically, unless developmental stage properties are intended, the species-normal properties are the properties of the normal *mature* members: e.g., humans have thirty-two teeth.) Whatever the importance of the conceptual machinery operating here (and it may be considerable), clearly a theory cannot match common belief by appealing to species-normal properties while denying the Standard Belief, since the predication of, e.g., rationality to certain human beings is based solely on their being human.

7. But then, if none of this matters, one might wonder what is at stake in the competition between rival traditional theories, for the arguments in their debates have generally been concerned at bottom only with how the implied verdicts of each theory compare with those of common belief. Any contrasts there may be on that score are controversial, with each side claiming coincidence with common belief. And if, as is rarely denied, the area of coincident verdicts is vastly greater than that of potential clash, a reputedly high-minded and deep-seated struggle would start to smack of petty wrangling.

8. So too for the philosopher: his acceptance of his theoretically derived principles (moral and extramoral) expresses itself in what he notices, attends to, etc., in his data, common belief. Yet actually philosophers virtually never bother to look at other people's beliefs anyway, in spite of their acknowledging common belief as evidence. Instead they look into their own heads, presumably on the assumption that their own considered judgments are as trustworthy as anyone's, so they have no need to look further—a dubious assumption since what is there to be seen may well be their philosophical theory or its effects in their beliefs. (Many philosophers liken philosophy to psychotherapy, but few have learned caution from the fact that patients in therapy often unconsciously manufacture symptoms to fit their therapist's diagnosis.) A more plausible assumption is that their own beliefs are no more and (for the reason just given) perhaps somewhat less trustworthy than the beliefs of other competent moral judges. Unfortunately, whether a philosopher looks at his own or at other people's beliefs, he is likely to look at them through the filter of his theory. And as psychologists tell us, look as you may, what you see is largely determined by what you believe and are thus prepared to see. To be sure, the alterations of the theorist's beliefs and perceptions may be an improvement, not a perversion, and it is possible to determine which they are. But it's not easy. Nor is it easy to be cognizant of such alterations—and this may help explain why philosophers don't notice the conflict of their theories with common belief.

9. For the nonce, a complete elucidation and defense of the essential-accidental distinction is not essential. For one thing, it suffices here that, in an unproblematic sense, it is less possible for you to be or have been other than

human than it is for you to be or have been other than rational or the like. For another thing, Saul Kripke has personally assured me that being human is an essential property.

10. An instructive pseudo-exception. Some cultures have cast out some of their members (e.g., the insane), denying them human status on the ground that they were possessed by demons. The logic of the explanation requires that the outcast was no longer himself, no longer a human being, and that this transformation was effected by supranatural powers.

11. More generally, this feature of rational principles explains why, for human beings unlike animals, the facts and possibilities of the past can be reasons for acting just as well as the facts and possibilities of the present and future can. A failure to appreciate this vitiates many a moral theory: utilitarianism's inability to make sense of punishment is only the most obvious example. A rational creature cannot live by consequences alone, and no creature can have an adequate comprehension of consequences or control his conduct by such comprehension without being rational.

12. The pro-abortionist's position can be only as plausible as this premise is.

13. Perhaps nothing said here can persuade the unpersuaded, since none of it is likely to dispel the pervasive and profound misconceptions about the very nature of morality that likely underlie their dissatisfaction. Let me here just give warning—however blunt and crabbed it may be—that morality, if it is to make any sense at all, can be only an aspect of rationality and neither a presupposition nor a consequence of it. Our moral principles are among our means of understanding our world, ourselves, and their relations. So our moral status is not something any of us deserve in consequence of some splendid trait, talent, or achievement. It's not a prized position of rights, privileges, and powers awarded for excellence in some cosmic competition. Nor is it a first-class citizenship in a community created for and confined to the protection and promotion of our interests. We are "entitled" to our moral status and animals to theirs only in the sense that we are entitled to our human nature and they to theirs.

14. Beliefs in transmigratory selves raise similar yet importantly different issues, because unlike the above, they do not suppose a change in the behavior of the beast or its physical (e.g., brain) structure. It is not clear whether such beliefs suppose or require that your self could be other than a human self.

15. Recently at least two philosophers have published defenses of abortion that allow as how infanticide is also at worst imprudent. Query: Will their essays create anything comparable to the public outrage generated by the now infamous work of Jensen and Herrnstein? Not bloody likely. Why not, for their assault on the conscience and intellect of civilized people is surely no less brutal and blundering? Well, without discounting numerable other salient differences, part of the answer is that Jansen and Herrnstein are social scientists, and, for good reasons and bad alike, we listen when social scientists, even those of minor distinction, speak out on matters touching upon public policy. Their counterparts in philosophy are not invited onto the stage. (It was eras ago, back when philosophers and social scientists were the same men, that the counsels of philosophers were sought and paid for.) Why is this? Just look at a typical philosophical performance: Abortion, an issue inspiring no unanimity among any random class of persons (as is evidenced by the turbulent condition of laws on the matter), that issue provides the occasion for a blithe dismissal of a prohibition endorsed by a monolithic consensus and enforced by every present

Western legal system. Once again a philosopher has thrown the baby out with the bath water (and the very premeditation of the performance only deepens the onlooker's despair); and once again, having walked upon the stage, the philosopher turns his back to his audience (and then walks off, for he has no responsibilities for what follows). And then, when the crowd remains unmoved except to laughter and derision, the philosopher deems it benighted. But the explanation of the crowd's response is not what the philosopher says, but *that* he says it. At least since Socrates philosophers have been regarded with hostile suspicion or amused contempt. They are not listened to because they do not listen. That may be an instance of a psychological law, but here the point is also that philosophers are not listened to because what they say is not worth listening to, and it is not because they do not listen (to anyone but themselves) and so they are in no position to speak (to anyone but themselves).

16. Probably the least discussed and most badly treated matter in the literature of moral philosophy is the one that matters most in most people's lives: familial relationships. That's not surprising since that literature lacks a theory that could say much about those matters that would be both interesting and true. The familiar philosophical models for understanding or justifying the special regard we accord familial relations are inadequate to the task. That regard must be treated as a phenomenon of rationality, for we don't take imprinting quite as well as ducks do, and neither do we have the mechanisms by which lost lambs are reunited with their mothers. Our natural family has a hold on us whoever brings us up, and we find out who our real relations are by being *told*. (It helps here to imagine your reaction if one fine day an elderly and utterly strange gentleman approached you with unimpeachable evidence that he is your real father.) But neither are our relatives like ordinary benefactors, business partners, or friends; the special regard goes beyond reciprocity, love, or likeness—as often as not, those things are lacking, and even when present they can't explain the special regard for natural parents as opposed to adopted, foster, or stepparents. Let us admit that a family forms a small (exogamous) caste system. It can be understood and justified in terms of the special role the family has in determining an individual's identity. We identify with our relations, not (or not just) because we are akin to them but because we are a kin to them. I, personally, am largely unmoved by the fact that the human race has got itself onto the moon or that blacks dominate in my favorite sports, but I can't imagine what it would be like to be immune to pride or embarrassment at the achievements and antics of those in my immediate family. (That is no sign of logical impossibility; it goes deeper than that, for there are logical impossibilities I can imagine.)

Abortion and the Social System

WILLIAM T. LIU

1. The Current Incidence of Abortion

In 1971, according to the International Planned Parenthood Federation figures, more than four abortions for every ten live births were performed throughout the world.[1] In California, during the same year, more than two out of every ten pregnancies were terminated by voluntary abortion,[2] but a higher figure was given by Tietze and Murstein, who placed the ratio of abortions per live births for California at more than one out of every three.[3] In New York, where many abortions were performed on nonresidents, the figure was more than twice the rate for California during that year.[4] In Hawaii, between March 1970 and December 1971, the ratio of live births to abortions was about four to one.[5] Given the problem of recordkeeping on such a difficult area of health statistics, plus the fact that data on illegal abortions are completely lacking, these reported abortion figures may be grossly inaccurate. This is not to suggest that abortion rates are actually much lower and deserve no more discussion or attention than other figures on infant mortality, stillbirths and spontaneous miscarriages. Statistics on abortions throughout the world indicate that abortion has increased in spite of the widespread use of modern contraceptives.[6]

Various papers in this volume focus on topics especially relevant to the Western Hemisphere. However, abortion is by no means an exclusive problem for the Western world; Third World countries in the Eastern Hemisphere have always been known for high rates of abortion.[7] But a trend toward an institutionalization of abortion is morally *more* offensive and therefore would have a greater influence on the judicial, social, and moral foundations of the Western world. Great Britain, for example, a country which had a rather conservative general public attitude toward abortion during the decade of the 1960s, reported an increase of nearly fourfold in abortions performed under

TABLE 1

Legal Status of Abortion by Country and by Grounds Mid-1975

Country	Population mid-1975 Estimate (in millions)	Illegal no exceptions	Medical Narrow (life)	Medical Broad (health)	Eugenic (fetal)	Juridical (rape, incest, etc.)	Social and social-medical	Legal grounds not specified
Algeria	16.8		X					
Argentina	25.4			X		X		
Australia	13.8			X				
(New South Wales)[2]				X			X	
(South Australia)[2]				X	X		X[3]	
Austria	7.5							X[4]
Bangladesh	73.7		X					
Belgium	9.8	X						
Bolivia	5.4	X						
Brazil	109.7		X			X		
Bulgaria[5]	8.8			X	X	X	X[6]	
Cameroon	6.4			X		X		
Canada	22.8			X				
Chile	10.3			X				
China, Peoples Republic of	822.8							X[4]

Columbia	25.9	X							
Costa Rica	2.0			X	X				
Cuba[7]	9.5			X	X			X[4]	
Czechoslovakia	14.8			X	X				
Denmark	5.0	X					X		
Dominican Republic	5.1			X					
Ecuador	7.1								
Egypt, Arab Republic of	37.5	X							
El Salvador	4.1			X	X		X		
Ethiopia	28.0			X	X		X	X[9]	
Finland[8]	4.7			X					
France	52.9							X[6]	
German Democratic Republic	17.2							X[4]	
German Federal Republic	61.9			X					
Ghana	9.9			X					
Great Britain	54.9			X	X		X	X[3]	
Greece	8.9			X					
Guatemala	6.1		X						
Haiti	4.6	X					X		
Honduras	3.0			X					
Hong Kong	4.2			X	X		X	X[3]	
Hungary[10]	10.5			X	X		X	X[4]	
India	613.2	X						X[3]	
Indonesia	136.0								
Iran	32.9		X						

Country	Population mid-1975 Estimate (in millions)	Illegal no exceptions	Medical Narrow (life)	Medical Broad (health)	Eugenic (fetal)	Juridical (rape, incest, etc.)	Social and social-medical	Legal grounds not specified
Iraq	11.1		X					
Ireland, Northern	1.5		X					
Ireland, Republic of	3.1	X						
Israel	3.4			X				
Italy	55.0			X				
Ivory Coast	4.9		X					
Jamaica	2.0	X						
Japan	111.1			X	X	X	X[3][11]	
Jordan	2.7			X		X		
Kenya	13.3			X				
Khmer Republic	8.1		X					
Korea, Republic of	33.9			X	X	X		
Lebanon	2.9		X					
Liberia	1.7	X						
Malaysia	12.1		X					
Mexico	59.2		X			X		
Morocco	17.5			X				
Netherlands[12]	13.6		X					
New Zealand	3.0		X					
Nicaragua	2.3		X					

Nigeria	62.9								
Norway	4.0				X	X[4]			
Pakistan	70.6		X	X					
Panama	1.7	X							
Paraguay	2.6		X						
Peru	15.3								
Phillippines	44.4	X		X	X	X[4 11]			
Poland	33.8								
Portugal	8.8	X		X	X	X[4]			
Romania[13]	21.2			X					
Senegal	4.4		X						
Sierra Leone	3.0								
Singapore	2.2	X		X					
South Africa	24.7	X		X	X			X[14]	
Spain	35.4	X							
Sri Lanka	14.0	X							
Sudan	18.3	X							
Sweden	8.3		X					X[15]	
Switzerland	6.5		X						
Syria	7.3								
Taiwan	16.0		X		X				
Thailand	42.1		X	X					
Trinidad and Tobago	1.0								
Tunisia	5.7								
Turkey	39.9		X		X			X[4]	
Uganda	11.4		X						
United States	213.9							X[4]	
USSR	255.0							X[3]	

Country	Population mid-1975 Estimate (in millions)	Illegal no exceptions	Legal on specified grounds [1]					
			Medical			Eugenic (fetal)	Juridical (rape, incest, etc.)	Social and social-medical	Legal grounds not specified
			Narrow (life)	Broad (health)				
Uruguay[16]	3.1			X		X	X[4]	
Venezuela	12.2		X					
Vietnam, Democratic Republic of	23.8							X[17]
Vietnam, Republic of South	19.7		X					
Yugoslavia	21.3			X	X	X	X[4]	
Zaire	24.5	X						
Zambia	5.0			X	X		X[3]	

NOTE: Table does not include countries under 1 million inhabitants and those for which information on legal status of abortion was not located.

[1] Abortion on medical and eugenic grounds is generally permitted prior to viability. Abortion on juridical grounds is generally permitted up to the same gestational period as abortion on social and social-medical grounds.
[2] Population included in Australia.
[3] Prior to viability of fetus.
[4] During first trimester (three months or 12 weeks).
[5] On request for married women with two living children, unmarried women, and women over age 40 with one living child.

[6] During first ten weeks.
[7] Abortion on request available in government hospitals.
[8] On request for women over age 40.
[9] During first 16 weeks.
[10] On request for unmarried women, for married women with three children, for *some* married women with two living children, and for married women over age 40.
[11] No formal authorization procedures required and abortion permitted in doctor's office; hence, abortion de facto available on request.
[12] Abortion on request openly available in non-profit clinics.
[13] Abortion on request for women over age 40 and women having four or more children.
[14] During first 24 weeks.
[15] During first 18 weeks.
[16] Penalty may be waived when abortion is performed for reasons of serious economic difficulty.
[17] Gestational limitation not ascertained.

Source: Christopher Tietze and Majorie Cooper Murstein, "Induced Abortion: 1975 Factbook," *Reports on Population Policy* (December 1975) pp. 8,9.

the National Health Service between 1961 and 1967.[8] The rate of legal abortions in England and Wales in 1967 was about ten times as high as the corresponding figures estimated for the United States in the same year when the first three states liberalized abortion laws.[9] The liberalization of abortion laws in New York and Canada, however, was thought to be responsible for the sharp decline of abortion figures for nonresidents in England at the beginning of the 1970s.[10] Similarly, the establishment of illegal, but officially tolerated, abortion clinics in the Netherlands reduced the influx from Belgium and the German Federal Republic. But women seeking abortions continued to come to England from Ireland, Scotland, and France as well as Italy.[11] In East European countries, liberalization of abortion laws began in the early 1950s, and the trend toward legalized abortion subsequently accelerated. Because abortion has been legal there since the 1950s, Hungary and Czechoslovakia have been regarded as having the most reliable statistics on abortion.[13] Abortion figures in these socialist countries outnumbered live births. In Asia, the nation which has the best and the longest series of abortion data is Japan, which legalized abortion at the end of World War II partly as a response to the alarmingly high birthrate encouraged by the pronatalist military government during the war and partly as an adjustment to the social and economic processes in postwar Japan.[13] In Korea, the sharp increase of abortion did not take place until the beginning of the 1970s, as was the case for the Republic of China (Taiwan), Singapore, and the People's Republic of China.[14]

Similar to the contraception campaigns during the decade of 1960s, the liberalization of abortion laws became a new social phenomenon in the 1970s. During the past ten years, there have been dramatic changes of governmental policies on abortion. In 1976 more than 60 percent of the world's population lived in countries where abortion during the first trimester was legal either for social and/or economic reasons, though the most common grounds are "medical." In addition, another 15 percent of the world's population lived in countries where an abortion may be obtained for medical and for humanitarian reasons. The remainder of about 25 percent of the world's population lived in countries where abortion laws were restrictive, though often these laws were not strictly enforced, such as many countries in South America, Taiwan, and the Philippines. Table 1 shows abortion's legal status by country and by grounds for abortion.

Among predominantly Roman Catholic countries, Austria permits abortion during the first trimester only, while France permits abortion during the first ten weeks. On the restrictive side, Belgium and Ireland consider abortion illegal. Italy allows broad medical grounds for abor-

TABLE 2
Estimated Number of Illegal Abortions, Abortion Rates, and Abortion Ratios: Selected countries, 1965–70.

Country	Number (in thousands)	Rate per 1,000 women, 15–44	Ratio per 1,000 births
Australia	40–80	16–33	150–310
Austria	70–300	50–210	620–2,670
Belgium	30–400	16–210	210–2,820
Canada	20–120	5–28	50–320
Chile	100–200	47–94	420–840
France	250–1,000	24–120	300–1,410
German Democratic Rep.	60–150	18–44	250–630
German Federal Rep.	50–3,000	4–250	60–3,790
Greece	60–100	29–48	410–690
India	2,000–6,000	16–48	100–300
Italy	500–2,000	43–170	560–2,220
Switzerland	20–50	15–37	200–500
United Kingdom	10–250	3–74	10–280
United States	300–2,000	7–47	80–540

Source: Tietze and Murstein, pp. 26–27

tion in contrast to Spain, which has narrowly restricted circumstances: danger to the life of the mother.

Most of the Catholic countries in Latin America legally restrict abortion. Among the twenty-two countries with more than 1 million population, one-third (seven countries) forbid abortion under all circumstances. Six countries allow abortion only when the mother's life is in danger, while nine countries permit abortion for rather broad medical reasons. Uruguay has the most liberal law and allows termination of pregnancy if the family suffers from serious economic stress. In socialist Cuba, abortion is allowed in all government hospitals. In the only Catholic country in Asia, the Philippines, abortion is illegal, but illegal abortions are commonly accepted by the medical and public health professions.

Thus Catholic countries have both liberal and restrictive laws regarding abortions. Where abortion laws are restrictive, such as countries in Latin America and the Philippines, illegal abortions are reported to be high. In Catholic Belgium, Spain, France, and Ireland, migration of women to nearby countries for abortion purposes is noted. Table 2 shows the estimated number of illegal abortions for

TABLE 3
Legally Induced Abortions of Nonresidents Obtained in England and Wales: By countries, 1969–73.

Country	1969	1970	1971	1972	1973
Belgium	200	600	2,100	2,500	1,500
Canada	400	300	100	100	*
Denmark	*	100	200	100	*
France	500	2,300	12,000	25,200	35,300
German Federal Republic	1,600	3,600	13,600	17,500	11,300
Ireland, Northern	*	200	600	800	1,000
Ireland, Republic of	100	300	600	1,000	1,200
Italy	*	100	200	500	1,200
Netherlands	100	800	800	200	100
Scotland	*	300	500	800	1,100
Spain	*	100	200	700	1,800
Switzerland	*	100	400	700	700
United States	1,600	1,600	200	100	100
Rest of world	500	200	700	1,100	1,300
Total	5,000	10,600	32,200	51,300	56,600

*Not available or less than fifty included in "rest of world."

Source: Department of Health and Social Security, *Report on Confidential Enquiries into Maternal Deaths in England and Wales, 1970–72*. (London: Her Majesty's Stationery Office, 1975). Also reports of earlier volumes. 1973 figures obtained from 1973 supplement on abortion.

selected countries around the end of the 1960s and the beginning of the 1970s.

If these figures are indicative of the abortion practices in these countries for which we have data, countries with high rates of illegal abortion are found among Catholic countries: Austria, Belgium, France, and Italy. Since the range of estimates is large, errors in such estimates must also be high. Table 3 shows figures by countries of origin for legal abortions performed upon nonresidents in England and Wales for the first three years in the 1970s.

Again, figures for Belgium, France, German Federal Republic, Ireland, and Spain are among the highest for countries where the data are available.

These figures indicate that problems of abortion are as serious in countries where the laws are restrictive as they are in countries where laws are liberal. Since illegal abortions are often the least reliable data reported, discussions on these figures would have to be based on the assumption that actual incidences of all abortions are higher. If, however, illegal abortions indicate that people are willing to risk breaking the law and to jeopardize their own physical safety, there may lie beneath the surface additional problems not directly related to abortion but rather to public health, the control and licensing of clinics, and so on. In short, the problem of abortion touches upon some of the most fundamental issues of public law, medicine, welfare, and the family.

2. The Push for Change

In the 1960s many considered abortion and sterilization to be an inevitable second agenda on the contraception issue which would surface sooner or later as the drama over population control unfolded. The anticipation was realistic, but few wished to tackle it head on. In the last ten years, as laws on abortion became liberalized the world over, with concomitant rise of abortions and a more serious effort to keep track of illegal abortions, there has been an expected movement to make abortion more readily available with as little as possible governmental control over abortion on one hand, and, on the other hand, a countermovement to keep the traditional conservative legal stance on abortion.

Militant and enthusiastic family planning promoters welcomed the opportunity since abortion in the past in many societies had served as an efficient last check on family planning. With abortion to back up contraception campaigns, the war against what was known as the population explosion might be won. Second, with the momentum of equal rights movement for women, there was an increasing awareness of the unequal degree of "penalty" when a couple has an unwanted pregnancy. This is particularly true if the pregnancy is conceived out of wedlock. Traditionally the man suffers less both in terms of social reputation and in the subsequent disposition of a child. A central argument in the liberation of women is that women should have complete control over pregnancy.[15] Finally, the *conditions* of many of the developed countries have changed, both as causes and as consequences of the liberalization of abortion laws, making abortion an easy alternative for women who perceived that having children was no longer one of the attractive feminine roles.

In the course of assessing various socio-economic and political forces which have shaped the milieu of the current abortion "movement," one can point to the Supreme Court's decisions as the primary force behind the change. If indeed the word "movement" is employed here, as it has been used elsewhere,[16] then singular acts of the highest court of the land could hardly come without many other factors already pushing for liberalization of abortion laws in the social system. As the push for change gains strength, those who held opposite views and those who are concerned about the ramifications of such legal changes on abortion practice would have to organize their forces in a collective and politically potent manner.

It is difficult to assess the social milieu within which the abortion issue was conceptualized and interpreted by various segments of the society. First of all, the social conditions surrounding pregnancy, conjugal relations, and contraception have changed so rapidly since the 1960s and these same conditions have so extensively affected the lives of individuals and their relations to their families that families, regardless of geographic region, ethnicity, and social class, are becoming alike in size, structure, consuming behavior, and aspirations and hopes. The similarities of family size, structure, and values, however, may be only superficial or even mythical. American society holds tenaciously to a pluralistic ethnoreligious ideal with a consequent wide range of views regarding the person's relationship to God and nature. Members of these diverse religious and ethnic groups have quite different views on family, on kinship relations, and on pregnancy as well as the avoidance of birth.

Roman Catholics have always found it difficult both to hold on to their religious and ethnic values on one hand and to achieve the ideal of a pluralistic society on the other. At the outset of its political and social establishment, American society had to confront conflicting and mutually challenging values: those of original settlers and immigrants, those of the people who were shipped from Africa, and those of the indigenous Indians. But both black- and red-skin minorities were dominated by the Anglo-European whites, a domination which worked also against those who later came from southern and eastern Europe and who did not bear the Anglo-Saxon moral and social values. The making of the dominating culture—that of Anglo-Protestantism—came gradually, in piecemeal fashion, through legislation both state and federal, and Anglo conformity seemed to be the yardstick of Americanization.[17] The fact that English became the *lingua franca* is taken for granted as part of the process of Americanization.[18] The current conflict concerning abortion on request is but another manifestation of a minority people who cherish traditional religious and moral values struggling against the tide of a more pragmatic and secular culture with different values.

The Conjugal Dyad

The American family, observed the French social historian, Philippe Ariès, has become the prisoner of love.[19] In contrast to many other industrial and Western nations, Americans regard conjugal bliss and marital exclusivity as the ultimate expression of happiness and the "good life." It is to this most sensitive and delicate and emotionally fragile relationship that all other personal commitments must take a lesser priority. Marriage, sex, and childbirth or the prevention of conceptions are, to a certain extent, the exclusive private concerns of the man and the woman, and so they are a sort of heterosexual expression of individualism. These relationships serve as instruments to achieve a mutually consenting and fulfilling relationship rather than functions of membership of the larger kinship or a collectivity. Human families allow eight sets of possible dyadic relationships: father-son, mother-son, father-daughter, mother-daughter, brother-sister, brother-brother, sister-sister, and husband-wife. Each of the eight dyadic relationships are different, and each may differ from culture to culture. Anthropologist Francis L. K. Hsu contrasted the American family with the Chinese family by pointing out that in the Chinese culture, the eight sets of relationships are dominated by the father-son relationship, since the Chinese family is patrilineal.[20] On the other hand, the American family is dominated by the husband-wife relationship. The father-son relationship differs fundamentally from the husband-wife relationship in that the father-son relationship is from generation to generation. At each generational level there are father-son relations, some of which may be grandfather and father relations and others may be son-grandson relations, depending on where you start. Inasmuch as such relationship is generational, it is continuous. On the other hand, husband-wife relations are not continuous: husband-wife relations do not repeat in the generational way. Second, the father-son relationship is asexual; and husband-wife relationship is sexual. Third, insofar as the father-son relationship may contain more than one dyadic pair, as in the case when the father has many sons, the relationship is *inclusive* of all the male offspring. In contrast, in the husband-wife relationship, insofar as it is a monogamous system, only one person can be the husband or the wife. It is therefore *exclusive*. Finally, the conjugal pair at least in theory does share family responsibilities, though such responsibilities may not be identical or even equal; the husband and wife relationship is symetrical. Francis Hsu argues that such relationships may be the fundamental unit of analysis for determining patterns of the cultural system. In the United States, the emphasis on conjugal bliss, a separate household for the nuclear family, and individual privacy (which owes its origin to conjugal exclusivity),[21] puts a premium on a highly valued sense of "freedom of choice," rather than on communal obligations, including the concerns of relatives or moral and religious values.

Sociologists have long posited that the emphasis on conjugal happiness and individual freedom has made the United States the most "married" country in the Western world.[22] Beginning from the turn of the present century, the medium age of first marriage has become lower each year from the previous decennial registration. At present, most women are married by the age of twenty-four. It is admittedly true that, at least during an earlier era, women derived their social status from their men and looked upon marriage as a source of the "good life" and a "station of life." Fewer alternative roles were opened to a woman in the American society without marriage and the role of homemaking. The recent upsurge of the woman's liberation movement and the equal opportunity employment campaign have made (or will make) marriage a less viable option. In the 1970s, there are 8 percent fewer women aged twenty to twenty-four who are married than were married a decade ago.[23] In anticipation of more alternatives and options, more women will take contraceptive measures to avoid having children too soon or having too many, lest such burdens may deprive them of the long anticipated career opportunities. But this "option squeeze" has a built-in time lag because of the amount of time needed to make reality keep pace with anticipations. Luker mentioned that even if medical schools began to admit a 50 percent female class this year, it would still be an average of eight years before there was a significant change in the number of women doctors.[24] The transitional period poses some of the greatest risks in terms of unwanted pregnancies and the taking of contraceptive risks. The lower figure of married women in the twenty-to-twenty-four age cohort does not, however, mean that fewer women today put premium on conjugal relationships, since this is the age group where we also have a large number of "living-together" relationships. In spite of the shifting of legal definitions of the relationship, it may still be argued that for young women marriage remains the "career" choice most favored by prevalent norms, even though having children may not be the concomitant expectation.

Inasmuch as marriage is a social institution and is, therefore, functionally related to other social institutions in reciprocal and significant ways, the legal definition of marital relationships affects property inheritance, mutual rights and obligations between the man and the woman, and the status of the offspring. Conjugal ethics strengthens, sustains, and interprets the authority of the church, but it also undermines that authority.[25] This means that we can understand the current family situation only if we take into consideration the wider sociocultural context within which American families operate. It is also within the context of contemporary requirement of conjugal exclusivity and happiness that American women come to define the meaning of personal experience when and if abortion is presented as a viable choice along with all significant elements of that context.

4. The Institutional Context of Social Change

The Christian tradition deemed abortion so unacceptable that it attracted little scientific or theological interest until there was increasing public recognition of the divergence of social norms from religious ethics. When such difficulties occurred, they were viewed primarily as indications of the lack of moral convictions or of poverty. Few, for instance, anticipated that the crisis and tensions connected with the abortion controversy might come from a multitude of pressures for the social system itself to change. A social system may respond to such forces without producing a stable mechanism to handle them. The process is so haphazard that it might be more correct to say that "this is the way things have become" rather than to say that this is the way things are or should be. This process of "becoming" must be understood both in its macro social milieu as well as in the micro processes whereby people alter their views of their world and come to redefine their relationships with one another.

There are, then, at least two ways to conceptualize the way people view the abortion issue: one deals with the issue abstractly as a moral and religious matter; the second concerns the specific circumstances and the sequence of events which lead up to the abortion decision and its consequences both with respect to the individual actor and the moral fibers of the community. There is no dispute about the consistency of the two approaches—each reflects the other. However, the resulting judgments may be quite different, primarily because of the contextual elements of the act itself.

It was during the period of industrial revolution and the advancement of biological sciences from the 1850s through the first half of the twentieth century that we witnessed the greatest demographic transitions. The Catholic church has only recently begun to come to terms with the consequences of such social change, perhaps because of the timidity of theologians and historians who hesitated to grasp the contemporary scene and its historical implications. Both preferred to give past events and ideas new meaning in light of their own standards and significance. Historical studies ordinarily cover the most important events as well as people of achievment or prestige. In a sense, historians study events to endow them with significance.[26] Thus, for example, social forces which shaped past instances of the sudden rise and fall of abortion ratios have by and large gone uninterpreted. Historical hindsight has been used to claim that the legal and theological principles that scholars were interested in studying, rather than social conditions, could explain the widespread recourse to abortion. Abortion, as ably shown in Davis's data,[27] was powerful and pervasive in shaping the demographic dynamics of societies in the past and has been significant in the lifetime of the present generation who witnessed the drastic check of rapid population growth during and shortly after World War II in Japan.

Contemporary history in its record of the rapid changes in two of our most traditional institutions—religion and the family—is as significant a public record as any of the great events of wars, elections, and civil strife. To date, however, little attention has been given to this problem. Social change is no more nor less than a shift in the thoughts and behavior of people from all segments of the society. Its focus is not just upon industrially advanced nations of Western Europe and North America but upon people everywhere. Abortion touches the basic conditions of life: birth, marriage, death, food, disease, material possessions, housing, work, the desire of improving one's lot, and the person's relationship to God and nature. All of these are interlocked and interwoven to become some of the most basic social institutions of humanity: the family, the economy, the institutional religious belief, and the polity.

It is clear that strong public reaction to the recent Supreme Court decisions on abortion reflects not merely a moral commitment but also a desire to maintain a traditional set of basic and dominant values as well. It seems that no matter how small a percentage of the public the abortion issue actually disturbs, the magnitude of the liberalizing effects has not yet been fully grasped. In this regard, it is regrettable that Catholic moral theologians do not seem prepared to assess the problem beyond the right-to-life argument and subsequently to take into consideration the impact of such new cross-class socio-cultural behavior as a significant dimension of the problem on which they are rendering judgment.

If indeed a given set of values is designed to achieve a set of objectives, it must also prescribe a number of instrumental conditions or exigencies. If abortion is wrong under all and any circumstances, then we must carefully study all and any of the circumstances under which violation of the principle may occur; and the system itself must be prepared to invoke a set of regulatory mechanisms to prevent certain conflict situations from occurring too often, lest constant repeated pressures become too burdensome for the system to bear. In the short run, such pressures may create deviant styles of response on the part of its membership. If the number of overt violations is small, the strength of the system can handle it without a great deal of strain. In the long run, however, the system must undergo structural modification or it will break down and collapse. In the case of the absolute standard of abortion ethics, the system can be weakened considerably as is now the case, yet still maintain outward operational viability, although at a very high cost.[28]

As a way of analyzing the needed system support of abortion, we use a parallel if somewhat dissimilar example: the taboo against incest. Rules against incest are universally observed in all societies even though the specific definition of the prohibited relationships may vary when it comes to members outside the immediate nuclear family. In all societies there are mechanisms and exigencies to prevent incestuous relationships from developing. When such relationships occur, they are not ignored. Strict boundaries of kinship relationships sustain universal rules against incest. The kinship structure is a complex form of lineal and lateral human groupings of both sexes and various age cohorts with carefully defined mutual obligations and specifically prescribed rights and privileges. These normative rules include the form of mutual addresses when communicating with one another, the display of emotional and affective attributes in any one of a number of dyadic ties, the residence arrangements, economic obligations and dependencies, inheritance rules, the assignment of status and ritual involving the birth and the departure of members. All of these are supportive mechanisms to sustain the rules against incest and to control and check what is called the "libido." If incestuous relationships were to occur frequently, the kinship system itself would be extremely vulnerable as a social institution. Although there always were important differences between the taboo against incest and the prohibition of abortion, the functional consistency and effectiveness of the incest taboo suggest the utility of the comparison.

5. Conclusions: The Problematic Status of Rules and Norms on Abortion

What are the requisite exigencies of abortion taboos in light of the Supreme Court decisions? Here we are faced with a set of moral dilemmas. If indeed the social system can tolerate a temporary and insignificant number of abortions on request, can the system tolerate a long-term liberal practice of abortions? Based on what circumstance? According to what rules? At what time frame after the conception of the human egg? Whose consent(s) must be obtained? Are such rules negotiable?

The polemical presentation of the abortion issue adds to the confusion surrounding the original issue of whose life was to be saved in the event that the pregnancy might endanger the life of the mother. Second, attitudes toward terminating pregnancy resulting from rape, incest, and other conditions raise additional questions about the priority of values which society holds. Third, a question is raised about the intrinsic rights of woman, her right to control her own body, and the communal claims of the life of the unborn child. The latter raises yet another question about membership (see Pincoffs's paper in this volume), still vaguely defined in a philosophical sense. In reality, an individual is subject to collective judgment of the legitimacy (rather than legality) of his membership in that group by virtue of universally corresponding rituals of birth announcements, naming, initiation rites, and, in religious traditions, baptisms, which tie many otherwise unrelated adult members in the community in fictive kinship bonds. Fourth, concern for what may be called "justice" dictates that the responsibility for abortion be equally assigned to the mother and the biological father. Perhaps restrictive abortion laws are intrinsically sexist laws.

Unlike the incest taboo, the prohibition of abortion, which for centuries has been supported by various institutional prerequisites and exigencies, has lost its weight as a social force in the past ten years and opposition to it has become so pervasive and powerful as to compel the withdrawal of some of the institutional supports from the traditional anti-abortion stance. The Supreme Court's decisions, for example, suggest that, at least for some people, there are other societal values which need to be protected and that abortion prohibitions must be qualified under the laws of the land.

There are those who believe that abortion under *any* circumstance is unacceptable. It may well be a minority group of people who hold such views for religious and moral reasons. Such religious minorities face a particularly difficult time under the comprehensive and powerful impact of social change. Catholic minorities in the United States do not have abortion statistics that are lower than other religious groups,[29] yet as a religious group, Catholics generally voice stronger objections to the liberalization of the abortions laws, and have consistently shown, as a group, a negative reaction to the Supreme Court's decisions. A serious problem remains in this case: that increasing discrepancies exist between a set of answers given to a survey pollster and actual behavior—a problem which suggests that pastoral counseling and marital therapists may have a particularly difficult time if such trends continue.

A whole spectrum of unanswered questions are raised with respect to some of the micro issues of man-woman relations—sexual intimacy, pregnancy, and the choice to contracept or not—which in some cases lead to the decision to abort a fetus. We have little systematic inquiry into the psychological aspects and the sequels of abortion. Judith Bardwick, well known for her work on the psychology of contraception, reported at the time of the Notre Dame conference that she knew of nothing significant to report to the conferees on the psychological sequels and suspected that any real trauma might come long after the usual six months follow-up period ordinarily used by researchers. Guilt about destroying life depends on, first of all, the cognitive awareness of the life being destroyed, which normally is embedded into the cultural heritage of the people and secondly, on the heightened awareness of her abortion's significance when the woman subsequently has a baby or, to some lesser extent, comes in close contact with someone else's baby.[30] Bardwick's assertions have not so far been tested by empirical studies.

In spite of the lack of any systematic data on this problem, many people have assumed that abortion is a traumatic experience for women. Many states have stipulated that one reason for legal abortion is that the unwanted pregnancy may be hazardous to the woman's mental health. Whether the requirement of psychiatric examination is the legal requisite, or a medical safeguard of the woman's subsequent mental well being, it is a social labeling process. Women who seek abortions are viewed negatively as "having problems," whereas women who seek contraceptive advice are the "intelligent planners." Hence, liberalization of abortion laws is a concerted effort to remove obstacles, legal or social, which currently remain as institutional barriers to elective abortion.

At this time, in the mid-1970s, I wish someone could show us that the abortion statistics as reported are all wrong and highly exaggerated and that the Supreme Court decision has met with such violent opposition from all segments of the society that the Court must retreat from its original position. I wish someone could say that the "precious life" being destroyed by the new liberalization of abortion laws all over the world has such profound ramifications in human societies that a countermovement is on its way. I wish someone could say that abortion is limited to a very minor and atypical subpopulation, and that it is nothing to be alarmed about even though, like other deviant behavior, it will always be a part of the scene. The reality of the situation is that the direction of change is toward further liberalization of the law. This is not to say that the liberalization of abortion laws does not constitute a serious incidence of the "clash of values" in societies where the taboo against abortion has had deep and historic-religious roots. In the United States, however, the political system is designed to absorb such a "clash of values"—a remarkable demonstration of how a system balances itself through conflicting sets of values.

It is still too soon to discern the consequences of the Supreme Court decisions on abortion for the various aspects of the American social system which are affected by abortion. The Court has both the legal responsibility to safeguard the value tradition of our society and to protect the rights of the individual members of our society. These issues, together with the disputed questions of the rights of the unborn and of the ownership of the fetus, are so interwoven and complex that the Court cannot be said to have settled them. On the other hand, those who maintain a militant demand for the total prohibition of abortion, based only on the right-to-life argument, appear to be isolated from the reality of massive social change. The Catholic church must find opportunities to address the question of abortion objectively and openly. If this is not done, the crisis posed by the abortion "revolution" will not go away by itself, and the theologians of the church will soon run out of answers.

NOTES

1. Margot Zimmerman, "Abortion Law and Practice: A Status Report," *Population Reports,* Law and Policy Series E, no. 3 (Washington, D.C.: George Washington University Medical Center, March 1976), p. E–26.
2. Christine Luker, *Taking Chances* (Berkeley: University of California Press, 1975), p. 181.
3. Christopher Tietze and Marjorie Cooper Murstein, "Induced Abortion: 1975 Factbook," *Reports on Population/Family Planning,* (December 1975), no. 14, pp. 1–76.
4. Ibid.
5. Roy G. Smith, P.G. Steinhoff, J.A. Palmore, and M. Diamond, "Abortion in Hawaii: 1970–71," *Hawaii Medical Journal,* 32 (1973): 213–20.
6. Tietze and Murstein, "Induced Abortion," pp. 15–26 *et passim.*
7. For selective countries figures are as follows (abortion per 1,000 live births): Korea (1972) 374; Singapore (1974) 149; Japan (1965) 1,974; and

Taiwan, according to L. P. Chow's study (citation in this paper), about one out of every five women reported having had at least one abortion. Those who are between thirty-five and thirty-nine years old, the ratio is one out of every three.

Legal abortion in India is low, compared with other countries, at about 4 per 1,000 live births, but illegal abortion is reported at between 100 to 300 per every 1,000 live births. In the Philippines, according to a large-scale fertility survey conducted by this author and a group of Notre Dame social scientists in the late 1960s, abortion is reported at about 300 to every 1,000 live births. Abortion is illegal in the Philippines.

8. P. Diggory and M. Simms, "Two Years after Abortion Act," *New Scientist* 48 (November 1970):261–63.

9. Tietze and Murstein, "Induced Abortion," p. 17.

10. Office of Population Censuses and Surveys (United Kingdom), "Legal Abortions," *OPCS Monitor,* October 1975.

11. Ibid.

12. A. Klinger, "Report on the Legislation, Practices and Statistics about Induced Abortion in the European Socialist Countries" (unpublished paper, 1973); C. Tietze and Hans Lobfeldt, "Legal Abortion in Eastern Europe," *Journal of the American Medical Association,* 175 (1961): 1149–54; and in D. Callahan, *Abortion: Law, Choice and Morality* (New York: MacMillan, 1970), pp. 242–43.

13. Cf. Irene Taeuber, *Population of Japan* (Princeton: Princeton University Press, 1972); M. Muramatsu, *Japan's Experience in Family Planning: Past and Present* (Tokyo: Family Planning Federation of Japan, 1967).

14. Cf. L. P. Chow, "Measurement of the Incidence of Induced Abortion: Preliminary Results from a Study in Taiwan," (presented at IUSSO Workshop on Abortion, Chapel Hill, North Carolina, March 1973); C. Djerassi, "Fertility Limitation Through Contraceptive Steroids in the People's Republic of China," *Studies in Family Planning* 5 (1974): 13–30.

15. Cf. K. Luker, *Taking Chances,* p. 6.

16. "Movement" is used here simply because the term has been used by many people. A. F. Guttmacher in a paper (December 1971) published in *Maryland State Medical Journal* used the title "Changing Attitudes and Practices Concerning Abortion: A Socio-medical *Revolution*" (italics added), suggesting that it was a revolution.

17. See Oscar Handlin, *The Americans: A New History of the People of the United States* (Boston: Little, Brown, 1963), 148–62.

18. Joshua A. Fishman, *Language Loyalty in the United States: The Maintenance and Perpetuation of Non-English Mother Tongues by American Religious and Ethnic Groups* (The Hague: Mouton & Co., 1966), pp. 29–31.

19. Jacques Mousseau, "The Family, Prison of Love," in *Psychology Today* 9 (1975): 53–58. Also see P. Ariès, *Centuries of Childhood: A Social History of Family Life,* (New York: Houghton Mifflin & Co., 1955).

20. Cf. Francis L. K. Hsu, ed., *Kinship and Culture* (Chicago: Aldine, 1971).

21. Cf. Philip Slater, *The Pursuit of Loneliness: American Culture at the Breaking Point,* (Boston: Beacon Press, 1971).

22. William F. Ogburn and M. F. Nimkoff, *Technology and the Changing Family* (New York: Houghton Mifflin & Co., 1955).

23. U.S. Bureau of Census, "Marital Status and Living Arrangements," *Current Population Reports,* Population Characteristics, Series P-20, no. 242 (March 1972), p. 3 Table.

24. K. Luker, *Taking Chances*, pp. 121–22.

25. Andrew Greeley compared data collected by the National Opinion Research Center on American Catholics' attitudes and religious behavior over the past ten years and concluded that a sizable number of practicing Catholics have not followed the church's teachings on contraception and the papal encyclical on *Humanae Vitae* perhaps was responsible for many Catholics leaving their religious faith.

26. This is not a peculiar judgment of sociologists. Jack P. Greene, a Johns Hopkins historian, wrote in the *New York Times*, stressing the importance of having a new history. "The New History: From Top to Bottom," January 8, 1975, p. 37:1.

27. Kingsley Davis, "The Theory of Change and Response in Modern Demographic History," *Population Index* 29 (1963): 345–66.

28. If indeed more than three-quarters of the world's population live in countries where abortion is either on request or easily justified or where proscriptive laws are conveniently ignored, the system is perhaps quite weak indeed.

29. Luker's data (in *Taking Chances*) showed that Catholic patients appear in the abortion clinic in a proportion about the same as the proportion of Catholics in the general population. In Hawaii, a report of abortion statistics made by Diamond et al. showed that Catholics are over represented in the abortion population as compared with the proportion of Catholics in the general population. Figures on Jews and Buddhists were too small to allow meaningful interpretations. See Milton Diamond, James A. Palmore, Roy G. Smith, and P. G. Steinhoff, "Abortion in Hawaii," *Family Planning Perspectives*, 5 Winter (1973).

30. Correspondence with Judith Bardwick, February 1975.

Philosophers on Abortion

DAVID SOLOMON

Academic philosophy in this century, especially in England and America, has been persistently criticized for refusing to discuss concrete normative problems. There has been an enormous increase, however, in the past ten to fifteen years, of philosophical discussion of questions of public policy and of normative problems generally. New journals have been founded, new societies started, philosophers have more frequently been included on the programs of conferences designed to discuss such topics, a much higher percentage of articles in "standard" philosophical journals have touched on these topics, and new, allegedly more relevant, courses have appeared in the curricula of philosophy departments. Topics discussed include sexual morality, civil disobedience, the rights of animals, the whole gamut of problems that arise within contemporary biomedicine, altruistic behavior, punishment, environmental questions, and educational practices. The explanation for this shift in attention on the part of philosophers is complex and undoubtedly impossible to give with any completeness at this time. Whatever may be the final explanation, however, there can be no doubt that a substantial change has taken place. And it might be thought that this change would satisfy those critics who have argued that philosophy generally, and moral philosophy in particular, has not contributed as much as it should to the resolution of the whole range of contemporary problems which some have argued constitute a value crisis.

These remarks are prompted partially by the reception given the papers presented by philosophers at the Notre Dame conference. Those participants in the conference who were not philosophers, a group which included persons with widely different views on abortion, seemed to feel, almost without exception, that the philosophical efforts contributed less than they might have to the conference. Indeed, there were those who would have argued that the philosophical contributions were both futile and obfuscating. The general feeling seemed to be that the philosophers started too far back, as it were, and would be unlikely to contribute significantly to any process of reasoned reflection on the abortion problem. This attitude calls for investigation, especially since anyone who is familiar with the recent philosophical discussion of abortion would agree that the papers read at the conference by philosophers are among the most penetrating and subtle to be found in the literature. Excellent philosophical discussion, presented and defended by first-rate philosophers, yet met with (almost) total disdain by fellow academicians. What went wrong?

2.

There are undoubtedly many possible explanations for this reaction. Some participants were unfamiliar with philosophical styles of argument generally and, consequently, unable to see the point of the philosophical exercises. They simply didn't understand. Others, who brought to the conference set views on some of the fundamental issues surrounding the abortion question, were unhappy at the sight of these questions being treated as if they were still unsettled. One participant, a lawyer, reacted to the philosophical presentations by remarking that "they talked about questions which most of us settled when we were much younger."

These reactions, of course, are of no particular interest, and if the negative response of all the participants were of this sort, no further comment would be called for. But there is another possible explanation for at least some of the uneasiness many persons seem to feel about the general philosophical approach to abortion; and this more subtle explanation is worth pursuing. Indeed, I will suggest that there is one typical philosophical approach to normative problems like abortion which *should* elicit uneasiness, and if the philosophical papers included in this volume had taken this approach the response they received at the Notre Dame conference would be fully justified. I will also suggest, however, that they do not take this approach.

One place to begin is by reflecting on the fact that there is not one simple and isolable problem which can be called the abortion question. There are any number of problems which arise for different persons and agencies, at different times and with different contributing circumstances. There is one question which presents itself, for example, to the pregnant, unmarried adolescent, confronted with the problem of whether to seek out an abortion. The teachings of her church, the laws of her state, and the attitudes of her parents and contemporaries are *features of the situation* in which this question arises for her. Her question is *not* one about how abortion laws should be written or how sacred texts should be interpreted. It is rather a question about what to do now, and she will have little time, and probably little assistance, in her attempt to answer it. The most important considerations in her situation have to do with the consequences for herself (and for what she may already think of as her unborn child). She will perceive these consequences, of course, through the filter of some conception of her self and of the idealized future she has set as her goal. Only the most rationalistic of persons would suppose that anything that goes on at an academic conference on "the problem of abortion" will be of any assistance to her, even indirectly.

A quite different question has presented itself to legislators of the various states in recent years: Should legislation be enacted which would remove the legal barriers to safe and easily available abortions for those women whose life or psychological well-being is not seriously threatened by giving birth? This question has a character completely different from the agent's question, although the certainty of the agent's question arising is one of the circumstances against the background of which the legislator's question arises. The legislator's decision will depend on a whole range of considerations quite irrelevant to the agent. Will such legislation promote the freedom of choice of women or further erode conjugal values upon which so much of our social system depends? Or perhaps both? And if both, which value is most worth promoting? How much of the pressure for liberalized abortion legislation is racist in origin? If a considerable amount, how is the legislator to take this into account? What are the attitudes toward abortion of persons within the community generally, and especially those medical workers who would be responsible for performing abortions? Would liberalized abortion legislation outrage the moral sensibility of most persons in the community so that any such legislation would be nullified by failure on the part of medical institutions to make legal abortions available? Finally, the legislator must ask what degree of care for the fetus is the state charged with insuring.

The legislator's question must also be distinguished from the judge's question. As Professor Kommer's sensitive comparison of the American and German supreme court decisions makes clear, subtle questions about constitutional interpretation come into play when judges are called upon to rule on the constitutionality of abortion legislation. Less concerned than legislators with the immediate impact of these laws on the community, they must insure that the legislation is consistent with basic constitutional guarantees.

A quite different question again arises for a physician who is called upon to perform an abortion. If abortion is at that time legal, he may query whether his own professional stance toward the care he owes his patient will allow him to perform an abortion. As someone has put it, he must decide whether he has one patient or two. If the abortion he is called upon to perform would be illegal, he must decide whether the care he owes his patient is sufficient to override his obligation to work within the statutory limits set for the practice of medicine. In either case, his difficulty (if he has a difficulty) will grow out of his conception of the commitments he makes in assuming his professional role.

This list of distinct questions concerning abortion, arising for different persons in different situations, could be extended almost indefinitely. And this should not be surprising since, as Professor Liu has emphasized in his comments, the fact of abortion has ramifications for almost every large-scale institution of contemporary life—legal, religious, familial, and professional. Persons whose roles are defined by these different institutions will inevitably confront "the problem of abortion" in a different manner. This inescapable complexity of the abortion problem provides one key to understanding both the approach philosophers have taken to it and the less than enthusiastic response their efforts have received.

3.

Moral philosophers, of course, are not unaware of the complexity of the abortion debate or of the diverse set of questions which arise surrounding it. They have attempted to accommodate this situation by defining one *crucial question* which, they allege, underlies the crazy-quilt of surface concerns. Their procedure is not unlike one that many historians of science have held to underlie the growth and progress of science. According to these historians of science, old scientific theories are standardly refuted by the construction of a *crucial experiment* which tests the theory as a whole. Given the complexity of many theories, the design of crucial experiments is alleged to be a task of great difficulty and its successful completion a work of genius.

In a similar fashion, moral philosophers have attempted to locate a crucial question within the abortion debate, the successful answer to which would provide a kind of Archimedean point on which they can elevate solutions to the various other questions that arise. Concerning this mode of approaching the abortion problem, one might wonder if there is such a crucial question to be found in the abortion debate. And if so, whether philosophers have correctly identified it.

There can be no doubt, at least, what philosophers have taken the crucial question to be. There has been virtual unanimity among those who have discussed this topic that the question of the personhood, or humanity, of the fetus is the crucial question.[1] The standard view, that is, is that if it were possible to determine whether the fetus is a person (or a human being), then the answers to all the other questions—i.e., the agents, legislators, judges, physicians, and many others—would fall into place. No one surely believes that these questions will be answerable without some hard thinking, but nevertheless it has seemed to many philosophers that at the bottom of each of these quandaries is some uncertainty about the humanity of the fetus. And this uncertainty is to be removed by a broadly conceptual investigation which will result in some set of necessary and sufficient conditions for ascribing personhood to some object.

Now part of the exasperation others feel at philosophical discussions of abortion can be explained by the manner in which philosophers quickly cut through what first appears to be an enormously complex issue to reveal a single, highly abstract question which, if successfully answered, could settle all difficulties. And this exasperation is surely understandable. One finds, for example, in the recent philosophical literature on abortion one article which attempts to answer the crucial question and more in under twenty pages.[2] Professor Tooley has argued in that paper that not only the fetus but also infants up to the age of a few weeks do not qualify as persons and hence have no right to life. They have, on his view, no more claim (and perhaps less) on our moral regard than the higher animals. No less surprising to most persons is Professor Brody's argument in his recent book in which he alleges to establish the humanity of the six-to-eight-week-old fetus by making essential use of certain esoteric doctrines refined in recent philosophical discussions of the semantics of modal logic.[3]

It is not my purpose (here) to criticize the positions of these philosophers, but one can understand how it might be supposed that the "problem" of abortion is not to be solved by application of the latest philosophical machinery or by intricate arguments seemingly more appropriate to dealing with the mathematical puzzle in the Sunday supplement. The problem of abortion is not a puzzle awaiting a solution; it is rather an enormously complex set of issues involving all the intricacies of large-scale social change, technological innovation, and changing patterns of human life. It would be surprising if legislative proposals, judicial decisions, or medical practices could be derived from some answer to the crucial question.

In Professor Liu's remarks above, one gets a perspective on the abortion issue quite different from the standard philosophical perspective. From Liu's sociological perspective, the abortion problem is essentially one of social adjustment. His data on abortion rates would suggest that we have already accepted, worldwide, something like abortion on demand. No matter what most persons might say about their attitudes toward abortion when queried by pollsters, there can be no doubt that their behavior indicates a broad and deep acceptance of abortion as a standard tool of the medical practitioner. He also indicates that this change in attitude toward abortion is not an isolated phenomenon, but rather one aspect of large-scale social change brought about by population pressures and the shifting conception of family life within modern technological societies. For Professor Liu, philosophical arguments designed to resolve the abortion debate would appear to be largely irrelevant to the future course of changing attitudes in this area. Where some philosophers have looked for a solution to a puzzle, some sociologists look for adjustment to an unalterable situation. Surely both perspectives are one-sided.

4.

The relevance of the preceding comments to the earlier remarks about the reception of the papers by Pincoffs and Wertheimer is somewhat complex. My suggestion is that a good deal of the negative reaction to the papers of Pincoffs and Wertheimer arose because many members of their audience understood them to be taking what I have characterized above as the philosophical perspective. That is, the audience understood them to be attempting to resolve the conceptual difficulties surrounding the attribution of personhood to the fetus as a step toward resolving the larger legal and social questions raised by the current abortion debate. But in fact this way of understanding their papers involves an important element of misunderstanding.

It is true that both Pincoffs and Wertheimer suggest that unresolved questions about the personhood of the fetus lie at the bottom of much of the contemporary controversy about abortion. Indeed, both papers are centrally concerned with understanding what is being asked when investigations of the personhood of the fetus are undertaken. But it is not true that either Pincoffs or Wertheimer argues that these difficult conceptual questions can be resolved by standard philosophical techniques. On the contrary, it is one of the main burdens of their papers to show why such a solution cannot be reached.

It would not be too farfetched even to say that in their papers it is possible to see how the philosophical and sociological perspectives might come together, avoiding the one-sidedness of each. While they emphasize the centrality of questions about the humanity of the fetus, they also never lose sight of the way, generally, perceptions of the human status of an object are a function of certain large-scale features of social life. For Pincoffs, decisions about the human status of classes of objects are made with reference to certain requirements on any human society to limit its membership in a clear and definitive way. For Wertheimer (as he argued more fully in an earlier paper), the human status of an object is determined by our perception of it, where this perception grows out of a history of normal relations with the object. Both eschew any *a priori* shortcut to settling the question of the humanity of the fetus.

It is unfortunate, I think, that in presenting papers which were essentially critical of certain standard philosophical approaches to the abortion problem, Wertheimer and Pincoffs received a response which would have been more appropriately made to those they were criticizing. They were not trying to resolve moral quandaries about abortion in a stroke; they were rather setting out, in quite different ways, reasons for supposing that one standard philosophical approach to a solution to the abortion problem will not work. Their critics at the conference were no harder on them than they are on some of their fellow philosophers.

5.

If Pincoffs and Wertheimer have at least partially succeeded in avoiding the one-sidedness of the philosophical perspective, it might be useful to note in a more systematic way, finally, some general considerations which suggest why they were wise to do so. Why is it that the conceptual investigations carried out by philosophers and the social descriptions attempted by sociologists are interdependent?

The dependence of the philosophical task on the sociological is explained by the role of social forces in determining the nature of our conceptual framework. The concepts with which we approach ethical dilemmas like abortion have been shaped and sharpened in social interaction and the communal attempt to provide a public vocabulary with which to work out our life together. It would surely be futile to attempt an investigation of these concepts without attending to the complex social relations out of which they have grown. Pincoffs shows special sensitivity to this feature of conceptual investigations when he compares determinations of the human status of an object to membership decisions. Part of the point he is making here is that the concept of a human being is not primarily to be understood as picking out a certain class of creatures on the basis of some set of natural properties. The concept of 'human being,' that is, functions within our conceptual framework in a quite different way than do concepts like 'canine' or 'insect.' These latter concepts are useful in identifying certain natural objects for purposes of classification or description. The concept of 'human being' has, however, a quite different point. We use this concept to pick out those objects which play roles similar to ours in the social, political, and moral orders. And in deciding to whom this concept has application, we are in effect deciding whom to treat as one of us. Hence, Pincoffs's illuminating discussion of the nature of membership decisions generally.

One might still wish, however, that he had gone a bit further in exploring the *nature* of membership decisions. In particular, one would like to know a bit more about what social consensus on such a question would be like, and how one arrives at it. As Pincoffs's paper stands, he leaves us with tantalizing suggestions about the role of the Supreme Court in reaching a consensus, but his position here is far from clear. While he surely holds that in a society like the United States a decision by the highest court on the moral regard owed the fetus is an important ingredient in a consensus on the humanity of the fetus, he makes it clear that such a decision does not *constitute* a consensus. What more is needed? And how are we to determine when that "more" has been achieved? Until these questions are answered, there remains a certain incompleteness in Pincoffs's account.

If a particular conceptual investigation requires attention to the social background for the use of the concept, it is no less true that attempts to describe the social reality of abortion implicate conceptual questions. One might pursue such an investigation through the use of polling techniques in an attempt to determine attitudes on the basis of verbal responses to explicit questions; or one might attempt to gather data more directly on the behavior of persons with regard to abortion. In either case, however, the data will be useless without some understanding of what the verbal responses *mean* and what the behavior actually *is*. It is a commonplace of contemporary philosophy that in order to understand what action a person performs on some occasion, it is necessary to understand his intention.[4] If a child throws a rock in the water on Monday just in order to see the ripples and throws another rock in the same place on Tuesday in an attempt to hit one of his playmates, he performs actions which are two, not only in number but in kind. He did something on Tuesday which was quite different from what he did on Monday; and it detracts nothing from this difference to point out that the same physical movements were involved in each action.

If what a person does is thus (partially) determined by what he intends, it is intentions on which it is necessary to focus in order to understand behavior. But the intentions with which someone acts are themselves a function of the conceptual material with which he works. Someone can only intend to checkmate his opponent if the conceptual tools of chess are part of his repertoire. A chimpanzee who moves chess pieces *as if* he were intending to checkmate an opponent is nevertheless not intending this. He can't have such an intention any more than he can intend to marry or intend to vote in the next election.

These points should make clear how conceptual questions are inevitably involved in attempts to explore the behavior and attitudes of persons toward abortion. It is not possible even to know (*really*) what actions persons perform when they undergo abortions (or advise others to have abortions or perform abortions themselves) unless we can understand the intentions involved in these actions. Of course, there is *some* sense in which all persons who perform abortions are doing the same thing. But to latch onto the sameness would be like approaching an investigation of violent behavior by supposing that all persons who shoot guns are doing the same thing. In both cases, there is a sense in which the same thing is being done; but in neither case is the similarity as significant as the difference.

Both the philosophical and the sociological perspectives must then be regarded as inadequate taken singly. Philosophers cannot reduce the abortion "problem" to a relatively simple crucial question, because any such question would have to be as complex as the social forces that have given rise to it. But neither can the sociologists eschew the conceptual difficulties of agents who have to deal with questions about abortion; to neglect these conceptual questions would render the sociological task—describing current behavior and attitudes with regard to abortion—impossible.

NOTES

1. Not complete unanimity however. See, for example, Judith Jarvis Thomson, "A Defense of Abortion," *Philosophy and Public Affairs* 1, no. 1 (Fall, 1971): 47–66.
2. Michael Tooley, "Abortion and Infanticide," *Philosophy and Public Affairs* 2, no. 1 (Fall 1972): 37–65.
3. Baruch Brody, *Abortion and the Sanctity of Human Life: A Philosophical View* (Cambridge, Mass.: The MIT Press, 1975).
4. For a classic statement of this view see G.E.M. Anscombe, *Intention* (Oxford, Eng.: Blackwells, 1958).

Conclusions

EDWARD MANIER, WILLIAM LIU, AND DAVID SOLOMON

The Notre Dame Conference on Abortion, Public Policy, and Morality was held at the University in March 1975 and from that time until August 1976 the three editors continued their own discussions of the many questions disputed by the conference participants. During this time, other duties called two of the editors to opposite ends of the country. Although this increased the problems of editorial communication, we think the book benefited from its relatively slow and deliberate preparation. However, we may owe our fellow conferees an apology for the resultant delay in publication and for allowing ourselves the benefit of so much hindsight.

We have mulled over all the papers presented at the conference, debated their methods and their implications among ourselves, and selected several of them for presentation in a context intended to provide a new focus and new directions for interdisciplinary research on abortion. What follows is a summary of our editorial conclusions. We do not pretend to speak for the contributors to this volume or those in attendance at the conference; we obviously do not speak for the faculty of the University of Notre Dame. The following four propositions express our *editorial* consensus on the current state of the many problems of abortion, our reservations concerning current public policy and the major alternative offered in opposition to that policy, and our goals for future research on the topic.

1. The Antinomy Concerning the Starting Point of Individual Human Life

It can seem equally reasonable either to assert or to deny that individual human life begins at the time of conception. The assertion that life begins at conception plausibly reflects the continuity of the process of embryological development; the denial that life begins at conception equally plausibly reflects the great disparity between the fertilized egg and the newborn child.[1] We conclude that present assertions and denials on this point respond to an improperly formulated question.

An unfortunate taste for misplaced abstraction is indulged by those who insist that biological evidence provides sufficient support for claims concerning the starting point of individual human life. We do not agree with John Noonan that

> the positive argument for conception as the decisive moment of humanization is that at conception the new being receives the genetic code. It is this genetic information which determines his characteristics, which is the biological carrier of the possibility of human wisdom, which makes him a self-evolving human being. A being with a human genetic code is a man.[2]

Since our general concept of humanity is more than a biological concept, no amount of biological evidence can provide adequate warrant for any claim concerning the starting point of individual human life. Noonan's view is on shaky biological ground as well. The view that membership in *any* biological species can be determined by checking off a list of conditions necessary and sufficient for membership is generally rejected by biological taxonomists and philosophers of biology.[3] Further, it is misleading to assert that "a being with a human genetic code is a man," as if there were special evidence from molecular biology warranting that assertion. In fact it has no more empirical significance than "a rose is a rose," since the only means of identifying genetic material as human is by direct comparison with DNA already identified as human.[4] Finally, the thesis that genetic information determines phenotypic characteristics fails to take account of the complex interaction between genetic material, developing organism, and the environment of that organism.[5]

Nor can questions concerning the humanity of the fetus be resolved by identifying an alleged "natural response" to the fetus on the part of human adults. Human reactions to pregnancy and childbirth are necessarily conditioned by culturally variable relationships between conjugal partners as well as those between parents and their live offspring.[6] Changing demographic and economic conditions also figure in the structure of these relationships and consequently in the social construction of the concept of humanity.

Social science alone is unable to describe and explain the social construction of the concept of 'humanity,' particularly within the ethically plural societies where the issue of abortion is subject to public debate.[7] What weight is to be given to verbal expressions of opinion? To actual behavior? At what point and on what grounds are we to say that opinion and behavior are in conflict? Can we accurately identify consensus or the absence of consensus on such a complex and fundamental issue?

The intradisciplinary research and analysis necessary if we are to understand our use of the concept of humanity has barely begun. No single academic discipline is adequate to this task. Resolution of the antinomy concerning the starting point of individual human life must take account of the intricate connections between the concept of humanity and the foundations of scientific and moral discourse in everyday language and experience. We cannot pretend to decide the limits of the concept of humanity without first fully comprehending the processes by which social groups construct their own "reality," particularly that portion of it made up of fellow human beings or 'human beings.'[8]

2. Liberal Individualism and the Question of Human Status

The political philosophy of liberal individualism, understood as the position that places individual freedom first among all social goals and values and regards that freedom as a necessary means for the attainment of every other valued end, is inadequate for the resolution of disputed questions concerning membership in the human species or status as a human being. One of the most cautious and comprehensive expositions of that position recognizes "liberalism's" inadequacy as a source of principles for fair dealing with those in a situation of complete dependency (the insane and children).[9] "Liberalism," used uncritically in such contexts, would always justify society's abandonment of a group unable to articulate or defend its own claims. "Tastes" differ, the matter is left to free decision in the market place, and the class whose humanity is in dispute is treated with legal indifference. If we do not trust the principle of liberal individualism to show us the way to deal fairly with children or with the mentally incompetent, however, how can we trust those same principles to determine the limits of membership in the class of human beings?

The literature on abortion makes extensive use of the principles of an individualistic and libertarian social and political philosophy, but it has yet to recognize the necessity of justification for such radical extension of the political philosophy of *laissez faire*. The political principles invoked in the Supreme Court decisions legalizing elective abortion place individual freedom first among social goals and values.[10] R. Wertheimer has argued that since conclusive arguments for or against the humanity of the fetus at some very early stage of development have not been forthcoming and since freedom should be limited only when there is a compelling rationale to do so, elective abortion cannot be legally prohibited.[11] But he does not hold that "liberalism" can justify a decision concerning membership in the class of human beings. This it cannot do, since the functioning of "liberal" principles *assumes* a domain of independent and voluntary agents.

Communitarian alternatives to liberal individualism have received scant expression in the course of the abortion debate and such social philosophies have had no influence on the outcome of that debate in the United States. The Supreme Court has given clear priority to the autonomy of the *individual* woman's decision on abortion, and it has given no attention to the impact of this autonomy upon the cohesiveness of the family. Nevertheless, the integrity of this basic social unit may well be on a par with individual human freedom at the foundations of morality and social life.

No political philosophy should go unchallenged in the discussion of abortion. If there is one point where our aspirations for individual human freedom must be conditioned and limited by principles of fairness, it is that at which basic questions of human status are resolved. Our use of the concept of humanity sets the context of all our moral dealings as a society.

3. Misreading of the Normative Consensus on Abortion

Neither the majority of the Supreme Court nor the most conservative opponents of legalized elective abortion can appeal to a normative consensus of American society which truly supports their position. The various provisions of *Roe* v. *Wade, Doe* v. *Bolton,* and *Planned Parenthood* v. *Danforth* depart from the expressed opinion of a majority of our society in

(1) permitting elective abortion,
(2) permitting abortion after the twelfth week of pregnancy,
(3) permitting abortion, in all cases, without the consent of the woman's husband.

Concerning (1), Judith Blake has found opinion opposing elective abortion hovering around 55 percent of the population.[12] Concerning (2), her data show that 67.6 percent of the population thought that legal abortion should be limited to the first three months of pregnancy and that about the same number thought that human life began by that point in fetal development.[13] Concerning (3), Blake notes that 61 percent of women and 66 percent of men express the opinion that abortion should not be lawful without the husband's consent.[14]

On the other hand, the unqualified characterization of voluntary abortion as murder or even as unjustified homicide reflects the opinion of a small minority of U.S. citizens generally and even of a minority of U.S. Catholics.[15] In January 1973, 11 percent of non-Catholics thought that abortion should *never* be performed, while approximately 25.6 percent of Catholics were of that opinion.[16] The percentage of Catholic men (42 percent) and women (48 percent) who set the point *after* which it should be illegal to perform an abortion at three months were almost identical to the figures (41 percent, 49 percent) for non-Catholic men and women.[17]

Moreover, if Kristin Luker's sample is at all representative, an increasing number of women are deciding to *risk* (by deliberately *not* using contraceptives) and then to abort unwanted pregnancy.[18] Abortions are also increasing among women who have never used contraceptives. More pregnant women below the age of fifteen obtained abortions than carried to term in 1974.[19] There is little reason to think that these trends will be reversed. Even if the legal situation were to revert to the *status quo ante Roe* v. *Wade,* no evidence supports the assumption that the annual total of abortions performed on U.S. citizens would significantly decrease.

In all respects save for its willingness to place a greater burden on the welfare system supported by the republic, the 1975 decision of the West German Federal Court is in closer apparent conformity with American public opinion concerning abortion norms than either the majority of the Supreme Court or the U.S. Catholic bishops and other conservative leaders of the opposition to legalized abortion in the United States.[20]

4. Exaggerated Partisanship and the Risk of Normative Chaos

All expert commentary on the subject of abortion is *inextricably* involved with its proponents' extradisciplinary assumptions and values, and *no* method provides or could provide the means of distinguishing a core of objective and value-free recommendations for public policy concerning abortion. Robert Gilpin's reservations concerning the general possibility of "expert" advice which is both scientifically objective and relevant to public policy have been fully borne out in the record of the abortion controversy.[21] The record of expert advice on U.S. population policy may show somewhat less balance than that reported by Gilpin for the controversy concerning the atomic test ban treaty with the Soviet Union. Peter Bachrach and Elihu Bergman have noted that official discussions of American population policy underrepresent dissenting views, particularly the views of those who will "consume" the services which implement U.S. population policy.[22]

The major contending parties in the abortion dispute risk the induction of a mood of anomie or normative chaos concerning human pregnancy and the institution of the family. Each of these parties has exhibited a penchant for misplaced abstraction, seizing upon some one normative principle or some one aspect of the evidence to construct a position which confuses and misstates the issues involved.

The majority position in *Planned Parenthood* v. *Danforth* extends the opinion of *Roe* v. *Wade* to secure the individual woman's right to an abortion against all considerations raised in the interest of the unity and quality of family life.[23] It is too soon to comment on the social "spin-off" likely to result from these decisions, but the liberal individualism upon which they are based will not of itself strengthen or protect the institution of the family. Kristin Luker notes that *Roe* and *Doe* have not resulted in an increase in shared responsibility, involving the parents of both sexes in the resolution of the problems of unwanted pregnancy. To the contrary, the women in Luker's sample for the most part found themselves alone with the decision to abort the pregnancy and equally alone with the abortion and its attendant costs.[24] Other evidence suggests that the legalization of elective abortion is being used to implement parental preference for offspring of a particular sex.[25] Neither of these consequences was intended by those feminists for whom liberalization of abortion laws is a *cause célèbre,* but these consequences do follow from the principles of liberal individualism which underlie *Roe* and *Doe*. Those principles will not directly promote items on the feminist agenda which call for equality or for means of *sharing responsibility* with male partners.

On the other hand, a comparable preference for misplaced abstraction is indulged by those who insist that biological evidence can establish the humanity of the fetus at conception. The Catholic church has generally been associated with the view that human life begins at the moment of conception or that "the unborn child is a person under the law in terms of the Constitution from conception on."[26] We cannot pretend to criticize all possible formulations of that position in advance. At this time, however, we conclude that efforts to defend the thesis that individual human life begins at conception have been methodologically naive and uncritical in their derivation of moral conclusions from biological premisses.

Our conclusions have not been inspired by a personal sentiment we might be presumed to have favoring some hypothetical middle ground. They have been based on our analysis of the evidence and on the general view that the abortion issue has been grievously distorted by excessive partisanship on both sides of questions set with far too little care. It is not likely that our society can soon achieve a true consensus on public policy concerning abortion.

The conditions for effective scholarly and interdisciplinary examination of the problems, however, are much more favorable now than in the recent past. We hope this volume will facilitate and focus a new direction for effort of this sort and that it will contribute to a more generous response by all sides to dissenting philosophical arguments as well as to sociological and cross-cultural evidence concerning abortion. It would be well to remember, however, that no legislative or judicial moratorium will be declared pending the completion of this tangled and difficult work.

NOTES

1. Roger Wertheimer, "Understanding the Abortion Argument," in *The Rights and Wrongs of Abortion*, ed. M. Cohen, T. Nagel, and T. Scanlon (Princeton: Princeton University Press, 1974), pp. 23–51. Also see the contributions by Wertheimer and Edmund Pincoffs to this volume.

2. John Noonan, "An Almost Absolute Value in History," in his *The Morality of Abortion: Legal and Historical Perspectives* (Cambridge, Mass.: Harvard University Press, 1970), p. 57. Noonan cites F. J. Gottlieb *Developmental Genetics* (New York: Van Nostrand Reinhold 1966), p. 17, in support of his position.

For a critical discussion of the "genetic school" concerning the starting point of individual human life, see D. Callahan, *Abortion: Law, Choice and Morality* (New York: Macmillan, 1970), pp. 378–83. Paul Ramsey's position seems to rely on biological evidence to an even greater extent than Noonan's. See Ramsey, "The Morality of Abortion," in *Life or Death: Ethics and Options* (Seattle: University of Washington Press, 1968), pp. 61–62.

3. Ernst Mayr, "Species Concepts and Definitions," in *Topics in the Philosophy of Biology*, ed. M. Grene and E. Mendelsohn (Dordrecht, Holland: D. Reidel, 1976), pp. 353–71; and David Hull, "Contemporary Systematic Philosophies," ibid., pp. 396–440.

4. Ursula Goodenough and Robert Levine, *Genetics* (New York: Holt, Rinehart & Winston, 1974), pp. 61–78, for a brief discussion of the relevant diagnostic technique.

5. C. H. Waddington, "Paradigm for an Evolutionary Process," in his *Towards a Theoretical Biology* (Edinburgh: Edinburgh University Press, 1969), 2:106–24.

6. See William T. Liu's discussion of the variability of the conjugal dyad in this volume as well as the work done under his direction on abortion in the Philippines, see pp. 149–51, and p. 157, note 7.

7. David Solomon argues this point, pp. 166–67. Also see Edward Manier's Introduction, pp. 22–25.

8. See Roger Wertheimer's contribution to this volume, pp. 128–32. P. L. Berger and T. Luckmann, *The Social Construction of Reality: A Treatise in the Sociology of Knowledge* (New York: Doubleday, 1966).

9. Milton Friedmann, *Capitalism and Freedom* (Chicago: University of Chicago Press, 1962), pp. 33–34.

10. Donald Kommers, this volume, pp. 106–12.

11. R. Wertheimer's "Understanding the Abortion Argument," p. 50.

12. Judith Blake, this volume, pp. 59, 61, Table 3.

13. Blake, this volume, pp. 64 and 65, Tables 4 and 5. Table 4 shows that 62 percent of 662 men and 73 percent of 696 women thought the legal limit for abortion should be set no later than the end of the third month of pregnancy. In April 1975, 57 percent of 679 men and 75 percent of 682 women expressed the opinion that human life begins no later than the time of quickening (47 percent of the men and 71 percent of the women said the unborn may be considered a human person no later than the time of quickening). See Table 5 of Blake's contribution to this volume.

14. Blake, this volume, p. 64, Table 4.

15. James T. Burtchaell, "Letters," *Newsweek,* July 26, 1976.

16. Blake, this volume, p. 70, Table 8.

17. Ibid., p. 71, Table 9.

18. Kristin Luker, *Taking Chances: Abortion and the Decision Not to Contracept* (Berkeley: University of California Press, 1975), pp. 1–17.

19. See the data set forth by William Liu, pp. 137–47. Also *Family Planning Perspectives* 8 (March/April 1976): 70, citing data from Department of Health, Education and Welfare Center for Disease Control, *Abortion Surveillance,* Annual Summary, 1974.

20. See the discussion of the West German decision by Donald Kommers in this volume.

21. R. Gilpin, *American Scientists and Nuclear Weapons Policy* (Princeton, N.J.: Princeton University Press, 1962).

22. Peter Bachrach and Elihu Bergman, *Power and Choice: the Formulation of American Population Policy* (Lexington, Mass.: D. C. Heath, 1973), and their "Participation and Conflict in the Making of American Population Policy: A Critical Analysis," in *Aspects of Population Growth Policy,* ed. Robert Parke, Jr. and C. F. Westoff, as volume 6 of The Commission on Population Growth and the American Future, *Research Reports,* 7 vols. (Washington, D.C.: Government Printing Office, 1972) 6:583–607.

23. See Appendix for a brief discussion of *Planned Parenthood* v. *Danforth.*

24. Luker, *Taking Chances,* pp. 112–37.

25. Richard A. Knox, "Doctors' dilemma: Abortion if fetus is 'wrong sex,' " *Boston Evening Globe,* August 11, 1976, p. 1:1, reports views expressed by faculty (including Dr. Park Gerald of Boston Children's Hospital) of a course in medical genetics taught at Jackson Laboratory, Bar Harbor, Maine, and sponsored by the National Foundation–March of Dimes and Johns Hopkins University. Physicians reported "no noticeable trend toward preference of male children over female, or vice versa."

26. National Conference of Catholic Bishops, *Documentation: Abortion and the Right to Life, II* (Washington, D.C.: United States Catholic Conference, 1976), p. 28.

Appendix

Comments on the 1976 Supreme Court Decisions:
PLANNED PARENTHOOD v. DANFORTH
and BELLOTTI v. BAIRD

On July 1, 1976, the U.S. Supreme Court's views on abortion were spelled out more completely in several new cases, including *Planned Parenthood of Central Missouri v. Danforth,* and *Bellotti v. Baird.*[1] Since these decisions were published when the manuscript of these proceedings was in the final stages of preparation, they cannot be discussed fully here. Nevertheless, aspects of these recent cases have such high relevance to our conclusions concerning abortion and public policy in the United States that some reference to them must be included. The sections of *Planned Parenthood v. Danforth* which are particularly relevant are those dealing with spousal consent and parental consent (for minors), but the Court's findings concerning the method of saline amniocentesis and the "standard of care" required for the aborted fetus are also significant.

The Missouri statute (Missouri House Committee Substitute for House Bill #1211, effective June 14, 1976) challenged in *Planned Parenthood v. Danforth* required the written consent of the woman's spouse for all abortions performed on married women except those certified by a licensed physician as necessary to preserve the life of the mother. The Court found this provision incompatible with the implications of *Roe v. Wade.* The keystone of its argument was the claim that the "State cannot delegate to a spouse a veto power which the State itself is absolutely and totally prohibited from exercising during the first trimester of pregnancy (44 LW 5202).

Justice Byron R. White's stinging dissent from this and other key elements of the majority opinion (written by Justice Harry Blackmun) was joined by Chief Justice Warren E. Burger and Justice William H. Rehnquist. White dismissed Blackmun's first argument as a *non sequitur* confusing a father's personal interest in his own offspring with an interest the state might delegate to him. White wrote,

> It by no means follows, from the fact that the mother's interest in deciding "whether or not to terminate her pregnancy" outweighs the State's interest in the potential life of the fetus, that the husband's interest is also outweighed and may not be protected by the State. A father's interest in having a child—perhaps his only child—may be unmatched by any other interest in his life. See *Stanley* v. *Illinois*, 405 U.S. 645, 651, and cases there cited. It is truly surprising that the majority finds in the United States Constitution, as it must in order to justify the result it reaches, a rule that the State must assign a greater value to a mother's decision to cut off a potential human life by abortion than to a father's decision to let it mature into a live child. Such a rule cannot be found there, nor can it be found in *Roe* v. *Wade*, supra. These are matters which a State should be able to decide free from the suffocating power of the federal judge, purporting to act in the name of the Constitution. (44 LW 5209)

In seeking to rebut this dissent, Blackmun appealed to a succinct dictum found in *Eisenstadt* v. *Baird*, an opinion written by Justice Brennan in striking down a Massachusetts law prohibiting the distribution of contraceptive materials to unmarried persons. Brennan had written that

> the marital couple is not an independent entity with a mind and heart of its own, but an association of two individuals each with a separate intellectual and emotional makeup. If the right of privacy means anything, it is the right of the *individual,* married or single, to be free from unwarranted governmental intrusion into matters so fundamentally affecting a person as the decision whether to bear or beget a child. (Emphasis in original.) (405 U.S. 453)

The core of Brennan's argument in *Eisenstadt* v. *Baird* had been that since the Court had already found, in *Griswold* v. *Connecticut,* that the distribution of contraceptives to married persons could not be prohibited, a ban on distribution to unmarried persons would violate the Equal Protection Clause of the Fourteenth Amendment. Brennan had formulated the dictum quoted above in order to support his claim that *Eisenstadt* v. *Baird* and *Griswold* v. *Connecticut* were analogous cases and that married and unmarried individuals should not be separately classified with respect to access to contraceptive materials. In *Eisenstadt* v. *Baird,* the proposition that "the marital couple is not an independent entity with a mind and heart of its own, but an association of two individuals each with a separate intellectual and emotional makeup" was not the point at issue. Correspondingly, it was neither elaborated, qualified, nor supported by evidence or further argument. The use of the dictum in *Planned Parenthood* v. *Danforth* shows the willingness of the current Court majority to include commentary on the nature of the *family* as part of its rationale for opinions concerning *abortion*. Its view of the marital relationship and of possible disagreements concerning the married couple's shared reproductive activity is impersonal and mechanical. Of the ameliorating choices that a couple might make when confronted with a pregnancy one of them does not want, only abortion is mentioned and the possibilities of conciliation are ignored. "In cases of disagreement between husband and wife concerning abortion, the view of only one of the two marriage partners can prevail." And, "Since it is the woman who physically bears the child and who is the more directly and immediately affected by the pregnancy, as between the two, the balance weighs in her favor." Justice White found, this last sentence in direct *conflict* with the majority opinion in *Roe* v. *Wade:*

> In describing the nature of a mother's interest in terminating a pregnancy, the Court in *Roe* v. *Wade* mentioned only the post-birth burdens of rearing a child, id. at p. 153, and rejected a rule based on her interest in controlling her own body during pregnancy. Id., at 154. (44 LW 5209)

Planned Parenthood v. *Danforth* also struck down the provision of the Missouri statute which required the written consent of one parent or person *in loco parentis* of an unmarried woman under the age of eighteen years unless abortion were certified by a licensed physician as necessary in order to preserve her life. The majority agreed with Justice Blackmun that "minors, as well as adults, are protected by the Constitution and possess constitutional rights" and that no significant state interest had been established sufficient to limit the rights of minors seeking an abortion. It concluded that this limitation would do nothing to strengthen the family unit (44 LW 5204). Justice Potter Stewart, writing a concurring opinion in which Justice Powell joined, identified the primary constitutional deficiency of this section of the Missouri statute in its "imposition of an absolute limitation on the minor's right to obtain an abortion." He found evidence in the record of *Bellotti* v. *Baird* (also decided by the Court on July 1) suggesting that it was unlikely that a pregnant minor would "obtain adequate counsel and support from the attending physician at an abortion clinic, where abortions for pregnant minors frequently take place." Stewart accepted Massachusetts Attorney General Francis X. Bellotti's statement in the brief for the appellants in that case:

> The counseling . . . occurs entirely on the day the abortion is to be performed. . . . It lasts for two hours and takes place in groups that include both minors and adults who are strangers to one another. . . . The physi-

cian takes no part in this counseling process. . . . Counseling is typically limited to a description of abortion procedures, possible complications, and birth control techniques. (44 LW 5208, 5209 and 5209 note 2)

Stewart also alluded to Justice John Paul Stevens's rationale supporting the state's interest in encouraging parental consent and dissenting from the majority finding against this section of the Missouri statute. Stevens found the "overriding consideration" to be "that the right to make the choice (concerning abortion) be exercised as wisely as possible" (44 LW 5213). He found that without a parental consent requirement, "many minors will submit to the abortion procedure without ever informing their parents," and argued:

> It is unrealistic, in my judgment, to assume that every parent-child relationship is either (a) so perfect that communication and accord will take place routinely or (b) so imperfect that the absence of communication reflects the child's correct prediction that the parent will exercise his or her veto arbitrarily to further a selfish interest rather than the child's interest. (44 LW 5212)

But while Stevens concluded that the state has power to select a chronological age as its standard for determining the point at which a minor can "independently make the abortion decision," Stewart and Potter sided with the majority in striking down the statutory requirement that the pregnant woman be eighteen or older before consenting to an abortion on her own behalf. Stewart did comment, however, that the Court's procedural findings in *Bellotti* v. *Baird* implied that

> a materially different constitutional issue would be presented under a provision requiring parental consent or consultation in most cases but providing for prompt (i) judicial resolution of any disagreement between the parent and the minor, or (ii) judicial determination that the minor is mature enough to give an informed consent without parental concurrence or that abortion in any event is in the minor's best interest. (44 LW 5208, 5209)

At issue in the latter case was Section 12P of "An act to protect unborn children and maternal health within present constitutional limits" passed by the General Court of Massachusetts (the legislature), over the governor's veto, on August 2, 1974. Section 12P reads in part:

> (1) If the mother is less than eighteen years of age and has not married, the consent of both the mother and her parents is required. If one or both of the mother's parents refuse such consent, consent may be obtained by order of a judge of the Superior Court for good cause shown, after such hearing as he deems necessary. Such a hearing will not require the appointment of a guardian for the mother. (44 LW 5221, 5222)

Appendix

While a three-judge federal district court found this provision created an unconstitutional "parental veto" over the performance of abortions on minor children, the Supreme Court unanimously found that the district court should have withheld judgment on the merits of the case and "certified to the Supreme Judicial Court of Massachusetts appropriate questions concerning the meaning of 12P and the procedure it imposes" (44 LW 5227). The appellants in *Bellotti* v. *Baird* had argued that the last paragraph of Section 12P preserved the "mature minor" rule in Massachusetts, a rule under which a child determined by a court to be capable of giving informed consent will be allowed to do so. The Supreme Court unanimously agreed that such an interpretation by the Supreme Judicial Court of Massachusetts would "at least materially change the nature of the problem" presented by Section 12P.[2]

EDWARD MANIER

NOTES

1. At the time this manuscript was submitted to the publisher, the text of *Planned Parenthood* v. *Danforth* and the two associated decisions handed down the same day (*Singleton* v. *Wulff*, and *Bellotti* v. *Baird*) was available only in a preliminary, unofficial version. All citations to these decisions will refer to the pages of *The United States Law Week: Supreme Court Opinions*, Vol. 44, no. 51, "Opinions Announced July 1, 1976." Citations will be included in the body of the discussion in the customary form: 44 LW 5181, referring to the forty-fourth volume of *Law Week*, page 5181. For the first newspaper account of these decisions, see Lesley Oelsner's "High Court Bars Husband's Power to Veto Abortion, . . . Parents Also Curbed," *New York Times*, July 2, 1976, p. A1:8.

2. The Court also found unconstitutional the Missouri statute's prohibition of saline amniocentesis in the second trimester and its requirement that the same degree of "professional skill, care and diligence" be used to "preserve the life and health of the fetus which . . . would be required . . . in order to preserve the life and health of any fetus intended to be born and not aborted." White's dissent concerning saline amniocentesis argued that it was within the state's right to change the practice under which second trimester abortions were performed and to make the "safer prostaglandin method generally available." His patience apparently exhausted, he closed with a rhetorical flourish: "That should end our inquiry, unless we purport to be not only the country's continuous constitutional convention but also its ex officio medical board with powers to approve or disapprove medical and operative practices and standards throughout the United States" (44 LW 5211).

Concerning the "standard of care" requirement, Blackmun found that the statute impermissibly required preservation of the life and health of the fetus, whatever the stage of pregnancy. White considered this provision of the statute constitutional and permissible under *Roe* v. *Wade,* since he read it to operate "only in the gray area after the fetus might be viable but while the physician is still able to certify 'with reasonable medical certainty that the fetus is not viable' " (44 LW 5211). *Roe* v. *Wade would* permit state regulation of this gray area, on White's account. Again, White's dissent was vehement, and he appended the following note of advice to Missouri courts.

> The majority's construction of state law is, of course, not binding on the Missouri courts. If they should disagree with the majority's reading of state law on one or both of the points treated by the majority, the State could validly enforce the relevant parts of the statute—at least against all those people not parties to this case. (44 LW 5212, note 4)

INDEX

Abortion
  as a contraceptive, 25n, 147
  cross-disciplinary discussion of, 2
  current incidence of, 137–47
  and the Democratic platform (1976), 28n
  and husband's consent, 53, 63, 68, 76, 177–79
  legal status of, 138–43
  and medicaid payments, 28n, 55
  as a moral problem, 31, 151, 160–64
  moral rule against, 32–38
  philosophical treatment of, 162–64
  prohibition of compared to incest prohibition, 153–55
  public support for, 54–81
  and the Republican platform (1976), 28n
  social system response to, 20–21, 151–53
  and women's liberation, 147, 150
Abortions, justifications for
  defective fetus, 56–57, 61, 85, 88
  desires of parents, 56–57, 61, 145
  financial, 56–57, 61, 145
  health of mother, 56–57, 61, 85, 88, 93, 101, 145
  pregnancy resulting from rape, 85, 88, 93–94, 154
Abortion Reform Act of 1974 (Germany), 87–91, 93, 101, 111
American Bar Association, 91
American Medical Association, 91
American Public Health Association, 91

Analytical jurisprudence, 110
Anscombe, G. E. M., 167n
Ariès, Phillipe, 149, 157n

Bachrach, Peter, 174, 176n
Baker v. Carr, 112n
Bardwick, Judith, 155, 158n
Barnsley, John, 29n
Bayh, Birch, 28–29n
Bellotti, Francis X., 178–80
Bellotti v. Baird, 177–82
Benda, Ernst, 104
Berger, P. L., 23, 29n, 176n
Bergman, E., 27n, 174
Bernardin, Joseph L., 27n
Bethe, Hans, 2
Blackmun, Justice Harry A., 11, 91, 108, 110, 177–80, 181n
Blake, Judith, 6–9, 11, 29n, 82n, 172, 176n
Blume, S. S., 27n
Bongaarts, John, 25n
Brandmeyer, Gerhard A., 26n
Brandt, Willy, 89
Brennan, Justice William J., 105, 178
Brody, Baruch, 167n
Bruenneck, Justice Wiltraut Rupp von, 99–100
Burger, Chief Justice Warren E., 93, 109, 110, 177
Burtchaell, J. T., 176n

Callahan, Daniel, 25n, 157n, 175n
Carter, Jimmy, ix

Index

Categorical imperative, 33
Catholic church
  bishops of, 1, 26n, 28n, 173
  attitude of members toward abortion, 67–70, 173
  members on West German Court, 105
  and social change, 151
Chow, L. P., 157n
Church amendment, 28n
Cohen, M., 25n
Confucius, 21
Constitutionalism, 103, 105
  American versus German, 106–7
  Madisonian view of, 11, 106
  tension with democracy, 84
Constitution, U.S., 91
  First Amendment, 109
  Ninth Amendment, 11, 91
  Fourteenth Amendment, 10, 11, 51, 91–92, 101, 108, 114n, 178
  Right-to-Life amendments, 26n, 53, 80
Constitution, West German, 13
Contraception, 19–20
Cook, Terence Cardinal, 27n
Crespi, Irving, 51n
Crichton, Michael, 49n
Culliton, Barbara C., 82n

Darwin, Charles, 4
Davis, Kingsley, 152, 158n
Declaration of Independence, 27n
Delahunt, William, 53
de Tocqueville, Alexis, 86, 113n
Diamond, M., 156n, 158n
Diggory, P., 57n
Djerassi, C., 157n
Doe v. *Bolton*, 8, 11, 12, 51–53, 68, 77–81, 84–86, 91–93, 172
Douglas, Justice William O., 93, 110
Dred Scott case, 111
Dryfoos, Joy G., 82n

Edelin case, 3, 29n, 48n, 53, 55
Edelin, Dr. Kenneth, 53

Ehrman, Henry W., 115n
Eisenstadt v. *Baird*, 178
Engelhardt, H. Tristam, 29n
Ensoulment, 101, 104
Epstein, Richard A., 86, 112n

Factunorm Principle, 120–23, 133n
Family relations, 136n, 149–51
Feinberg, J., 25n
Fishman, Joshua A., 157n
Freedom of speech, 106–8
Friedman, Milton, 176n
Friedrich, Carl, 105, 115n
Furman v. *Georgia*, 105

German Draft Penal Code of 1962, 88, 113n
Gilpin, Robert, 2–3, 27n, 173–74, 176n
Golden Rule, 33, 128–29
Goodenough, Ursula, 175n
Gottlieb, F. J., 175n
Gray, V., 27n
Graymer, LeRoy, 51n
Greeley, Andrew, 158n
Greene, Jack, 158n
Griswold v. *Connecticut*, 178
Guttmacher, A. F., 157n

Haberer, J., 27n
Handlin, Oscar, 157n
Heidenheimer, Arnold J., 114n
Heller, Joseph, 41
Helms amendment, 29n
Helms, Jesse, 26n
Hesburgh, Theodore M., ix
Hippocratic Oath, 91
Hobbes, Thomas, 31, 47
Hsu, Francis L. K., 149, 157n
Hull, David, 175n
Human being
  and genetics, 5, 40, 170
  identification of, 44
  membership in class of, 4–5, 13, 38–43, 63, 65–66, 72–73, 92, 94, 102–4, 123–24, 162–64, 168–71

Index

distinguished from persons, 123–24
species-normal properties of, 134n

Indications solution, 113n

Jaffe, Frederick, 82n
Janowitz, M., 11
Joint Commission on the Accreditation of Hospitals, 52
Jones, Elise F., 82n
Judicial review, 52, 78–81, 84, 86–87, 99–100

Kant, I., 33
Klinger, A., 157n
Knox, Richard A., 176n
Kommers, D., 10, 176n
Kripke, Saul, 135n

Landman, Lynn C., 82n
Larson, Eric, 51n
Lecky, W. E. H., 49
Legal culture, 102–3
Leibholz, Gerhard, 103, 115n
Lemon v. *Kurtzman*, 109
Levine, Robert, 175n
Liu, William, 19, 29n, 163–64, 175n, 176n
Lobfeldt, Hans, 157n
Luckmann, T., 23, 29n, 176n
Luker, Kristin, 3–4, 25n, 26n, 150, 156n, 157n, 158n, 173–74, 176n

MacIntyre, Alasdair, 20, 22, 27n, 29n
Manier, E., 176n
Marshall, Justice Thurgood, 105
Mayr, Ernst, 175n
McCormack, Ellen, 26n
Meltsner, Arnold, 51n
Migratory abortions, 78

Model Penal Code, 84
Moral agency, 35
Moral rules
and the abortion problem, 32–36
and moral conflict, 33
primary versus secondary, 33
Moral status
of animals, 130–31
dependent versus independent, 117
human, 117, 124–25, 135n
Mousseau, Jacques, 157n
Muramatsu, M., 157n
Murphy, Walter, 83n
Murstein, Marjorie Cooper, 156n, 157n

Nagel, Thomas, 25n
National Conference of Catholic Bishops, 27n
National Right to Life, 26n
National Socialism, 98, 104
Nebel, Heidi, 51
Nimkoff, M. F., 157n
Noonan, John T., 25n, 48n, 170, 175n
Notre Dame Conference on Abortion, 27n, 51n, 155, 159, 169
Notre Dame, University of, ix–xii, 23, 169

Objective values (in German constitutional law), 115n
Ogburn, William F., 157n
Osofsky, H. and J., 25n

Palmore, J. A., 156n, 158n
Perkins, Robert L., 25n
Peterson, William, 51n
Pfeffer, Leo, 112n
Pilpel, Harriet, 51n
Pincoffs, E., 4–6, 8, 22, 51n, 164–66, 175n
Planned Parenthood v. *Danforth*, 29n, 172, 174, 176n, 177–82

Pomeroy, Richard, 82n
Powell, Justice Lewis F., 179
President's Commission on Population Growth, 85
Primack, J., 27n
Pro-abortion movement, 54, 80–81, 118, 135n
Prostaglandin, 3, 29n, 181
Prussian Penal Code of 1851, 86
Public policy formation
  and expert advisors, 2–3
  and normative assumptions, 2–3, 173–75
  and social change, 8–9

Racism, 132–33
Ramsey, Paul, 175n
Rehnquist, Justice William H., 92–93, 177
Right to life, 27, 104, 172
Right-to-Life movement, 1, 53, 80
Right to privacy, 11, 91–92, 101, 108
Roe v. *Wade*, 8, 11, 12, 51–53, 68, 77–81, 84–86, 91–93, 106, 108, 172, 174
Rorty, A., 27n
Rosoff, Jeannie I., 53, 82n, 54

Saline amniocentesis, 181n
Scanlon, T., 25n
Schaar, John H., 116n
Self, 121–22
Shearer, Bruce, 25n
Simms, M., 157n
Simon, Helmut, 99
Singleton v. *Wulff*, 27n
Slater, Phillip, 157n
Smith, Roy G., 157n, 158n
Solomon, W. D., 22–24, 176n
Spicker, S., 29n
Standard Belief, 118–33
Stanley v. *Illinois*, 178n

Steinhoff, P. G., 156n, 158n
Stewart, Justice Potter, 93, 179
Subjective rights (in German constitutional law), 115n
Substantive due process, 93
Supreme Court, U.S., 5, 24, 27, 48, 83–86, 172–73
Supreme Judicial Court of Massachusetts, 181

Taeubner, Irene, 157n
Teller, Edward, 2
Term solution, 113n
Thomson, Judith Jarvis, 176n
Tooley, Michael, 176n

U.S. Coalition for Life, 26n

Verweyen, Hans, 83n
Viability, 52, 56, 92–93
von Hippel, F., 27n

Waddington, C. H., 175n
Wahoske, J. J., 83
Weinstock, Edward, 82n
Wertheimer, Roger, 13–19, 22, 164–65, 171–72, 175n, 176n
West German Federal Constitutional Court, 10, 19, 24, 83–85, 102–4, 173
  abortion decision of, 10–13, 83, 86–91, 93–101
Westoff, Charles F., 82n
White, Justice Byron R., 92, 177–78, 181–82n
Wildovskt, Aaron, 51n
Winch, Peter, 29n

Zimmerman, Margot, 156

WITHDRAWN
From Bertrand Library

HQ767.5 .U5A23

DATE DUE			
MAR 4 1985			NOV 6 1984
APR 1 1985			
NOV 3 1985			
JUN 2 1986			
MAY 2 0 1987			
MAY 23 '88			
NOV 15 '88			
JUN 2 '90			
NOV 2 0 '90			
NOV 2 4 1991			
NOV 1 4 2002			
APR 1 1 2006			

45230
Printed in USA